B
PENN

Fantel, Hans

76-54

Penn;

B
PENN

Fantel, Hans

76-54

William Penn;
apostle of dis-
sent

DATE DUE	BORROWER'S NAME	
OCT 1 5	Dale Karp	8th (Wiles)
NOV 2	Dale Karp	NOV 8 Wiles
NOV 1 5	Ben Duroen	8-B.
MAY 2	L. Digg	
OCT 1 4 1981		
JAN 7 1982		8.5

DATE DUE

WILLIAM
PENN

By the same author

THE WALTZ KINGS

WILLIAM PENN
Apostle of Dissent

by HANS FANTEL

William Morrow & Company, Inc.
New York 1974

Printed in the United States of America.
1 2 3 4 5 78 77 76 75 74

Book design by Helen Roberts

Library of Congress Cataloging in Publication Data

Fantel, Hans.
  William Penn; apostle of dissent.

  Bibliography: p.
  1. Penn, William, 1644-1718.
F152.2.F36   974.8'02'0924 [B]   74-10626
ISBN 0-688-00310-9

For my friends in America,
who took me in

Acknowledgments

Writing, as an act of self-assertion, rests upon inner confidence. In this respect, the encouragement and companionship of Shea Fantel have sustained the creation of this book.

A person can have his own ideas no more than he can have his own language. Others form our horizons. Among those who have immeasurably expanded my reflective range, I want to give particular thanks to Trent Schroyer, Benjamin Nelson, etti de Láczay, and Urs and Eva Jaeggi. As teachers and friends, they illuminated my vision and vitalized my thinking.

I also feel lastingly grateful to Carol Coe Conway, who long ago directed my interest and imagination toward deeper concern with meaning in history.

They all had part in this, though none is accountable for my opinions.

Hillel Black, my editor, strengthened my work by his critical judgment, and his generous patience let this book grow at its own pace.

The New York Public Library provided most of my sources and aided my research by allowing me the use of the Allen Room.

H.F.

Mill River
Massachusetts
Spring 1974

CONTENTS

In times of change and danger, when there is a quicksand of fear under men's reasoning, a sense of continuity with generations gone before can stretch like a lifeline across the scary present.

—JOHN DOS PASSOS

We may and must lay hold of ideas in history if we want to gain meaning for our life in community.

—KARL JASPERS

Nothing is finally understood until its reference to process has been made evident.

—A. N. WHITEHEAD

A VIEWPOINT

As one looks toward remote horizons, distance seems to draw things together. Mountains miles apart or stars separated by light-years appear next to each other.

So it is with human events as they recede in time from the observer. Centuries merge into each other like hours of a single day. Detail fades but design emerges.

When one looks at William Penn from our point in time, he seems to be standing spiritually close to the Reformation, which began some hundred years before him, and to the American Revolution, which occurred nearly a hundred years after. It is in this perspective that I want to tell of his life.

Penn's genius lay in translating moral values into social reality by political means. Moved to outrage and compassion by the anguish of his era, he envisioned a new kind of society in Pennsylvania, radically deviant in principle and life style. His colony prospered, but his plan failed. Yet the gist of his scheme—the politics of individual conscience—endured in the American tradition and emerged more sharply than ever in the American present.

In Quakerism, Penn had a firm religious underpinning for his "Holy Experiment" in social engineering. Today, we are not so well equipped. The secularization of philosophy has left us only reason. Yet rationality has disenchanted our vision, and in turn we have become disenchanted with rationality. Early in this century Max Weber diagnosed this dilemma: ". . . an epoch which has eaten from the Tree of Knowledge discovers that we cannot learn the meaning of the world from the results of its analysis, be it ever so perfect. Rather, we must be in a position to create its meaning."

In returning to America's origins we can perhaps, as T. S. Eliot puts it, "arrive where we started and know the place for the first time" and so come closer to a creation of meaning in Weber's sense.

WILLIAM PENN

The only contemporary, though not authenticated, portrait of Penn shows him in armor during his military exploits in Ireland at the age of twenty-two.

One

PASSAGE AT SEA

> By the good providence of God, a Country in America
> is fallen to my lot.
>
> —WILLIAM PENN

In the fall of 1682, a small three-masted sailing ship plied westward in the Atlantic. With her short, stubby hull, the *Welcome* moved awkwardly in the open sea. Unlike the sleek clipper ships of later times, she did not cut the waves but bobbed in choppy waters like a cork. Even when her sails filled with wind, her progress could only be described as a kind of purposeful waddle.

She was riding low, her hold filled to capacity with wrought iron, nails, window glass, horse collars and saddleware, glue, candles, and shoes—the usual cargo for the newly settled lands in America. Only the passengers were unusual. To the crew, they must have seemed an odd change from the flinty traders, roughneck adventurers, and stolid Puritans normally met on the westward passage. On dark, low-ceilinged decks, where no lamps could be lit for fear of fire, huddled more than a hundred Quakers. Driven from England for their beliefs, they entrusted themselves to the uncertainties of a new life in a distant land, and the combined burden of their despair and their hopes seemed to load the vessel more heavily than the cargo.

With her pitch-sealed oak planking, 248 tons gross weight,

1

and a massive stern-post rudder jutting down from her poop, the *Welcome* was as seaworthy as any ship of her day. But that was scant assurance. A squall might break her masts and leave her drifting to oblivion. Sometimes the sea reached out for ships of her kind, with a high wave closing over the vessel like a giant hand. Even experienced sailors never quite lost the feeling that the great water somehow longed to draw them down, and they spun their legends of mermaids and monsters in fearful awareness of what Yeats called "the murderous innocence of the sea."

The Quakers, most of whom had never traveled more than a few miles from their towns, were terrified by their isolation in the vastness of water, so far beyond reach of the ordinary world. Seasickness churned their stomachs as the little ship rolled between wave crests, and, to make matters worse, they often felt as afraid of the crew as of the ocean. Most sailors at that time were little better then derelicts, just barely checked by the whip. They taunted the passengers, picked fights with the men, and took liberties with the women.

Only the most prominent passengers enjoyed grudging respect from the crew or the privacy of a cabin. The rest were quartered on cramped dormitory decks that offered no amenities except straw-filled sleeping pallets. With no way to preserve fruits and vegetables, small children in particular suffered from lack of fresh food; but thanks to several goats sharing the journey, the children at least had milk, and some pets to play with.

The crowding and the lack of adequate facilities for washing made the *Welcome* a floating invitation to disease, and when smallpox broke out aboard it spread like an inescapable fire. In their suffering, the Quakers drew comfort from the presence of William Penn among them. If any man could inspire confidence amid disaster, it was he. Not only did he have that compelling strength of character that enables others to find the resource of their own courage; he was the focal point and motive force of the whole venture. The Quaker exodus to America—the "Holy Experiment," as Penn called it—was his design, and his unrelenting faith in their common purpose heartened the others.

Immune to the pox thanks to a touch of the disease in childhood, Penn spent most of the voyage caring for the sick. There was little he could do except cool the fevered sufferers by washing them. It was an agonizing procedure, for the limited supply of fresh water was needed for drinking and cooking, and the salt water used for washing the sick burned on their erupted skins. Had a doctor been present, he might have applied the standard therapy: opening a vein to let the patient bleed. Draining off "bad blood" would release the evil influences that were causing the disease—a plausible theory that made this form of treatment widely accepted for almost any illness. Luckily, no doctor was aboard, so the sick were spared the additional strain of blood loss. Even so, thirty-one of them—nearly a third of their total number—died and were left to the waves.

This was a dark beginning for a venture inspired by profoundest hope, and for a while it seemed that even Penn could not sustain the spirit of the survivors. The epidemic spent itself, but grief, doubt, and dejection remained in its wake. Those who looked to the stars for portents anxiously watched the nocturnal sky. That year, a strange appearance in the heavens caused widespread alarm. It didn't matter that Edmund Halley, using Mr. Newton's new theory of gravitation, had calculated the orbit and explained the nature of the great comet now bearing his name. Scientific dispassion was not yet a widely shared attitude. As far as most people were concerned, the fire-tailed visitor in the night forboded disasters. The firmament announced the imminence of God's wrath. Perhaps it had been foolhardy to sail at such a time.

Yet on the fifty-third day of the voyage, on October 22, 1682, these fears dispersed with the first signs that the *Welcome* was nearing shore. The smell of land unmistakably

mingled with the sea air, and now and then a coastal bird
streaked over the masts. The ordeal of passage was almost over.
Ahead lay a land where none would be imprisoned because
God appeared to him differently than to the government.

The nearness of landfall intensified Penn's vision of America. Here, on a continent unburdened by the past, he would
set up a new order of life—in the boldest social experiment
ever carried out. This land was to be a testing laboratory for
new concepts of spiritual and political freedom—ideas that in
Europe were still considered criminal because of their radical
implications.

The new continent of America had never before been seen
in such a light. The early settlers of Virginia and the Carolinas
had come mainly for purposes of colonial exploitation. The
Puritans, who had settled New England some decades before,
regarded America as a sheltered preserve for their dry orthodoxies. Penn, by contrast, never conceived America as an
enclave for dogma. He already saw America as it appeared to
later generations: an open frontier not merely in the geographic
sense but also an ongoing expansion of the boundaries of
human existence. He saw America in terms of civilizational
change.

A century before the founding of the United States, Penn
pioneered a libertarian republic at the edge of the wilderness.
He set up new institutional models for man's most fundamental
relations: his relations to God and to the state. Penn's political
imagination furnished Jefferson and the later framers of the
Constitution with a bold and persuasive precedent for democracy in America. Penn's personality and values marked the
American venture at its very outset with traits that have ever
since shaped America's self-image as well as her basic conflicts: politics as the expression of moral concern, and defiance
of authority in the name of justice.

"By the good providence of God, a Country in America is

fallen to my lot," Penn exulted after the King of England had granted him the territory of Pennsylvania. As outright "Proprietor" of his province, Penn had almost limitless power over his realm, more power in fact than the King had over England. For the King was constrained by Parliament, by a truculent merchant class contesting his royal monopolies, and by the religious factions struggling for dominance in England at that time. Paradoxically, Penn, the pioneer of democratic rights, had virtually unchecked authority. Within his own domain, Penn was more absolute than his monarch. He was completely free to map the future of a land yet untouched by history. The canvas was still blank.

Politicians and artists are presumed to inhabit separate spheres. Their minds and imaginations seem differently structured. Yet this difference may be more apparent than real. The creative politician, the seminal reformer, looks at the social world in much the way a painter looks at a canvas: as a field for creative design, an area for generating new forms and meanings to lessen the eternal tension between the real and the ideal, to narrow the gap between what is and what should be.

So Penn conceived the still unseen land to the west. The sails billowed behind him and the wind sang in his ears.

Two

A SAILOR'S BOY

Penn was born on October 14, 1644, at his father's town house on Tower Hill in London, just a few steps from the great fortress whose dungeons he would come to know so well. His father, an ambitious young naval captain, had just received his first important command. At twenty-three, William Penn, Sr., had charge of the *Fellowship,* a vessel of 300 tons, which at the time happened to be anchored a short way down the Thames. When word reached the captain that his wife was about to give birth to their first child, he ordered all oars into action to take him upstream to London and arrived at his house just in time to learn that Margaret and her little boy were doing well. In those days, fewer than half of all children born reached maturity, but the baby seemed strong and healthy enough for a fair chance at survival.

Captain Penn had orders to sail for the Irish Sea to deal with those troublesome Irish Catholics, who still would not willingly accept English domination, even though Cromwell massacred their garrisons, on the ground that "this was the righteous judgment of God upon these barbarous wretches." But Captain Penn had wrangled a brief stay of orders so that, on October 23, 1644, he could attend little William's baptism. The ceremony took place at All Hallows, Barking, a squat, square-towered church built of great stones in the style of early English Gothic. A day or so after the christening, Captain

Penn left for his dangerous mission against Irish blockade runners, not to see his wife and little son again for almost two years.

As a sailor's wife, Margaret was accustomed to her husband's long absences. In any case, she was used to being by herself, having been widowed for a while before meeting Captain Penn. Her first husband, Nicasius van der Schuren, had been a Dutch merchant with whom she had lived in Ireland, at Kilrush on River Shannon. She herself may have been of Dutch ancestry, descended from a merchant family of Rotterdam. But this lineage is not clearly established, and her maiden name of Jasper could be either Dutch or English.

Margaret was widowed after only one year of marriage to Nicasius, and shortly thereafter Irish Catholics raided the Protestant settlement at Kilrush. She and her father escaped with little but their lives and took refuge in London, and in her new marriage she regained stability after the unsettling experience of widowhood and exile. Captain Penn's salary was modest, but since Cromwell had removed the administration of the English Navy from the King's personal caprice, at least the money came regularly. The house on Tower Hill was quite comfortable, and, according to an official building census, "consisted of one hall and parlor and kitchen with a divided cellar . . . and above stairs in the first story two fair chambers and in the second story two more chambers and two garrets over the same with a yard before."

While the captain blockaded the Irish, Margaret tended little William and supervised the servants. An unremarkable woman, with no particular interests or talents of her own, she was completely overshadowed by her flamboyant husband. A neighbor and friend of later years, Samuel Pepys, describes her in his famous diary as a "well-looked, fat, short old Dutch woman, but one who hath been heretofore pretty handsome." This rude comment may reflect a measure of chagrin on Pepys's part. Earlier, Pepys seems to have been rather taken by Mrs. Penn's "heretofore" prettiness, and gossip persisted that Margaret's notoriously ribald neighbor found many ways to console her for her husband's absence at sea. In view of Mr. Pepys's reputation, this was not an unlikely assumption. In view of Margaret's character, it was. Though, by one description, she appeared "happy-go-lucky, fond of a frolick, and remarkably untidy," the little information available about her suggests a woman of sturdy decency, not apt to be led astray by Mr. Pepys's persuasions. Besides, Mrs. Pepys was her best friend.

As for the captain, he was even at early age noted for his maritime skill and stood out among the well-born bumblers who infested the naval officer corps. He had such sure command over his crew that he could reliably execute complex maneuvers in all kinds of weather and, according to one contemporary report, "was not equalled for knowledge of navall affayres."

He had learned his trade young. From the age of ten he had sailed with his father, Giles Penn, the owner of a merchant ship. Fascinated by anything having to do with ships and the sea, the boy learned quickly. At seventeen he was competent to assume command of his father's vessel and plied the Atlantic and Mediterranean coasts.

From his many trading trips to the Mediterranean, Giles Penn, the ship owner, had a thorough knowledge of local conditions, and King Charles I entrusted the old merchant sailor with a consular mission to the Barbary Coast. It is likely that on this occasion the old sailor's son came to the King's attention as a teen-age shipmaster. The King was looking for such young men. He was building up his Navy for possible use as a counter-force against his domestic opponents in Parliament, who had marshaled a rebel army under a Puritan general named Cromwell. The King needed naval officers who were unquestioningly loyal as well as technically competent. He wanted to catch them young, before they had a chance to become embroiled in the political struggles then rampant in England. Young Penn filled this particular bill perfectly and was offered a commission in the Royal Navy.

Contrary to the King's expectations, the young officer knew more than one way to trim sails to the prevailing wind. He retained his commission even after the Royal Navy ceased to be royal. The Puritan rebels under Cromwell, with the blessing of Parliament, had occupied London and taken over the Admiralty. Yet the King and his Cavaliers were still holding out at Oxford, and the final outcome of the great Puritan uprising was by no means certain. Captain Penn, despite his youth, was a prudent man who hoped that if he just followed orders, no matter who gave them, nobody would get particularly angry at him. His courage was mostly military. This may explain why the captain was so amenable. Almost everybody liked him, and one report describes him as "mild-spoken" and "easy of accesse so no person went from him discontented."

It must have been hard for Captain Penn to leave his family so soon after little William's birth, but the assignment to Ireland brought him at least one consolation. He headed for the region from which his wife had been forced to flee some years before, and staged a land raid during which his sailors burned "all the villages and houses along that bay." After this personal contribution to the pacification of Ireland, he turned to more important tasks in the service of his new master. The guns of his ship, deployed at point-blank range, scattered the soldiers of the King who were laying siege to Cromwell's men at the castle fortress of Youghal. The captain's particular combination of technical competence and personal courage was noticed by his superiors, and on his return, in 1645, he was rewarded with a promotion: Now he was Rear Admiral of the Irish Sea.

The resounding new title didn't keep him from landing in jail the following year. There were no specific charges, but Penn seems to have made the wrong friends in Ireland. He had been the guest of such influential Royalists as Lord Iniquin and Lord Broghill. Besides, for all his cautious blandness, Penn apparently could not quite hide his own conservative leanings. Taught since childhood to recognize rank and order aboard ship, he was temperamentally inclined to accept authority. The idea of absolute monarchy, desperately defended by the beleaguered King, appealed to him more strongly than the new parliamentary government. In the politically roiling London of the time, feverish with intrigue and treason, there was just one thing to do with a man of doubtful loyalty: lock him up.

But within a month Cromwell ordered the Admiral set free. England could not afford to keep her most capable naval commander in jail, and, while Cromwell didn't really trust Penn, he wanted to use him where he could do the most good and no particular harm. So he sent him off with a task force of three squadrons to harass the Dutch, who had been taking advantage of England's domestic troubles to drive her merchant ships from Europe's coastal waters. Chasing the Dutch all the way down to Gibraltar and beyond would keep Admiral Penn busy and far away.

The assignment marked the beginning of nearly twenty years of intermittent naval warfare against the Dutch, from which the elder Penn emerged as a national hero, a man of great wealth, and a Knight of the Realm. In short, the Admiral was now set on the course that was to bring him into direct collision with his son.

During his long absences, the Admiral worried about leaving Margaret and little William alone in London. The city was hardly safe at the time, and certainly not a good place for bringing up children. True, the civil war was over. The King had been captured and Cromwell's victory was complete. But the crisis persisted. Too many lives had been disrupted. Uprooted men from the provinces, hapless veterans from Cromwell's "people's army," unable to find work or fit themselves to urban ways, prowled the streets of London, living by theft and robbery. Because many farmers had been driven from the land, the crops were neglected and the food supply for London had become unreliable. Even though Cromwell was taxing rich Royalists into poverty to pay the cost of his having defeated them, he could neither halt the rampant inflation nor provide the social services needed to deal with the human blight that always follows in the wake of war.

The Puritans' main program for improving moral conditions and public safety had the advantage of costing nothing. They simply banned all public sports and amusements. Ignorant of history, they didn't understand that in the absence of bread people must have circuses. At any rate, the Puritan scheme for moral uplift didn't work. Deprived of sports, music, dancing, and theater, the lower classes lacked suitable outlets for their natural exuberance, and their energies became increasingly diverted into brawls and other forms of surly violence. A gentleman walking in the street might have a chamber pot emptied on him from one of the overhanging balconies of London's half-timbered houses, and some disgruntled castoff from Cromwell's army—cheated of earlier hopes and no longer believing anyone's promises—might even address a rude remark to a person of quality. And with its theaters closed and all music silenced, London was as dull as it was dangerous.

Even basic sanitation failed under the mass influx of displaced persons. Large parts of the city had become warrens none too careful about waste disposal. The great fire and the plague, that broke out some years later, merely capped this long period of municipal decay.

Under these conditions, the Admiral thought it best to move his family to the suburbs. After all, little William had already caught the pox in the filthy city. Aside from making all his hair fall out, it had done no lasting damage. But the boy felt very self-conscious about wearing a wig, and who knew what might happen next in Cromwell's rotten capital?

With his now ample salary, the Admiral bought an estate at Wanstead, near the village of Chigwell, in Essex. For little William, it meant escape from a London back yard and his first experience of country life. It must have been a delightful and durable impression, for throughout his later writings Penn extolled the pleasures of rural living, and even in his plans for the city of Philadelphia he specified an ample garden for each house. It was probably at Wanstead that he first conceived his passionate love for trees, shrubs, and flower gardens, which he later indulged at extravagant expense.

The Penns' house was fully staffed with servants, and the estate produced its own supplies of grains, groceries, and livestock—an important consideration in those uncertain times. Yet Wanstead lay only eleven miles beyond the thirty-five-foot wall that still encircled London, so Margaret could visit her old friends occasionally. And if the weather was good she would sometimes send a servant into the city to fetch a pound or so of little William's favorite dish—a venison paté from a certain pie shop in Fetter Lane.

The nearest villages, Wanstead and Chigwell, were both typical of the region. Bay windows and balconies jutting from half-timbered houses, and the wide eaves of thatched roofs, created many sheltered places in the narrow streets where one might duck in for a while if the English drizzle encouraged itself to the point of actual rain. The larger houses, set back on well-tended greens, were mostly of stone and conveyed a comfortable feeling of solidity. The setting seemed to neutralize the turmoil of the times with the reassurance of sturdy beams and thick walls.

It was here that William received his primary education, at Chigwell School, one of the better institutions of its kind. As yet there was no public education in England, and virtually all schools, from primary schools to universities, were affiliated with the Anglican Church. For the most part, these schools enrolled only children considered teachable—which meant that they had parents who could read and write. In effect, this practice excluded the lower classes. As a rule, a child from a poor family could gain an education only if a wellborn sponsor took an interest in his abilities. Among Penn's contemporaries, Isaac Newton, for example, obtained his education by attracting the attention of a generous neighbor who at his own expense sent the exceptionally bright farm boy to school.

With its high ceilings, supported by stout beams, the main classroom at Chigwell resembled the great hall of a baronial castle. The furnishings were sparse, consisting mainly of long desks and benches, and the high stone walls were bare. But, as seen on an old engraving, the atmosphere of the school was by no means somber. Light streaming into the tall windows gave the lecture hall an aura of cheerful spaciousness, enhanced in winter by an open fire.

Each weekday morning from six to eleven and afternoons from one to six, William sat here, copying passages from books —still rare and costly items at the time—while the master, seated on a raised platform, expounded the text.

The curriculum at Chigwell reflected the classical taste of Dr. Samuel Harsnett, Archbishop of York, the school's founder. Even before the age of ten, William was fluent in Latin and Greek. He read Cicero and Terence to improve his prose. Homer and Vergil were his models for poetry. Modern literature was banned from the shelves at Chigwell. It just wouldn't do to expose the young to the corrupting influence of Shakespeare, a man without dogma and an unblinking skeptic who saw, behind all human passion, man's fate as the "quintessence of dust." And Milton, the main contemporary writer, whose *Paradise Lost* was still in the making, seemed even worse in his arrogant struggles with God. Penn's heroic optimism and unbending rectitude may have been instilled by the cast of this curriculum, with its consistent stress on classical writings in praise of uncomplicated virtues. By the same token, the neglect of English literature beyond Chaucer left Penn with a certain clumsiness in the use of his native language.

The class schedule allowed little time for sports, but William managed to find a regular outlet for his abundant physical energy. The special pride of Chigwell School was a large bell donated by the founder, who also left an annuity of twenty shillings a year to the man who rang it. Each morning the bell would summon the students from the village. At the peal of the bell, William—who was a remarkable runner even then—would sprint the distance of more than three miles from his home to school. Foot racing was his favorite sport, and it probably put him into the sound physical condition that later helped him withstand the rigors of prison without serious damage to his health.

Chigwell was just the kind of school the Admiral would have chosen for his son. Soundly conservative, it was not at all hospitable to current Cromwellian notions of governmental reform. Apparently, the Admiral never abandoned hope for a return of the monarchy, and was educating his son for some future court position. He wanted William to have the formal manners and classical erudition deemed suitable for advisors to the King.

Though Chigwell described itself as "neither Papist nor Puritan," the school was evidently influenced by the Puritanism prevalent under Cromwell. A teacher, for example, was supposed to exhibit "only grave behavior" to his pupils, to be "severe" in discipline, and "no tipler nor haunter of alehouses, no puffer of tobacco." Above all, he was to "stir up the buds of virtue in his pupils' youth." No humor was to be allowed, for the Cromwellian era reveled in unrelieved earnestness—a "long divorce of wit from virtue," as Addison called it. A proper school was expected to squelch any natural levity its pupils might have.

William was lastingly marked by all this gloom. As far as is known, he never told a joke and would not have understood one. Though he later opposed the Puritans on theological as well as political grounds, he remained essentially Puritan in personal conduct, and despite his own later doctrine of "soul freedom," he sometimes overstepped the line between probity and priggishness.

During William's years at Wanstead, a momentous event took place. At the age of five he was far too young to understand it, but in retrospect and in consequence it shaped his thought and destiny. On January 30, 1649, King Charles I was beheaded. On the scaffold the King undoubtedly made a far greater mark upon history than his rather dim wit and obstinate temper would have allowed him to make on the throne. Of course, kings had been killed before, regicide being one of the oldest strategies either for power grabs or for genuine radical reform. But the execution of Charles I marked the first time a king had been subjected to legal process in his own realm by elected representatives. The feudal faith in the holiness of kingship had been shattered. Mere mortals had sat in judgment over a royal person, a creature hitherto presumed sacrosanct, holding power by divine right. Nothing comparable had happened for almost a thousand years—not since 695 A.D., when the extravagance of the Byzantine emperor Justinian II so annoyed his council that they sentenced him to have his nose cut off. But few Englishmen knew about that. To them, the events of the day were singular and overwhelming. For a generation who still believed that the mere touch of the royal hand could cure illness, it was as shocking as it was liberating to discover that even an anointed head could be severed. That stroke of the ax, more than anything else, raised the crucial questions of freedom and authority to which Penn devoted so much of his mature reflection.

After the King's death, Cromwell's power was so secure that the politically unreliable Admiral Penn could now be allowed to come home more often. One result of his more frequent visits was little Peggy Penn, who was born about 1652. She grew up into a notably charming and sprightly girl, a point not lost on the lecherous Pepys. It seems that he pursued Pegg as eagerly as he had once courted her mother, and with as little success. Stung by these romantic disappointments, he grew more and more peevish toward the Penns, filling his diary with scurrilous slurs about them. He complained of Mrs. Penn's "sluttishness" and accused the Admiral of advancing through bribery and enriching himself by plunder. Pepys himself liked to dip into Navy funds while serving at the Admiralty, and perhaps he was furious at Penn for getting there first on occasion. Penn was later accused of having conducted treasury raids on his own behalf, but the charge was never made to stick. More likely, Pepys simply felt that by running down the Admiral's reputation, he justified his own pursuit of Penn's daughter. By seducing Miss Penn, according to this logic, Pepys punished the wicked Admiral. Lechery was thus ennobled and malice made praiseworthy.

Pepys carefully buried these psychological explosives in his diary. Outwardly, the two families remained friendly throughout the years, and the Penns and Pepyses continued to invite each other for dinner. Pepys, who was as much a snob about food as about anything else, huffed about the plain cooking at Penn's house. True to form, he railed at Penn in his diary as a boorish sailor unable to appreciate refinements of cuisine. As for young Pegg, who loosened this avalanche of chagrin by being so exceptionally pretty, she married at fifteen, moved to Yorkshire, and subsided into obscurity.

By 1653 the frequent but indecisive skirmishes with the Dutch had burst into open war. The newly formed Republic of the Netherlands, bolstered by the Treaty of Westphalia and full of mercantile verve, earnestly challenged Britain's power at sea. More than a hundred ships were now deployed in the opposing navies, and Penn, whose courage matched his pugnacity, was eager to engage the Dutch in a full-scale battle. As a fighter, Penn had the ability to combine sound strategy with blind rage—a rare and winning combination. Indeed, the father of the world's first great political pacifist had the temperament and method of a successful barroom brawler. Once, while walking home from a dinner with Pepys, the Admiral suddenly hurled himself against a stranger on horseback to avenge some imagined slight. Time and again he leapt up at the rearing horse to strike at its rider, until he had unseated his adversary and pinned him to the ground.

On the crucial day of the sea battle of Texel, Penn was similarly inspired by an insult. The Dutch commander, Admiral van Tromp, had tied a twig broom to the top of his mast, betokening his intent to sweep the English from the sea. When that upturned broom loomed in Penn's spyglass before the battle, he took grave offense. That broom wasn't just a case of misplaced symbolism; other factors added to Penn's indignation. It was just then becoming customary for opposing military commanders to act as gentlemen, to spar for tactical positions—to yield on points, as it were—without actually inflicting too much damage. But this style of warfare was a serious game and did not allow for mockery. If the Dutch couldn't observe proper etiquette, the war would have to be fought differently.

At any rate, the Dutch paid dearly for van Tromp's whimsy. With the recklessness inspired by outrage, Penn vowed to have his men board the Dutch flagship and haul down that broom. After sinking or otherwise disabling thirty Dutch escort vessels, Penn's guns came within range of van Tromp's ship, hammering it with broadsides until its masts broke and the broom trailed in the water. Incapable of maneuvering, van Tromp was now an easy prey, and Penn's crew soon succeeded in grappling his crippled ship. Swarming aboard, the English sailors slaughtered most of the Dutch survivors by forcing them below hatches and blowing them up with their own powder. It was, at last, a decisive victory.

Sea couriers in swift vessels took the good news of the battle to shore. From there, relay riders carried the message to London. By the time Admiral Penn's flagship, the *James,* slowly moved up the Thames toward the capital, a triumphal welcome had been prepared. Even with her battle scars, the *James* was a thrilling sight as she came into view for the waiting Londoners. With a thousand gross tons, she had a massive hull with a high and richly carved poop, surmounted by three tall masts each fitted with square sails, and from her sides gaped the mouths of seventy cannon.

English national pride, shattered in the civil war, now surged once more. For Penn had proved that the new Commonwealth of England was as formidable as the old English monarchy that had sent the Armada to the bottom. Once more, as in the days of Elizabeth, Britannia did in fact rule the sea. To a people largely perplexed by their own revolution, guilt-ridden for killing their king, fearful of their freedom and confused about their aims, Penn's victory was a tonic to self-esteem. Overnight the Admiral had become a popular idol, and not even the grudging Cromwell could any longer withhold public honor.

It was also a banner day for a little boy waiting for his father to come home. His father was so often away, doing daring and dangerous things. One never knew if he would come back. And when he did come to the house at Wanstead for a brief stay, he was irascible with the servants and formal and remote toward his family. After all, he had been at sea since an early age and wasn't used to intimacy. Little William must have found his father difficult.

But this day made a difference. At the age of nine, William was able to sense the feelings of the crowd. His father must be a dear and good man, after all, if all these people admired him so. William was proud of his father. Even in later years, when the conflict between the military hero and his pacifist son became something of a national embarrassment as well as a source of deep personal distress to both Penns, William preserved an attitude of affectionate regard for his father despite their disagreements.

Since Penn was already an admiral, Cromwell had to invent a new rank to reward him with a promotion. He made Penn "General of the Sea." As a bonus, he bestowed on him a large estate in Ireland, at Macroom, some twenty miles west of Cork. At one stroke, Penn was rich beyond all his hopes.

Cromwell's generosity was part of a plan. Officially, the Irish estate was given to Penn as restitution for the loss suffered by his wife during the Irish rebellion, though her own holdings never approached the princely magnitude of Cromwell's grant. In fact, the award to Penn was just one more item in Cromwell's pacification policy for Ireland.

Having failed to daunt Irish resistance, Cromwell tried to uproot a population that ravage alone could not subdue. He seized Irish landholdings and parceled them out among Englishmen he wanted to reward or buy off. The estates were then to be settled by their new owners with reliable Protestants from England or Scotland, the latter forming a new ethnic group known as the Scotch-Irish. By such means Cromwell drove the Catholic Irish from their communities, dispersed them to assure their political impotence, and made them homeless captives in their own land. In short, Cromwell was teaching the British their first lesson in colonialism.

Admiral Penn had no objection to accepting his bounty on these terms. As a military man, he was accustomed to dealing woe to the vanquished, and he believed in the principle of loot. And Cromwell could be sure that a man like Penn would know just how to deal with any local insurgence.

The Admiral's lawyers were still busy transferring to him

the title to the ancestral lands and castle of the Catholic Earl of Clancarty, when Cromwell urged him on a new mission. Penn was to raise Britain's flag over the West Indies.

The discovery of the Caribbean had triggered a colonial frenzy among western Europe's seafaring nations. Those islands would make convenient strongholds from which to extend Europe's westward reach toward the yet unmeasured riches of America.

Colonizing was prompted not by the need for raw materials or controlled markets. These classical motives of colonizers gained force only after the industrialization of western Europe and the consequent pursuit of mercantile policies. What inspired the earlier colonizers was the simple fact that Europe had run out of land. Since about 1500, almost all the land in Europe had been owned, drained, and cultivated. The frontier had vanished. With land ownership still regarded as the only basic source of wealth and the only badge of privilege, European rulers needed more land to parcel out to their aristocracies and became ravenous for new territory. France, Holland, Spain, and Denmark were scrambling for possession of Caribbean outposts. Emboldened by Penn's triumph over the Dutch, Cromwell now dispatched his victorious admiral to garner the island of Hispaniola. His ships were to carry an army of seven thousand, and so eager was Cromwell to get the expedition under way that Penn couldn't even spend Christmas with his family. On December 25, 1654, his fleet put to sea from Spithead.

Margaret and the two children now were alone again at Wanstead, much to the relief of the servants, whom the Admiral had treated like a mutinous crew. Even little William may have felt easier now that he was no longer awed by his father tromping about the house in his wide-topped sea boots. Up to this time, William had shown no signs of uncommon qualities, but after the Admiral's visit following the victory at Texel, a change came over William. Perhaps it was his father's

sudden prominence and wealth, along with the public adulation bestowed on him, that awakened some reflective trait in
the boy. Or he may have been struck by the contrast between
the dignified ceremonies honoring his father and the coarse
seafaring company his father brought to the house to regale
with mutton, beer, and bloody tales of battle. At any rate,
something in the boy's experience evidently prompted his
search for deeper explanations.

In his eleventh year he began to read seriously on his own.
Among the books that fell into his hand was a volume entitled *Sparkles of Glory,* the work of an eccentric recluse
named John Saltmarsh, who wrote mystic rhapsodies about
the immanence of God in all things. Years later Penn recalled
that "the Lord first appeared to me" while he meditated on
the murky effusions of Saltmarsh. Whatever this experience
may have been, it seems clear that the boy's religious sensibility had somehow been awakened. The world would no longer
appear to Penn merely as things, people, and events. From
here on, his young mind would penetrate beyond appearance
in search of essence and meaning.

It has been said that thought is born of failure and perplexity. If that is so, young William soon had plenty of motive
to develop his newly formed tendency to contemplation.
Trouble suddenly fell upon the family.

The Caribbean venture ended badly. Unused to jungle
warfare, the British were routed by Haitian natives, who did
not fight in military formation but staged hit-and-run assaults
from ambush. The English commander, General Robert Venables, was unprepared for such ungentlemanly tactics. His
forces suffered heavy losses and failed to occupy Hispaniola.
Unwilling to return empty-handed, Penn sailed for Jamaica,
and succeeded in claiming this island for Britain. But Cromwell did not graciously accept this consolation prize. It didn't
matter that Jamaica was in many ways a more valuable

island. The orders had called for the occupation of Hispaniola, and when anything went wrong Cromwell considered treason to be the most likely explanation. Admiral Penn and General Venables expected honors and rewards for their capture of Jamaica, but they had no sooner landed in England than Cromwell cast them both in the Tower. For returning to England without specific orders Penn was accused of having "deserted." But this was patently a pretext. Cromwell's real suspicion was that Penn had conspired abroad with exiled Royalists to stage an invasion of England.

Given the Admiral's secret royalism, Cromwell's hunch may well have been true, but he couldn't mobilize evidence against Penn. No formal charge of treason was filed, and Penn was too prominent a person to let rot in jail without trial. He was soon set free, but stripped of his command. With his career apparently at an end, Penn thought it wiser to leave England and retire with his family to his Irish lands, which Cromwell didn't dare reclaim from the once popular hero.

Macroom Castle, judged by its present ruins, was sturdy and square, built of large gray stones, with heavy battlements and a crenellated roof. A company of soldiers was stationed within the castle walls to protect it against possible assault from the resentful Irish. Just outside the walls stood a small village, now housing the newly imported Protestant peasants who worked the thousands of acres belonging to the estate. Young William, already given to much quiet reflection, must have thought a great deal about the conditions surrounding him. Certainly the context of Ireland contrasted sharply with the placid environment he had known in Essex. Laid waste by Cromwell's fury, the villages were in ruins, the fields neglected, one-third of the population killed or maimed, and the survivors embittered by the systematic suppression of their faith and their native language.

The shattered and hostile land with its grieving people seems to have kindled in young William those impulses toward compassion and justice which marked his entire religious and political life. Later he recalled that during his stay in Ireland, between the ages of twelve and fifteen, "the Lord visited me, and gave me divine Impressions of Himself."

In this frame of mind young William encountered Thomas Loe, a missionary traveling in Ireland to preach the newly formed precepts of the Society of Friends, commonly called the Quakers. Because of his unconventional views, Loe was maligned by both the native Catholics and their Protestant conquerors. Admiral Penn was warned about the presence of this heretic near his estate. Normally, he might have ordered his hounds to be loosed on such a stranger. But his own imprisonment and humiliation seem to have mellowed him. "Let us hear the man before we judge him," the Admiral said. In an untypical gesture of tolerance, the Admiral invited the Quaker missionary to Macroom Castle. Before the assembled household, Loe discoursed on the doctrine of the Inner Light— of direct mystical communication with the Infinite.

That kind of talk was just what young William needed to hear. He had been having secret, private conversations with God, and here, for the first time, was another person to confirm his own experience. What must have been to William a lonely and even frightening encounter with his own spiritual potential was now validated by another. If William had suffered the self-doubt that often accompanies religious sensibility, this new sense of sharing must have lifted a great burden from him.

Of course, William was too young and too shy to confide to the wandering preacher his own religious intuitions. But something in the back of his mind must have clicked into a conceptual pattern that later disposed him toward serious theological concerns.

Less than a year later, the Irish exile ended. Cromwell had died. Royalism was resurgent. The Admiral promptly returned to London to join his influential friends in a plot to bring the son of the executed King, Prince Charles, back to England's empty throne.

The time seemed ripe for such a move. Charismatic leaders like Cromwell had never been able to solve the problem of succession. Without him, England's political imagination could not find a focus. The Parliament fumbled, and many who had once sided with the revolution now turned against it.

The poor felt betrayed. Lured to Cromwell's cause by the vague socialist hopes that often set the tone of utopian movements, the lower classes had formed Cromwell's "people's army." They pitted the courage of their despair against the professionalism of the King's soldiers. But they had won Cromwell's victory, not their own. Once in power, Cromwell drew his main support not from those who had actually fought for him but from another group who had also opposed the King: the new middle class, the businessmen and entrepreneurs wanting to break the trade monopolies the King had reserved for himself and his favorites. This aim had now been accomplished; free enterprise had been assured.

The liberated merchant class soon tired of drab Puritan government. Having money and status, they also wanted display. They chafed at the Puritan curbs on luxury and longed to recover the delights of art, fashion, and frivolity. Feeling certain that a constitutionally revised monarchy would no longer interfere with business, they would just as soon have the King back. The middle class, having successfully taken its measure against the aristocracy, now envisioned itself as the backbone of a restored monarchy, and rich burghers began lusting after titles.

Sensing the favorable climate and counting on his fame as a patriot and hero, the Admiral ran for Parliament and won a seat in the House of Commons. From this position of influence he quickly made himself a key figure in the plot to bring Prince Charles back from exile. His spacious new house on

Tower Hill, just outside the Navy Office Gardens, was alive with intrigue, secret meetings and furtive messengers, and elegant dinners with important persons. Young William watched these machinations with the observant detachment that increasingly marked his character. He was probably not too surprised when, in April, 1660, his father suddenly disappeared.

Almost everyone in England guessed the purpose of Admiral Penn's "secret" voyage. With thirty-one ships, he set out for Scheveningen, on the Dutch coast, to fetch the son of the slain King. It was typical of Penn that he had not taken official command of this excursion, leaving that honor to General Montagu. His own role was strictly unofficial. He had learned to be cautious. But when the future King stepped aboard, he knew who was his true friend. He bade Penn to kneel before him, laid the royal sword upon the sailor's shoulder, and when the Admiral rose to his feet, he was a Knight of the Realm: Sir William Penn.

There was yet another name change on that trip. The ship itself, the flagship of the English Navy, was called the *Naseby*, after one of Cromwell's victorious battles—clearly an unsuitable name for the occasion. So in mid-Channel the ship was rechristened the *Royal Charles*. News of her impending arrival had preceded her to England, and when she docked at Dover her illustrious passengers were welcomed in triumph by "twenty-thousand horses and foots, brandishing their swords and shouting with inexpressible joy; the wayes were strew'd with flowers, the bells ringing, the streets hung with tapistry, fountaines running with wine."

Sir William was now one of the most famous and powerful men in England, and his son, just setting off to Oxford for his education, clearly enjoyed splendid prospects.

Three

THE FIRST REBELLION

> Everything which is known is known not according to
> its own nature but rather according to the capacity of
> the knower.
>
> —BOETHIUS

October mist already hung over the towers of Oxford when
William arrived at the university in the fall of 1660. The
broad meadows sloping from the quadrangles of Christ Church
down to the Thames had already turned autumnal brown, and
the forked Gothic of bare trees framed the pinnacles of the
city. The town within its walls seemed to be drawing into itself
against the oncoming winter, seeking shelter in its own countless nooks, arcades, and archways.

But the somber cast of gray stone and gray sky could not
daunt William's exuberant anticipation. He came with a hun-
gry mind and expected a feast. He had been away from school
for years. During his exile in Ireland, and later in London,
his education had been in the hands of private tutors. No
doubt they were competent enough, but hardly equal to
William's intellectual eagerness. Precocious and intense reading had left him with large questions he did not yet know to
be unanswerable. This innocence, this trust in knowledge,
raised high his expectations of Oxford.

In contrast to his febrile intellectual tension, his outward life was comfortable enough. From his window in the great quadrangle of Christ Church, he could look out on one of the most splendid and harmonious vistas ever achieved by English architecture. As a gentleman scholar, he was assigned a servant to take care of his rooms and see to his clothes. He took his meals in the great dining room of the college, seated with the other students at long tables running the full length of the hall, while the masters of the college dined at the transverse high table under the cathedral-like vaulting. The glitter of these banquets was only slightly dimmed by the use of pewter for table settings. The late King Charles had melted Oxford's famous silverware into coin to pay his troops.

Unlike the setting, the meals were prosaic. The English manner of cooking was already well established, and everyone hacked away at thick joints of beef or mutton, which were accompanied by leeks and cabbage. Great tankards of beer and ale were swilled, water being considered unhealthy. With sewage constantly seeping into the wells, there was good reason to distrust water.

The students divided into two groups, easily distinguished by attire and length of hair. The older students, who had entered the university under Cromwell's regime, were mostly Puritans, with close-cropped hair, dark-brown cassocks, and worsted stockings. They were a quiet, studious group, old beyond their age, their manners reflecting sternly Presbyterian attitudes. Students entered since the recent upswing of Royalism came mostly from aristocratic Cavalier families. With their brightly colored coats, embroidered vests, lace-trimmed breeches, silk stockings, and flowing locks, they presented a provocative contrast to the Puritans, who were greatly vexed at this change in the student body. Of all the irritant habits of the Cavaliers, nothing irked the Puritans as much as the long hair. For ever since Puritans had come into conflict with the English Establishment, they had regarded long hair on men as the badge of loose morals.

The two groups were as alien to each other as species from different planets. The Puritans were disciplined and earnest. The Cavaliers, by one contemporary account, "had no aim but to live like gentlemen, keep dogs and horses, to turn their studies and coleholes into places to receive bottles, and to swash in apparell."

These elegant gentlemen seemed out of place in the ancient university, which had been a center of Scholasticism since the days of Abelard and had later become a focus of humanist learning. The Cavaliers also created more tangible problems. Always itching for a fight or chasing after women, they were stirring up trouble in town, and for a while it seemed as if the old warfare between Town and Gown, between the local population and the university, might flare up again in all its bloody violence.

Social groups just freed from suppression tend to be intemperate, and these fashionable young men, gloating over their return to power, were notably nasty. Their swashbuckling was often a façade for vengeful cruelty and cowardice. They took special pleasure in baiting members of nonconformist sects, mainly Quakers, who were trying to win support for the cause of religious freedom at a time when the Royalists were once again tightening the shackles of Anglican orthodoxy. To the delight of bemused bystanders, these young academicians would pounce upon some hapless Quaker expounding his views, beat him senseless, and then revive him by a dunking in the icy Thames.

They indulged such sports with immunity. For one thing, they were gentlemen, and no constable mindful of his career would interfere with them. Besides, the new Royalist government discouraged religious dissent and discussion. By thrashing nonconformists, the young Cavaliers did precisely what the police themselves wanted to do but felt constrained from doing for reasons of political discretion.

Penn was in an awkward position. He didn't like to see

Quakers, or anyone else, get beaten up. He had no official connection with the sect. He was as Anglican as the snottiest of Cavaliers. But he recalled that night in Ireland when Thomas Loe, the Quaker missionary, had come to talk at his father's castle. He remembered how that moment had flooded his inner perceptions with a new light, and he knew that these insights sustained his continuing quest for deeper knowledge. Perhaps he also knew that Thomas Loe, the man who had so inspired him, was in Oxford, too—not among the illustrious faculty but in the town jail, kept there for his nonconformist views.

Penn's natural compassion went out to the Quaker demonstrators when he saw them go down under the fists and clubs of his fellow students for thinking as he himself was thinking privately and for speaking as he himself would speak, had he yet found the words.

To add to his confusion, he himself was regarded as a Royalist. As the Admiral's son, he belonged to the foremost rank of the newly risen Establishment. The very clothes he wore marked him as a member of the new ruling class that so blatantly asserted its power and its style against Oxford's somber tradition. In temperament he was actually closer to the scholarly Puritans. But in their own way the Puritans were as narrow and intolerant as the boisterous Cavaliers, and they were deeply suspicious of the son of Admiral Penn, whom they considered a traitor to the Commonwealth. Thus the tensions between the student groups mirrored the conflict of world views that had sundered England. William, at seventeen, was lost between them both. Apparently, he had no friends and for a while withdrew into solitude and books.

The curriculum at Oxford was certainly more than enough to keep him occupied, and his studies were thorough, if one-sided. Science, just then awakening in Newton's physics and Boyle's chemistry, was not yet part of the general plan of study. This was also true at other universities, and, in consequence, even educated men of the period were often as ignorant of scientific methods for testing truth as the most superstitious peasant. This may explain why witchcraft, magic, and demon possession still passed as likely explanations for otherwise puzzling occurrences or irksome personality traits.

The general curriculum placed single-minded stress on the traditional mainstays of scholarship: history and philosophy. Students wormed through a staggering reading list. They plowed through classical historians from Thucydides to Plutarch. And starting from the lucid peaks of Plato, Aristotle, and the Stoics, students trailed into the thickets of medieval philosophy, to arrive finally at more recent writers such as Hobbes, Erasmus, and Descartes.

As a reader, Penn had the knack of quickly extracting essences. He gulped this heavy fare without notable indigestion and with perhaps deeper understanding than one normally expects from undergraduates. In any case, he acquired a life-long taste for disciplined reading, and his own later writings bear witness to a panoramic literacy.

Luckily, Penn escaped the scholar's fallacy of believing that reality resides in books. He took to heart Montaigne's admonition that "we must drink the spirit of the classics rather than learn their precepts," and remained free of the pedantry that so often defeats the purpose of learning. "More true knowledge comes by Meditation and Just Reflection than by Reading," he once advised a young man who had asked him for a list of works "most valuable for a moderate library."

The main effect of Penn's classical readings was to stamp him with that equable temper so valued in antiquity—that spirit of moderation that underlies the rich orchestration of Greek thought. Without this grounding in philosophy Penn's religious and political fervor might have degenerated into querulous bigotry. As it happened, he achieved the rare feat of turning his passion into a motive for tolerance.

Penn's first holiday from school turned out memorable in many ways. The journey home was not difficult. There was enough traffic between Oxford and London to make the road safe from highwaymen, and the coaches were of the latest type, with the passenger box hung on leather straps within the carriage frame. This suspension cushioned the bumps, though the horses sometimes had to slow down to keep the free-swinging coach from lurching too much. Still, unless the mud got too deep, the stagecoach covered the fifty-seven miles down to London in a day and a half, allowing for an overnight rest at Reading.

William had a special reason for this trip. The Royalists had prevailed. Prince Charles, the disputed heir to the throne whom the Admiral had fetched from exile, was at last to be crowned. The Admiral had been assigned a place of honor from which to watch the procession. Nearly two decades had passed since the Admiral had first been commissioned as a servant of the Crown—two distasteful decades during which the principles cherished by the Admiral had been reviled and flouted by radicals and revolutionaries. Now, at last, things would be set right in England once again. Once more there would be a Crown to serve.

By his own lights, the Admiral had been faithful to England in betraying its Government. He had virtually stolen England's fleet, sailing off to Holland to bring back the exiled Prince. Now that Prince was to become King, it was the Admiral's vindication; his own supreme moment. And he wanted his son to share it with him.

Proceeding through the Strand from St. Paul's to Whitehall, the coronation parade brought back to London the color and pageantry so sadly missed during the years of Puritan drabness. "So glorious was the show with gold and silver that we were not able to look at it, our eyes at last being so much overcome," notes Pepys in his diary. Another chronicler, John Evelyn, comments on the "magnificent traine on horseback, as rich as embroidery, velvet, gold and silver and jewells, could make them and their pransing horses." Triumphal arches, specially built for the occasion, rose above the flower-strewn streets, and rich tapestries hung from the windows along the way.

When the King and his brother, the Duke of York, reached the place where Admiral Penn and his son stood, on a raised platform among the onlookers, the King and the Duke, high in their saddles, turned toward them. Then the royal brothers raised their hands in greeting to the Admiral. It was an unprecedented gesture, a signal honor.

Exuberant over this sign of royal favor, the Admiral and his son spent several days together in their house on Tower Hill. Walking in the garden, the Admiral told William of his good fortune. He had been appointed Commissioner of the Navy, a post of cabinet rank with the munificent salary of £500 per year. As a further token of royal pleasure, the King had generously increased the Admiral's Irish estates, giving him the castle and lands of Kinsale, "with a foot company there for the defence and safety thereof . . . together with all fees, profits and advantages thereunto belonging." The Admiral was evidently unaware how odd it was that he now held grants from both Cromwell and the King. Proudly, he spoke to his son of the brilliant future awaiting him, and in their shared elation a new closeness sprang up between father and son. Fondly, they said farewell, as William set off again for Oxford.

Almost immediately after William's return to the university, his mind began to take adventurous turns. His classical readings apparently did not fully satisfy him, and he seemed to be casting about for other kinds of knowledge. His first exploration, strangely enough, took him briefly into medicine. The state of this art was still such that epidemics were sometimes blamed on the presence of Jews in a community, who were then executed as a sanitary measure. But like other sciences, medicine was just entering a more rational phase. William Harvey's discoveries of the pumping action of the heart and of blood circulation, published some years earlier, had alerted the medical faculty at Oxford to the merits of experimental research. Curiosity about this new method drove William into the dissecting room. There he may have encountered John Locke, another medical student at Oxford at the time. Slicing at cadavers, the two young men could hardly have foreseen how soon their interests would shift, or that both of them would have a lasting influence on the new continent of America.

Penn had his own way of looking at biology: "If Body and Soul were intermixedly and inseparably generated by Man," he wrote, "it would be no more difficult to find the Soul than any other Part. In case of operating or dissecting of living men, as I have at the University seen living Beasts [dissected] by Anatomists, it would be but rational that one should behold the very Thoughts, Purposes and Intents of such Men's Hearts and Souls."

The philosopher was forming within the biologist. Like Descartes before him, Penn searched for the anatomical soul and, by extension, for the rational God. Unlike Descartes, who mistook the pineal gland for the soul and logic for God, Penn found neither in these scientific pursuits. The physical body did not yield him the knowledge he yearned for. He had to search elsewhere.

The next turn was decisive. It took Penn right to the point where his genius caught fire: the intersection of religion and politics. The man who led him there was Dr. John Owen.

Owen streaked through Oxford like a shooting star—a brief illumination extinguished in a hostile atmosphere. Appointed dean of the university by Cromwell, Owen quickly cleared away the medieval cobwebs lovingly preserved by his predecessors, and ventilated Oxford with the fresh air of Erasmian humanism. Though a staunch Puritan, Owen evidently had some maverick notions. He believed that a university should permit the open encounter of ideas.

Now, for the first time, Oxford scholars could think out loud about two startling discoveries: First, that the earth is not the center of the universe, which made the location of heaven uncertain; second, that new stars were still forming in the sky, which meant that creation is going on all the time.

These fairly recent discoveries by Copernicus and Tycho Brahe cast doubt on the entire body of traditional thought embodied in scholastic philosophy. Christian cosmology was shaken to its roots. John Donne, churchman and poet, dispairingly exclaimed: " 'Tis all in pieces, all coherence gone . . ."

By admitting the new knowledge gained from astronomy and physics into the academic precincts of Oxford, Owen made bitter enemies. They could not forgive him that he invited to the faculty physical scientists—the ultimate radicals of their day—and encouraged them to delve by experiment into "The Book of Nature," which Owen believed might be read as profitably as the book of Revelations.

To make matters worse, the scientific "heresy" was spreading to other fields. Already men like Thomas Hobbes and James Harrington were picking up cues from physics and tried to lay the groundwork for a rational analysis of history and economics. They even had the gall and irreverence to probe into such troublesome subjects as the legitimacy of government and the nature of authority. Oxford under Dr. Owen was evidently breeding termites in the structure of traditional society.

When the Royalists regained power, one of their first acts was to fire Dr. Owen. They replaced him with Dr. John Fell, a pious Anglican with a genuine abhorrence of free inquiry. He earnestly relished his job as the new King's hatchet-man and swiftly decimated the faculty. As for Owen, it was hoped that he would fade quietly into genteel retirement.

But a man of Owen's enormous vitality couldn't live buried

in his library. He needed sparring partners. He had spent his life at the cutting edge of current issues; he longed for the stimulus of debate and for the interplay of personalities and ideas. A handful of the brightest students remained loyal to him, reviling the new dean in doggerel beginning "I do not love thee, Dr. Fell." Soon a permanent seminar developed around the fireplace of Dr. Owen's mansion. In effect, Owen was running an alternate university where topics shunned or twisted under the new Royalist regime received a free and thorough discussion.

How a Cavalier scholar like Penn, an acknowledged favorite of the new King, ever came to join Owen's underground movement remains uncertain. Very likely, it was through the custom of notebook-sharing that he first encountered members of the Owen group. Students seldom kept private notebooks. For one thing, before the invention of the continuous paper mill, paper was expensive, having to be pressed and trimmed sheet by sheet. Besides, in the absence of pencils, note-taking was too cumbersome to be done easily in class, requiring inkpot, quill, penknife, and drying sand. Instead, a group of several students would meet after class to reconstruct the lecture in a joint notebook by pooled recollection. As each student offered his own remembered version, those sessions often proved more stimulating and spirited than the lecture itself, and students naturally tended to seek out notebook partners of scholarly acumen comparable to their own. Penn probably didn't find many academic equals among the Cavaliers, and this may have led him into the circle of Owen's dissenters.

It was in this group that Penn first experienced the pleasure and exhilaration of informed, competent discussion. In Owen's mansion, Penn discovered his natural habitat. This was the kind of milieu he had longed for without even realizing it. For years he had been absorbed in private thoughts far more intense and systematic than the usual adolescent attempts to make sense of the world. Until now, these tendencies had isolated him from others. Now, suddenly, he found himself in a setting where his intellectual interests were no handicap. Penn's earlier loneliness must have been painful at an age when young people naturally yearn for companionship and acceptance. All the greater his joy at the discovery that thoughts and ideas, rather than being a silent hoard in his head, were actually a medium of exchange, and that deep pleasure and enrichment were to be drawn from such a trade.

His intellectual profit was at least equalled by his emotional gain. The open exchange of feelings and ideas led the seventeen-year-old Penn to a deeper understanding of himself. Formerly isolated, he now gained self-knowledge through interaction with others, recognized his own competence and strength, and rid himself of adolescent self-doubt.

He also gained the practical skills that would make him such a convincing advocate and polemicist. He learned the essential techniques of reasoned discourse: to crystallize his own thoughts and to test their validity. He also learned how to examine—or demolish—opposing arguments with fairness and courtesy.

Such discipline was particularly important for a young man with Penn's rather woolly leanings toward mystic religiosity; for people attuned to their own intuition tend to offer unsupported statements as truth. Prodded by Owen's exploring questions, Penn learned to marshal evidence and to avoid the common self-delusion of being uncritically in love with one's own notions.

Owen taught Penn to respect factual knowledge as the necessary basis for theorizing—an idea quite new at the time and never very popular with young students. It was probably from Owen that Penn learned to regard skeptical questioning as a way to arrive at truth, even religious truth. This attitude affected Penn profoundly. It made him resist all pressure toward orthodoxy, resolved to let religious doubt guide him toward a supportable faith.

During Penn's second year at Oxford, the administration clamped down on Dr. Owen. The university faced a dilemma. Under the new Royalist regime, education had two contradictory functions: One was to expose students to ideas; the other was to protect them from improper thoughts. It was difficult to do either; to do both was impossible; and Dr. Owen only complicated matters.

They couldn't fire him. He already had been fired. To proceed against Owen as a private person would have been awkward. He was, after all, a widely renowned scholar, and any attempt to muzzle him would have been poor public relations for England's new monarchy. Besides, what charge could be brought against him? That he was corrupting the youth of Oxford? Such an accusation would have raised eyebrows and maybe even opposition in a college town where people knew about Socrates. Where nothing can be done legally, administrative measures are called for. The new dean declared Owen's home off limits for matriculated students. Penn received a personal warning from his faculty advisor to stay away.

Thus Penn faced his first serious moral challenge. But by now he had the inner strength to meet it. He decided on the basis of principle, even though he knew that his career might be ruined. He ignored the warning and kept on visiting Owen. It was his first rebellion.

The university imposed a formal fine and reprimand and notified the Admiral of his son's misconduct. The Admiral was stunned. Everything had been going so well, with William obviously slated for a high court position after completion of his studies. Now suddenly William was showing traits that threatened his father's ambitions. Of course, the Admiral had noticed that William tended to be rather peculiar at times, too thoughtful perhaps, and reading too much. But he had assumed this behavior was just part of growing up. During the Admiral's boyhood, the other sailors had often taken him into port to share their entertainments. Young William had lacked such opportunities, so it was understandable that he was a bit moody. Once away at school, surely young William would find himself a wench and that would settle his mind. But this trouble at Oxford was of another kind which the Admiral didn't really understand. With pain and anger, the Admiral began to suspect that something was basically wrong with his son.

The trouble, he gathered from the Oxford report, had something to do with religion. This puzzled the Admiral. He had always thought of religion as proper and becoming to a gentleman. Piety, he felt, was part of good manners. After all, he himself was a member in good standing of the Anglican Church. He would have been shocked at the thought that Christ died as a condemned criminal, which is why this probably never occurred to him. He abhorred the kind of questioning that had captured the imagination of his son. Such questions, he suspected, were perils to order and decency.

Most galling of all, the trouble arose at Oxford, the very place where he had sent William to learn gentility. After all, the Admiral himself had never had an education, and he had expected the university to teach his son fine speech and good manners and give him just enough learning to keep from being vacuous. Now all had gone awry. The boy was infected with heresy.

But perhaps it was not too late to root out this contagion. Maybe William had been studying too hard. Perhaps he needed diversion. What better antidote to the pitfalls of philosophy than a taste of the pleasures in store for a young man mindful of his advantages? The Admiral summoned William down from Oxford and immersed him in a round of entertainments.

London had changed since William had been away. Gone was the last trace of Puritanism. As if making up for lost years, the city had turned itself into a nonstop carnival. Its theaters were alive with racy comedies, and music rooms once more resounded to madrigals and "consorts." For the first time, women appeared on stage to portray female roles, an immensely popular innovation that scandalized conservatives, the more so since many of the new actresses were professionals who also enlivened the town in other ways. "Almost any coffee-house," notes one contemporary account, "could be a house of joy in disguise."

Color, display, and extravagance marked the fashions of the rich, who dressed in "furs, laces, embroidery, slashed sleeves, doublets, silk stockings, and high-heeled shoes with silver buckles." Yet this elegance was but glittering skin stretched over hardened depravity. Manners were bawdy, sentiments crass. In its frantic search for pleasure, society seemed propelled by an eros brutalized through past repression. Unbridled appetite obscured the distinction between love and sex. In consequence, the social climate was bereft of tenderness, consideration, and restraint.

This shift in tone had been signalled by the King himself. Nowhere was licentiousness more firmly enthroned than at the palace. Charles II even had a secret stairway built to his bedchamber, and sometimes the traffic there got so heavy that the King had to appoint a Page of the Backstairs to keep his appointments on schedule. Life at court quite openly revolved around such royal companions as Marguerite de Carteret, Lucy Walter, Elizabeth Killigrew, Catherine Pegg, Eleanor Needham, Barbara Palmer, Louise Kéroualle, Hortense Mancini, Moll Davis, and the uproarious Nell Gwynn, whose names are preserved in history for their services to the Crown, and whose complacent husbands were elevated to nobility by the grateful monarch.

Under Charles II lechery ranked as a political virtue. Lord Chancellor North, a prominent jurist of noted sobriety, was earnestly advised "that he should keep a whore . . . because he was ill looked upon for want of doing so." Dutifully, the

Lord Chancellor installed a hussy. On one occasion, another member of the court, having taken a sudden and impetuous fancy to someone else's wife, simply ran his sword through her husband when the latter had the ill grace to object. The lady in question willingly bedded down with the murderer immediately afterward, undeterred by the bloodstains on his shirt, which he kept on for the occasion. In its less drastic forms, Charles admired such style. The rake became the role model for Restoration males, and women accommodated themselves to the prevailing standard with no apparent reluctance.

The King's taste for minor outrage isn't really surprising. After all, his father had been executed by the Puritans. The murder of his father would be a shock to any boy, the more so perhaps for a prince, who forms his self-image in dynastic terms. It is not likely that Charles ever forgave the Puritans for the death of his father or his own experience of exile. When fate restored him to the throne, he would punish the Puritans in the most devastating way possible: by undermining the basic tenets of their entire culture. He used the influence of the court to make a national fetish of the very things the Puritans detested most: sex and sensual spontaneity.

Of course, this was not a reasoned policy. Had he been conscious of what he was doing, Charles would have been appalled by his own actions. In many ways, he was a decent, sensible, and competent monarch, and he was quite certainly unaware of the underlying motives that made him a paragon of lust. He thought of his pastimes as personal pleasure, not as an act of retribution. Still, to revenge himself on the Puritans, the King surrendered himself and his capital to debauchery.

Many young men found this ambience very agreeable, and young squires from the provinces eagerly flocked into London to avail themselves of these cultural opportunities. But this kind of lure had no appeal for William. He had been to the parties, the plays, and heaven knows what else. But nothing in this empty tragedy of manners attracted him. The Admiral had miscalculated.

What, after all, were parties and parades to someone in search of inner illumination? Like most young men intent upon the private ecstasies of understanding, William was a bit of a prig. His mind might leap high over the fences of convention, but his feelings were held in rein. They had to be, not to distract his thoughts.

William may have tried to explain his interests to his father. For all their differences, he cared deeply for his father and hoped to gain some understanding from the Admiral. Apparently, the two had long and serious conversations. Pepys, always snooping on his neighbor, observed the Admiral and his son walking together in the garden, looking dismally unhappy with each other.

William was probably too young and too impetuous—too set in his own ways of thought and expression—to credit his father with much comprehension. But in fact the Admiral may have understood a good deal of what William was telling him. After all, he was an intelligent man, able to extract a kind of wisdom from his worldly experience. Like most fathers who had attained prominence by their own effort, he wanted his son to be an ornament to his position. In his gruff way, the Admiral loved his son. Very likely, he sensed William's dilemma and wanted to protect him from what seemed an excess of virtue. As a warrior and politician, the Admiral had learned much the same thing that William had learned as a philosopher: that innocence invites its own destruction. They agreed on the need for armor and weapons but differed in their choice. William had chosen knowledge and integrity; the Admiral relied on wile. The two attitudes lacked a common denominator. The discourse faltered. Father and son could not affirm each other.

Back at Oxford, William tried to mend the cracks in his career. His father's cautions had left some impression. Besides, he was not the kind of radical who prefers self-immolation to objective achievement. He could serve his principles better by being circumspect and completing his studies. Of course, he'd have to be discreet about his contact with Dr. Owen. Up to a point, tact is not hypocrisy.

But William was not yet adept at walking around obstacles. Within months of his return to the university, he ran headlong into another confrontation. Dr. Fell, the new dean, was thinking about public relations. He was anxious to give visible signs of orthodoxy. Under his administration, Oxford would be a showplace of piety. He passed a new rule: Daily chapel attendance would be compulsory for all students. Moreover, all students would have to dress in religious garb.

Penn protested. This was a charade. The purpose of religion, he felt, was to generate meaning and value from human experience. Enforced worship was a contradiction in terms— an outright blasphemy. He pointedly stayed away from chapel and refused to wear the prescribed surplice.

Theologically, Penn's protest was more orthodox than the dean's order. After all, St. Paul himself recognized that faith cannot be compelled. But Dr. Fell, for all his piety, seemed unconcerned with St. Paul. What impressed him far more was that now, at last, he had a clear and uncontestable case against that troublesome William Penn. Hobnobbing with Owen was bad enough, but nothing too drastic could be done about that, considering Owen's great reputation and the fact that the meetings took place at Owen's private residence. Now, however, the boy had walked into a trap. This was a simple matter of willful, obstinate, and persistent infraction of the rules on the university's own grounds—exactly the kind of disrespect for law and order that would no longer be tolerated at Oxford. Penn was summarily expelled.

The Admiral was not sympathetic when William arrived home. The boy had deliberately and foolishly shattered his own career and the Admiral's fondest hopes. William, on his part, was too incensed at his new discovery of the ways of the world to listen patiently to his father's reproaches. For days they glowered in mutual frustration.

The Admiral knew about disobedience. Aboard ship, among his drunken, half-criminal sailors, he had dealt with insubordination many times in his own way. At last, these memories broke through the Admiral's frustration. He seized his cane and, shouting at William to leave the house forever, dealt blow after blow upon the cringing body of his son, who luckily managed to reach the door and drag himself into the street.

Four

THE PLEASURES OF PARIS

Lady Penn retrieved her son several days later. How and where she found him is not known; she overruled the banishment pronounced by her husband and took William back to the house to nurse his bruises.

Margaret Penn didn't like her son's conduct any more than the Admiral did. If anything, she liked it even less. The Admiral feared that William's nonconformity might damage his political standing. That at least was a rational objection. Lady Penn objected on strictly passionate grounds. She had become rather snobbish, and it irked her that William's attitude was so unfashionable. Taking moral positions just wasn't very chic in Restoration London. The chance of William's getting crossed off some elegant guest list worried her more than his removal from the student roster at Oxford. Still, she wasn't going to have her son traipsing about London, all beaten, sore, and without money.

Grudgingly, the Admiral let William stay in the house. But there was no real reconciliation. William stayed in his room. The servants brought his food. He did not come downstairs. The Admiral did not go upstairs.

In his perplexity, William secretly wrote to Dr. Owen for advice. But the Admiral intercepted Owen's reply. Outraged at William's persistence in this perilous friendship, the Admiral unburdened himself to his neighbor.

"Sir W. Pen much troubled upon letters come last night," notes Pepys in his diary. "Showed me one of Dr. Owen's to his son, whereby it appears that his son is much perverted in his opinion by him; which I now perceive is one thing that hath put Sir William so long off his hookes."

The Admiral had reason for worry. It just wouldn't do for the son of Britain's highest naval officer to keep company with subversives. There was only one solution: send the boy abroad.

France, then as now, served as a convenient receptacle for wealthy young Englishmen too embarrassing to keep at home. Foreign travel, after all, was part of a gentleman's education. Besides, being footloose in France might help William forget all this odd philosophizing. At least the Admiral hoped so. At any rate, William would improve his French—a decided asset, since French was just beginning to replace Latin as the common language of the educated. Lady Penn agreed that her son's going abroad was an excellent idea. A touch of Parisian manners would make William a great social success. Thus, in July, 1662, at the age of eighteen, William set off for Paris, equipped with ample funds, letters of introduction, and a slightly older cousin named Robert Spencer as a travel companion.

Paris was already Europe's foremost city, having surpassed both Rome and Florence since their Renaissance heyday. Yet it bore little resemblance to the glittering metropolis of later years. The broad, tree-shaded boulevards with their balconied façades still lay far in the future, as did the spacious vistas of the Place de la Concorde and the Champs de Mars. In Penn's day, the massive towers of Notre Dame, like a pair of stocky sentinels, looked upon a welter of narrow streets extending eastward from the Ile de la Cité toward the newly completed Place des Vosges.

Adjoining this harmonious square, the town houses of France's noble families dotted the district of *le Marais,* then the fashionable center of the city. These mansions combined massive dignity with geometric grace. Unlike anything Penn might have seen in England, the French Baroque, with its richness of form and varied textures of stone and marble, must have seemed as exotic as the pale Paris sunlight after London's persistent fog.

In other respects Paris seemed more like home. The narrow streets reeked with filth. Open gutters were the only sewer system, and garbage dumped in the street was eaten by pigs, chickens, and dogs that freely foraged through the city. Shortly after Penn's visit, an energetic police prefect named LaReynie ordered the streets of Paris to be paved to make them easier to clean. But in Penn's day, travelers reported that they could smell the mud of Paris for miles as they approached the town. As a countermeasure, elegant Parisians perfumed their lace cuffs and went about sniffing their sleeves.

Only in the newly laid-out western part, where the great horseshoe of the Louvre opens toward the Tuileries, did Paris offer its vaunted opportunities to the casual stroller. Along the Rue Rivoli, the *haute monde* promenaded in the afternoon, showing off their elaborate fashions, which made dressing and undressing almost a full-time occupation for the rich.

Elsewhere the streets were less inviting to saunterers. The narrow lanes were clogged with pushcarts, horse vans, coaches, and sedan chairs. Every crossing was an impasse where pedestrians and drivers cursed each other. In this respect Paris was similar to other cities whose old medieval core could not accommodate the traffic resulting from the rapid growth of its outskirts.

In its social forms, however, Paris was unique. Behind the heavy gates of the elegant town houses, the *maisons particulières,* life had already taken on refinements far in advance of the rest of Europe. This was not merely a matter of outward *politesse;* rather, it sprang from a new vision of life as a work of art to be designed by one's own sense of style. Elsewhere, people might take life as it came. Parisians insisted on shaping existence to their own taste. They had the knack for it—the *savoir faire*. Paris was an attitude, a sense of being.

Thanks to the letters of introduction the Admiral had secured for him, William soon found himself swept into the life of the Parisian aristocracy. His own upper-class background had prepared him at least for the outer form of such encounters. For example, while ordinary Englishmen still ate with their fingers and cut their meat with daggers, Penn was already adept in the use of knife and fork. Also, he was accustomed to have his own place setting at table rather than reach into the common bowl. Though he had lived much of his life in the provinces, he was no yokel.

Still, there were new manners to be learned. In England, for example, hostesses prided themselves on tablecloths of Dutch linen, big enough to reach down to the floor on all sides. The overhang served as a common napkin for all diners. In France, elegant households sported separate table napkins as the latest fad—an innovation that seems to have fascinated elegant Parisians. One contemporary book on etiquette, de Courtin's *Nouveau Traité de la Civilité*, seriously discusses twenty-seven different ways of napkin-folding.

There were other differences. At Parisian dinner parties the quality of the conversation was considered quite as important as the quality of the food, while in England little attention was paid to either. And Penn must have been surprised to hear women join in the table talk quite as readily as the men. For unlike the British, Parisian women had already proved that wit and intelligence were not exclusively male attributes. Mme. de Rambouillet had already established the first of the Paris *salons*, those splendid enclaves of civilized talk through which a small vanguard of Parisiennes created a new phase of European culture. In similar settings, the eminently presentable Penn surely met a number of young ladies more adroit in conversation than he might have found at home, and, given such incentives, he soon gained fluency in French.

Still shaken by the quarrel with his father, Penn eagerly lost himself in the flood of new impressions. There would be visits to the theater, perhaps to see a play by Corneille or to sample the work of those promising new writers everyone was talking about—Molière and Racine. Penn had no ear for music, but his fashionable friends probably persuaded him to hear one of those new operas by Monsieur Lulli—grandly staged spectacles that were the musical rage of Paris.

Back in London, the Admiral meanwhile cooled his anger and once again began to think of his son as a future courtier, high in the circles of government. As long as the boy was in Paris, wouldn't it be an asset for him to be received at the court of France? With the help of friends close to the royal family of England, the Admiral wrangled the necessary introductions. William was to appear before Louis XIV, *le roi soleil.*

Not much older than Penn himself, Louis had already gained a remarkable reputation at the age of twenty-four. Having subdued the *Fronde*—a group of rebellious aristocrats —the King was obsessed with the idea of forestalling future challenges to royal power. As a result, he carried the doctrine of royal absolutism to preposterous lengths. With the aid of his enormously capable prime minister, Colbert, Louis proclaimed that all public power rested in his own person and that all France was but a metaphoric extension of his own body: *L'état, c'est moi!* No evidence exists that Louis really spoke those famous words; yet they epitomize the style and spirit of his rule. As a symbol of his personal supremacy, the King was building an enormous palace at Versailles. The massive structure was the visual device by which the pudgy little King projected himself into a figure of grandeur. Like a gigantic seal imprinted on the land, the new palace sat upon its sloping grounds—the colossal sign of one man's will.

Since Versailles was still unfinished, the King received William at Fontainebleau, some thirty miles southeast of Paris, where he liked to hunt stag in the surrounding forests. At the chateau William entered into a world of almost unimaginable sumptuousness. The Sun King moved in an ambience of jewels and satin, ivory and gold. This splendor was no mere extravagance; it was a calculated statement of the absolutist cult; the idolization of the King.

In tune with this visual opulence, court ceremony was elaborate to the point of fetish. Gestures, manners, and speech were stylized into ritual. Every aspect of daily routine became an official occasion. Even the King's sojourns on the toilet were announced with proper pomp and circumstance. At times this obsession with ritual verged on the grotesque, as on the occasion when the King's famous kitchen master, Vatel, slipped up in his timing. The fish wasn't ready at the proper moment in the sixteen-course royal dinner. Vatel was disconsolate. The shadow of imperfection had fallen upon the King's table. And it was his fault. The devoted cook saw only one way to atone for such a mishap. He killed himself.

Had Vatel overdramatized? Not by the standards of the royal court. On the contrary. His suicide was widely praised as a gesture of stylish appropriateness. Such excess of manner over matter gave the court of France an air of almost laughable contrivance. Fitting himself into such protocol must have been rather trying to a straightforward person like Penn. How long he stayed at Fontainebleau, or what conversations he had with the King, has not been historically established. But it seems certain that he left the royal presence with considerable relief.

Soon after, Penn experienced a chance encounter in the nocturnal streets of Paris that left a deep impression. He was walking home, at about 11 P.M., when he was challenged by a man brandishing a rapier. The French at that time were notably fond of swordplay. The lower ranks of the aristocracy —commoners were not permitted to carry weapons—were constantly hacking at each other for the preservation of their honor. In the absence of real provocation, an imagined insult sufficed to set off murderous sport. The stranger accused Penn of having failed to return his greeting. Penn quickly assessed his opponent. The man was obviously spoiling for a fight. Perhaps he was drunk. It would do no good for Penn to explain that he hadn't seen the man doff his hat in the dark street. An apology would have incensed him even more. Penn drew his own sabre, none too soon, for without awaiting Penn's reply the stranger thrust at him. Penn parried. Like most upper-class boys of his era, he had been well schooled in fencing. Besides, he had the advantage of being sober, and after a few passes he succeeded in disarming his adversary.

Now the stranger was at his mercy; for by law and custom Penn was entitled to stab his opponent to the heart. Most men, angered by an unprovoked attack, might have taken this chance for retaliation. But an innate generosity kept Penn from pushing his weapon through the defenseless man. Even in the flush of fighting for his life, he maintained his compassion. He sheathed his rapier and let his attacker go.

From this point on, Penn's life in Paris was no longer carefree. The moment of his own mortal danger and the experience of holding another person's life in his hands reawakened his speculative tendencies. Once again the urge toward reflection, the search for meaning, took hold of him. He did not see the street assault as a purely personal encounter. In his mind, the incident became a springboard for more general thoughts about the nature of violence—thoughts that prepared the ground for his later pacifism. The violence he met in the street, he recognized, was merely a convention—another kind of stylized behavior, as senseless as the ritual he had seen at the King's court. The act of aggression did not spring from authentic human necessity. "I ask any man of understanding and conscience," he wrote later, "if the whole ceremony were worth the life of a man, considering the dignity . . . and the importance of the life of man, both with respect to God, his creator, and the benefit of civil society?"

His thoughtful mood led him back to his religious concerns. Four months in Catholic France had given him a new perspective on the topics he had once so fervently discussed at Dr. Owen's. At Notre Dame, Penn had felt the hypnotic power of religious ritual as never before. Under the high and austere vault of the great cathedral, the chanting of the choir and the spectacular celebration of the Mass conveyed with almost bodily impact the strength and coherence of tradition. Yet Penn's own piety did not harmonize with that kind of religion. He could not accept a ready-made faith. Doubt and search were the chief elements of his religious impulse. Once again he was troubled by inner disquiet. The pleasures of Paris grew pallid. Again he longed for the effort and the concentration of serious study.

The most famous Protestant theologian in France at that time was Moise Amyraut, a man of stupendous learning whose *Traité des Religions* marked a new departure in the philosophy of religion. It was one of the first treatises that did not depict religion as a revealed entity, rigid and fixed forever. Amyraut ventured the idea that religious precepts were changing in different historic situations—in short, that religion was an open-ended process of development. He had been a major influence in liberalizing French Protestantism, steering the Huguenots away from the grim severity of Calvin. Amyraut taught at *l'Académie Protestante,* the foremost Huguenot university in France, located in the picturesque city of Saumur, overlooking the Loire.

Penn journeyed south to the Loire valley and, with his usual directness, presented himself at the Academy at the beginning of the fall term in 1662, asking to be accepted as a student. Amyraut was so impressed by the eager and erudite young Englishman who already spoke such excellent French that he invited Penn to stay at his own house. For more than a year, the young student and the old professor lived in each other's constant company. In some ways, Amyraut must have seemed like a father to Penn, whose real father had always been so remote from him. Now, at last, he had the experience of daily life with an older person whom he profoundly admired and who shared his deepest concerns.

Like Erasmus a century before, Amyraut was a Christian humanist. His effort to reconcile Christian faith and Greek philosophy led him to a broad tolerance of different approaches toward the mystery of faith, a tolerance quite rare in that period of brutal religious conflict. It was this undogmatic attitude that endeared Amyraut to Penn, whose own religious style favored an open mystical awareness rather than a logically structured creed.

"I never had any other religion in my life than what I felt," Penn recalled. "From the age of sixteen I have been a great sufferer for it. . . . I never addicted myself to school learning to understand religion by, but always, even to their faces, rejected and disputed against it."

But as a serious thinker, Penn could not simply discard dogma. He had to come to terms with it, disprove or transcend it. Together, Amyraut and Penn were chipping away at the dictates that confine the spirit. Dogma was a narrow window that admitted only a thin shaft of light. They wanted a faith that illuminated the whole world, a faith that did not exclude but embraced.

Like most Protestants of his day, Amyraut keenly felt the thorn of Calvin's theory of predestination. According to Calvin, every person is predestined by God either to salvation or to perdition. Nothing of his own doing can alter his fate. He is either one of the elect or one of the damned. This was not the kind of notion to appeal to William's compassionate temperament. Obvious questions troubled him: Why would a loving and omnipotent God allow creatures to be born whom he knows to be eternally damned? Is God's will but a whim? Where then lies justice?

Neither could Amyraut accept a wanton and capricious God. In *La Morale Chrétienne* he develops the view that personal liberty is the key to a morally responsible life. Only if there is a free choice can personal integrity develop. That was the meaning of Christ's choosing the cross. The human will must be free. Self-determined acts—not externally imposed rules—mark the moral character of man. He is neither saved nor damned by divine prearrangement, but through freedom he becomes the maker of his own moral destiny. The role of religion, then, is not to compel obedience but to provide ways of contemplation which lead to closer communion with God. In this private communion—not through institutions—man finds charity for others and guidance toward the Good.

Amyraut's liberality freed William from the earlier Puritan influence on his mental development. Spiritual fear, the haunting torment of the Puritans, no longer shackled him. He was now a free agent, master of his own spirit, and therefore open to the promptings of his own ethical intuition.

Gradually Penn's doubts resolved in the gentle strength of his teacher's mind, and he gained confidence in his own capacity for creative thought. All through the summer, the sojourn at Saumur was for Penn an almost lyrical journey of self-discovery. But with the coming of the cold season the old professor took sick, and early in 1664 he died.

For Penn it was almost like the loss of a father. Without Amyraut, the Academy no longer had any meaning for him. He left Saumur and traveled about the Continent in spring and early summer, leaving no record of where he went or whom he saw. But the footloose life was not to his taste. As always, he wanted to be engaged in something. He needed purpose and direction, a serious pursuit.

More than two years had passed since that fateful quarrel with his father. He had changed since then. He was no longer a rebellious adolescent, full of self-righteous impudence. The edges had been smoothed. At twenty, he had learned to temper forthrightness with tact. Now, he felt, he could get on with all kinds of people—even his father. Perhaps it was time to go home.

Five

AN ACCEPTANCE

> We know that in religion . . . all the enigmas of the
> world are solved, all the contradictions of deeper
> reaching thought have their meaning unveiled . . .
> and the voice of the heart's pain is silenced.
>
> —G. W. F. HEGEL

Sir William and Lady Penn were delighted with their son on
his return to London in August, 1664. Of course they had
expected to see him changed. After all, William had been gone
for two years. And of course they had hoped the change might
be for the better. But the suave and self-possessed young man
now come back surpassed their fondest wish. Dressed in the
colorful, brocaded style of a French aristocrat, with a matching
adroitness of speech and manner, William bolstered his mother's pride and renewed his father's confidence in the future.

William had to become reacquainted with his family. His
young brother Richard hardly remembered him, having been
only five when William went away to Oxford. And Pegg, now
thirteen, looked with shy admiration at her big brother in his
fancy foreign clothes, all scarlet, blue, and yellow. Even the
neighbor's wife, Mrs. Pepys, noticed that William was "a most
modish person, grown a fine gentleman." Her husband, of
course, had nothing good to say of any member of the Penn
family. William "hath a great deale, if not too much, of the

vanity of the French," he observed, and was "affected of speech and gait." In all, Pepys concluded, "I fear all profit he has made in his travel will signify little."

A portrait of young Penn stems from this period. If the picture is authentic, the Admiral and Lady Penn had reason indeed to be pleased with their son's appearance. It shows an oval face of almost girlish prettiness but with strong features, the brusqueness of the straight, short nose in counterpoint to the almost sensuous mouth. What gives the face its dominant character are the eyes, burning with a dark, luminous insistence. The portrait shows only the head. But it is known from verbal descriptions that Penn was fairly tall and athletic. Altogether, the young man must have been both handsome and impressive.

William had so much to tell. Time and again he had to relate his travel adventures and then repeat it all again when the family went to have dinner with Pepys. "Home pretty betimes and there found W. Pen and he staid supper with us," reads Pepys's diary for September 5, 1664. "And mightily merry talking of his travels and the French humours." They ate "a barrel of oysters," and Pepys undoubtedly tried to flirt with Pegg and, as was his custom, pull her into a corner. Later in the evening, Mrs. Pepys sang a French ditty she knew "un air tout interdit"—asking William for a translation. Querulous, Pepys pitted his wobbly French against William's fluency. "I laid twenty to one against him which he would not agree with me, though I know myself in the right as to the true sense of the word, and almost angry we were." That broke up the party.

The Admiral also had much to tell during those first weeks of reunion. To his delight, he found William quite easy to talk to. At last the boy seemed to have developed some practical sense. He understood the difficulties the Admiral had with his job. He was trying to build a fighting navy. But since the new King had come into power, there had been nothing but peace, which was obviously bad for military morale. The whole officer corps was infested with highborn bumblers holding their positions as political plums. Some captains turned their ships into cargo boats for their own profit. Dockyard officials sold naval supplies to commercial distributors as if they were running a private wholesale business. Indeed, the Admiral himself had been secretly accused, probably by Pepys, of running such a sideline.

The ships themselves were more beautiful than practical. Carved from bowsprit to poop with rich tracery, they looked like palatial furniture drifting in a flood. But their rigging was frayed and the rudder hinges rotted. Sailors were incompetent, which was hardly surprising, most of them being petty criminals rounded up by press-gangs. Their officers defrauded them of their pay, so they supported themselves by robbery in port, for which—if caught—they were flogged or tied to the mast and left there to starve, setting a proper example to their mates.

For officers, life aboard was much more pleasant. Many of them kept mistresses in their quarters. In fact, under the permissive reign of Charles II, the Royal Navy was in effect a fleet of floating harems. In his effort to convert these pleasure craft into a fighting force, the Admiral ran constant risk of stepping on aristocratic toes. It was all so frustrating, and he was glad that in William he at last had a confidant to whom he could speak freely.

The Admiral was still concerned about his son's education. He didn't think much of William's studies at Saumur. Too much theology. A future statesman had to know law. As a person of influence, the Admiral had no difficulty enrolling William at Lincoln's Inn, England's foremost law school.

Located just off Chancery Lane, in what was then London's West End, Lincoln's Inn was laid out as a vast quadrangle of regal Gothic to be entered through massive gate towers. The heart of the school was a high-vaulted library with tall stained-glass windows where England's best collection of law books lined the walls in huge leather-bound tomes. In this impressive if drafty setting William would pore over unwieldy volumes of case law piled before him on the hand-hewn oak reading pews. During the winter semester he would get up every so often to warm himself by the open fire in the center of the hall whose smoke rose up nearly thirty feet to an overhead cowling and chimney. As a practical part of his legal training, he participated in mock trials staged by the students. Alternately taking the parts of prosecutor and defender, he became versed in courtroom strategy, never suspecting how soon he would need these skills in his own efforts to keep out of jail.

But William's law studies were interrupted almost as soon as they began. Another war with Holland seemed imminent. Rankling from their earlier defeat, the Dutch again harassed English shipping, and hostilities once more approached the point of open conflict.

The Admiral was pleased. With the threat of war hanging over England, he finally received the authority needed to deal with the Navy's discipline and manpower problems. Now he was entitled "to press and take up carpenters, shipwrights, caulkers, smiths, joiners, sawyers, gunners, soldiers, &c. &c., to repair and set for the king's ships." A royal order compelled all magistrates to assist Penn in his recruiting campaign and specified that "all who refuse to obey be imprisoned." The fact was that the royal Exchequer was too poor to pay for its Navy and so had to rely on conscript labor. But thanks to his organizational talent and sheer ruthlessness, the Admiral managed to ready the fleet even with unwilling workmen.

Throughout these hectic preparations, William was constantly at his father's side, learning executive skills and perhaps musing privately about such matters as freedom and compulsion. When the Admiral had finally refurbished his fleet, he assembled one hundred and three ships in the waters off Harwich and asked William to come with him aboard his command vessel, the *Royal Charles*.

Taking William aboard served a double purpose. For one thing, it gave the boy a taste of military life at the level of high command. As a future man of decision, William should feel at home in this atmosphere, the Admiral calculated. Secondly, he planned to employ William as confidential messenger between the naval command and the royal court. By making William his secret emissary, the Admiral virtually assured a face-to-face meeting between William and the King. It was the Admiral's way of introducing William at court: no formal presentations. He wanted the King and William to meet on business.

William succeeded at first try. In May, 1665, the Admiral dispatched him with an "urgent" message. Setting off in a small courier vessel, William ran into foul weather and didn't reach the port of Harwich until nightfall. Making up for lost time, he took a horse and rode right through the night, arriving at Whitehall in the early morning.

The King, a late riser, was still asleep when William panted up the palace stairs to the royal antechambers. Breathlessly, he told Lord Arlington, the royal chamberlain, that he had come with sealed dispatches from the commander of the fleet at sea.

Arlington was in a quandary. The King had been busy at night, after his fashion, and needed rest in the morning. Normally, Lord Arlington would not wake him for anything short of popular rebellion. But this was different. The King's own brother, the Duke of York, shared command of the fleet with Sir William and was also aboard the *Royal Charles*. So this was perhaps a family matter. Besides, there was this war. Arlington had to choose: risk the displeasure of the King or perhaps risk a naval disaster. At last, he knocked at the door and entered the royal bedchamber.

Almost immediately, the door opened again and William was ushered in. If the Admiral wanted William to meet the King informally, he could have hoped for nothing better. As

William later described it, the King was "earnestly skipping out of his bed, he came only in his gown and slippers."

Despite his grogginess, the King was cordial. "When he saw me he said, 'Oh! is't you? How is Sir William?' " William reported to his father. "The king asked how you were three several times. He was glad to hear your message about *Ka* [evidently a code designation]. After interrogating me above half an hour, he bid me go now about your business, and mine too."

The Admiral's stratagem had succeeded. Surely the King would remember the young man presented to him under such unusual circumstances.

William did not return to the ship. The fleet was now ready to sail against the Dutch, and the Admiral had no intention of exposing his son to danger. William continued his law studies but was much distracted by worry about the Admiral facing the uncertainties of war. He had grown deeply fond of his father. Working together in the preparation of the fleet had given William and the Admiral a shared context and a chance to know each other. One of William's letters to the Admiral clearly reveals his care and concern:

> I never knew what a father was till I had wisdom enough to prize him. . . . I pray God, after all the dangers you are exposed to . . . that you come home secure. And I bless God; my heart does not in any way fail, but firmly believes that if God has called you to battle, he will cover your head in that smoky day. . . . I pray God be with you and be your armour in the day of controversy! May that power be your salvation, for his name's sake! And so will wish and pray, that is, with all true veneration,
>
> > Honoured father,
> > Your obedient son and servant,
> > William Penn

The "day of controversy" came within a month. A sea battle was joined on June 3, 1665, near Lowestoft, a mere 120 miles from London. Once again the Admiral was victorious. He routed the Dutch and returned to London triumphant, with a bounty of four Dutch warships and ten captured merchant vessels.

But London was in no mood to celebrate. The plague had struck. Sick rats, the carriers of the disease, crawled out from their holes and hiding places by the thousands, tumbling through the streets and convulsing in the gutters as they played out their grim dance of death. In almost every house, fevered men and women lay prostrate with their boils. The town rang with the cry "Bring out your dead!" as open carts trundled from door to door to collect corpses. Before the pestilence abated, more than 70,000 Londoners had been thrown into hastily dug mass graves.

The Penn family was spared by the epidemic. But the horror and grief pervading the city had their effect on William. As once before, in devastated Ireland, he felt haunted by the primal question: What is the meaning of suffering? With Amyraut, his old teacher, he had speculated on the nature of compassion and the links between sorrow and human sympathy. Now, again, his thoughts circled about the lasting perplexities of the human condition, drifting away from the practical preoccupations he had lately shared with his father. "In the time of the Great Plague in London," he wrote, the Lord "gave me a deep sense of the Vanity of this World, of the Irreligiousness of the Religions in it." Deep within himself, apparently, he was preparing for some basic departure from the established religions.

During the plague, he observed the variety of human responses to disaster: some selfishly seeking nothing but their own protection and advantage, others offering whatever help and solace seemed possible, even at risk to themselves. In particular, he noticed that the Quakers, regardless of their own

danger, would enter the houses of the sick to bring them food
and comfort.

These works of charity placed the Quakers in double jeop-
ardy: first from the epidemic and secondly from the police.
Following the King's policy of suppressing all religious nonconformists, the constables arrested Quakers on sight as they
went about the city on their errands of mercy, often recog-
nizable by their dress. Moreover, opponents of the Quakers,
both Catholic and Puritan, started the rumor that the plague
was caused by the presence of the Quakers, whose bold heresy
was evidently offensive to God. As a result, the Quakers faced
viciousness and danger not merely from the plague and the
police but even from those whom they wanted to help. The
absurdity of their plight was not lost on Penn, who was developing a fine ear for grotesque disharmonies of this sort. Again
the Quakers had touched his imagination, as they had once
before in Ireland, and then again in Oxford. Unconsciously,
perhaps, Penn was filing away these impressions for future
reference.

On reaching the age of twenty-one, in October, 1665, William could act legally in his father's behalf in the management
of the Irish estates. This was fortunate, for the Admiral was
housebound with an attack of gout, which forced him to sit
in his chair all day, with his painfully swollen foot perched on
a pillow.

The situation in Ireland had become complicated. The former owner of the confiscated estate of Macroom, which Cromwell had given to the Admiral, had been a good Royalist all
along. Now he was pestering the King to get his property back.
This put King Charles in a quandary, and he was looking for
a way to make everyone happy. Would the Admiral mind returning Macroom to the Earl of Clancarty? the King asked
politely. In exchange, the King would give Penn Shanagarry
Castle, with some seven thousand acres of land near Bally-

cotton Bay. Of course, Admiral Penn didn't mind in the least. William would go to Ireland to settle the formalities.

So, in January, 1666, William once again took leave of his law studies and set off for Dublin, braving winter storms in the Irish Sea. He spent much of his time at the Viceroy's court, befriending the Duke of Ormonde, Lord Lieutenant of Ireland. As a landed gentleman, William was received by the Duke as a social equal, especially since his stay in Paris had given him a certain elegance of manner much admired at the provincial court of Ireland.

William's ties to the Irish court involved him in a military adventure, which stands out as an inexplicable and discordant episode in his career. The garrison at Carrickfergus rose in rebellion against the English occupation of Ireland. The Earl of Arran, whom William had met at Dublin, invited him to join an armed contingent under the Earl's command to quell the riot. Surprisingly, William accepted the challenge and bravely fought against the insurgents. The Earl quickly spotted officer material in William and suggested that, as the first step toward a military career, William might assume command over the garrison at his father's estate in Kinsale.

William was so heated by his first experience of combat that all his pacifism evaporated for the moment. It was as if some suppressed anger, some frustration, had broken to the surface in the fury of battle. Suddenly the gentle student of theology, the bookish seeker of God's mercy, relished blood and craved violence. Eagerly he wrote to his father for permission to take over the offered command.

Surprisingly, the Admiral was not at all pleased by his son's sudden turn toward the military. After all, he knew William. Even if he couldn't fathom his son's learning and philosophy, he could sense the nature of his temperament. He had seen all kinds of men at war and knew how mild persons, who habitually suppress their aggression in normal life, are sometimes overcome with a fierce blood-lust in battle. The Admiral under-

stood that this probably happened to William. But such states
are a passing intoxication. They do not make a soldier. On the
contrary, a good soldier does violence with dispassion. And
William was not that kind of person.

To William's request for permission to accept command at
Kinsale, the Admiral replied with unusual restraint:

July 17, 1666

Son William:

. . . I can say nothing but advise to sobriety. As for
the tender . . . concerning the fort of Kinsale, I wish
your youthful desires mayn't outrun your discretion.
. . . God bless, direct and protect you.

Your very affectionate father,
W.P.

That put an end to William's military ambitions. After settling legalities about the new estate at Shanagarry, William
went to the old estate at Kinsale to set up a lucrative little
business there. The Admiral, always eager for an extra pound,
had arranged that his own estate would supply provisions for
Navy ships in nearby waters. William was named in the contract as the official "victualler" for the fleet. Of course, as a
gentleman, he could not be expected to attend personally to
any details of business, but he did stop by to see that these
matters were properly taken care of by his stewards.

He enjoyed his new status as Lord of the Manor at Kinsale
and had quite comfortably settled down at the estate when
catastrophic news came from London. Almost half the city
had burned down.

As if to cleanse the ground after the pestilence, the great
fire of 1666 had turned the center of London into a charred
desert. Beginning near London Bridge, spreading to the north
and driven westward by the wind, the fire cut a black semi-
circle out of the city, hemmed in on the south by the river. The
tall Gothic tower that surmounted St. Paul's was gone, and

with it a vast expanse of half-timbered houses whose beams burned like matchsticks in the conflagrations. More than ten thousand families lost their homes, and most of them, unable to obtain carts, fled before the flames with nothing more than they could carry on their backs.

Once again, as William returned to London, he found himself surrounded by misery beyond imagination. And once again his family had escaped unscathed. Their house on Tower Hill lay east of the fire's origin, in Pudding Lane, and remained undamaged as the flames traveled in the opposite direction. William stayed long enough to assure himself of his family's safety and to attend Pegg's wedding.

For Pegg, just turned fifteen, the prospect of marriage seemed like a child's play of Let's Pretend. How nice to be a grown-up lady with all these lovely clothes and all these many things. She had always liked the fanciful—including the flatteries of lecherous old Pepys—and now she could go about in the gilded coach her future husband had given her, and visit her friends utterly forgetful of the charred ruins, and have the train of her dress carried by her own page. Life has such moments, and that is good. Let the city smolder.

William didn't stay long after the wedding. The blackened ruins depressed him. To be sure, London would rise again. Christopher Wren, whom he had often seen at Oxford, was already drawing plans for rebuilding the city. That huge dome he envisioned for St. Paul's would rival the magnificence of St. Peter's in Rome.

But it wasn't just the visible aftermath of the fire that disquieted William. He could no longer hit that note of comradeship with his father that had bound them together during those weeks aboard the *Royal Charles*. Something almost like tenderness had sprung up between them then. Perhaps it had been the sense of imminent danger that united father and son. Now there was only diffidence and distance. Harried by the pain of gout, the Admiral had grown irritable and short-tempered.

Political intrigue at the Navy Office made him suspicious and withdrawn. William felt uneasy in his company.

He was eager to leave. He longed for Ireland, for solitude and long walks, and soon he returned to Shanagarry. Many things were somehow coming together for him. How strange it had been, his stint of soldiering, his pleasure in the fight. What would Amyraut have said? Or Dr. Owen? And what, after all, would he himself say if he were to sum it up? Sum up Paris and Ireland, Oxford and London, the books and the parties, the ships and the King—all the things that didn't quite fit together. He needed time—unbroken days, the long horizons, and the sea.

For the fortunate, there comes a confluence of time, a moment in which all that has passed is gathered. Sometimes it takes the form of love, when the light from all the stars falls upon a single face. Sometimes it takes the form of an idea in which all reality seems encompassed. Such moments do not come at random. One grows ready for them.

It is the moment when for the first time one understands what one already knows, and recognizes in new ways what is already familiar. It is the time when the innate becomes explicit.

It began simply enough. Penn was riding into Cork to buy some clothes. Approaching from the gentle rise flanking the River Lee, he could see the whole town spreading over a cluster of islands between branches of the river. Penn crossed one of the drawbridges separating the island city from the main shore. Passing through a massive gate into the walled town, he searched out a haberdashery that happened to be owned by a Quaker woman. She didn't know her customer and may have been suspicious of the young man whose elegant attire marked him as a Cavalier, a possible enemy of her sect.

But Penn chatted quite amiably with the Quaker shopwoman. After all, as owner of the nearby castle he wanted to get to know some of the townsfolk. The woman's distrust was quickly overcome when he mentioned that he himself had known some Quakers and recalled how deeply touched he had been many years before when, as a boy, he had heard Thomas Loe speak at his father's estate at Macroom.

The woman's face brightened. Thomas Loe? What a coincidence! It so happened that the Quaker leader was in Cork that very day to speak to the local Society of Friends. If the young gentleman would care to come, she would gladly take him to the meeting with her.

It sounded like just a friendly invitation. In fact it was a risky undertaking. The King, resolved to establish supremacy of the Anglican Church, had outlawed all nonconformist creeds. Catholics and Presbyterians were powerful enough to resist effectively, but the many Protestant splinter groups that proliferated during the Puritan period were drastically suppressed. A new set of laws, the so-called Clarendon Code, forbade all religious gatherings except those under the auspices of the official Church of England. The penalty for unauthorized worship was imprisonment or deportation. The code was enforced with particular virulence against the Quakers, whose libertarian and politically progressive views made them dangerous subversives in the eyes of the Royalists. Religious and political liberty were linked, in the thinking of the times, and Charles II, still reacting against Cromwell, would permit neither.

The Quakers found no sympathy in their plight. To most people they seemed godless heretics who richly deserved their misfortunes. Thousands of Quakers had already lost their property through confiscation, and countless others were cast into prison. Local bullies everywhere knew that it was open season on Quakers and that they could beat the men or importune the women with the blessing of the constabulary.

But William saw no reason why he shouldn't accept the woman's invitation. He was, after all, a gentleman, Lord of

Shanagarry, and the son of Admiral Penn. It was inconceivable that a person of such rank should be in any danger from commoners, constables, or any such lesser folk. Of course he'd go.

The meeting was held in a private home so as to attract no attention. It had not been advertised, except by word of mouth to trusted members of the Quaker underground. Participants spaced their arrivals so not too many would be seen entering the house at one time. With luck, the gathering would remain unnoticed and there would be no disturbance.

Penn immediately recognized Loe, though the great Quaker had aged much in the ten years since Penn had last seen him. The physical strain and nervous toll of an illegal existence, combined with passionate devotion to a cause, had marked Loe's gaunt but gentle face. The look of pain long endured lent conviction to Loe's words as he stood up and quietly announced the topic of his talk: "There is a faith that overcometh the world, and a faith that is overcome by the world."

As Loe developed this theme, Penn felt a growing inner agitation. Loe was exploring the tension between World and Spirit, between the Real and the Ideal. Exactly that had been the central conflict in Penn's own life: a tension between his worldly expectations and his spiritual search. As Loe spoke, Penn suddenly perceived how his social role as a young Cavalier clashed with his true inclinations. He had been the Admiral's courier and Amyraut's disciple. The split had gone through his center. It had to be healed.

As if he were reading Penn's innermost thoughts, Loe was speaking of just such a reconciliation of seeming opposites. The bridge between World and Spirit, between what is and what should be, is formed by a faith that transmutes reality—a faith that becomes a creative agent shaping the world.

Tears came to Penn's eyes. With a sudden impulse to show how deeply Loe's words had moved him, Penn stood up, and remained standing in silence. Loe noticed him. Later in the

evening he talked with William for a long time. The former
student of theology quickly grasped the meaning of the ideas
Loe was expounding to him. All these years William had been
searching for a creed, often without even being aware of his
inner quest. Now, at last, everything seemed to fall into place.
Here was a Christian faith free of both Calvin and Rome—a
faith consistent with the open and accepting humanism that
Penn had inherited from Amyraut. It was a faith in the
spiritual worth of the individual person, not a creed to marshal
coercive force against the individual. It was not a church to
dominate the soul or to mingle the love of God with the love of
power. It was, at last, a religion without terror.

Like all true forms of faith—and many forms of faith are
"true"—it rested on reverence: on the stunned and grateful
wonder at existence which men call God. But it did not
enchain the mind in dogmatic shackles. Nothing was pre-
structured, no beliefs were compulsory. There was no cate-
chism. The mind remained free to question, to explore, and
above all to listen to its own innermost promptings and
thereby to worship.

This was the synthesis toward which Penn himself had been
tending. He had rebelled against received dogma and searched
for individually authentic beliefs. He had longed for some link
to the Eternal Being that yet allowed freedom in the temporal
realm. He knew that solitary contemplation was not sufficient,
that faith had to be expressed within a social framework to
become capable of social action. In this perspective, Penn saw
the Quaker Meeting as a community through which a free
faith of separate individuals could take on socially effective
forms. He recognized the Quaker Meeting as a religious
group structure without the mechanism of conformity or
church bureaucracy—and therefore capable of continuous
self-renewal and spontaneity. In sum, Penn had found what he
had searched for ever since his discussions with Dr. Owen: a
practical intersection of faith and society.

But such analysis came later. At the meeting with Loe, Penn had no need to itemize these arguments or array his reasons. They all merged into a single intuition, into a readiness for acceptance. He felt a concord with those around him, as if nothing in the world was separate any longer, and people, thoughts, and things were come together in unison.

Penn knew that evening that he had found his faith. By doubting, he had reached the point where he could no longer doubt. Feeling and reason now chimed together for him, and his faith gained strength from the depth from which it was drawn. Inescapably, he made an inner commitment to an attitude, and thereby to a mode of action. He had become a Quaker.

He made no declaration and said very little after talking with Loe. Later in the evening, someone mentioned that Loe needed a horse to continue his journey, his old mount no longer being fit for the road. Penn sprang up. Impulsively, he offered the magnificent Arabian mare he had brought with him from France. Loe understood. He looked long and gratefully at the young man. But he declined the offer, saying that so fine a horse would not be suited to his mode of travel.

The next day Penn rode back to Shanagarry, deep in thought and much downcast. He felt that Loe had spurned the gift of his horse because he had not yet proven his spiritual worth.

Six

COMMITMENTS

Now all the days were like a single sunrise. Even the coastal dunes of Kinsale looked different to Penn, and the line of grassy hills held the signature of a new meaning. For a person's vision of the earth takes on new dimensions when he feels himself touched by God.

Penn's inner perspectives widened as he immersed himself in his new recognitions. Now everything sprang into focus. The aching rift between what is experienced and what is expressible gradually closed. Penn felt that he had grasped a central wisdom by which to render himself an adequate account. As the new balance developed, former contradictions resolved themselves toward a harmony. The matchstick structures of theology, to which Penn had devoted so much anguished learning, now recessed in his mind, as the essence of a simpler faith emerged.

The poet W. H. Auden once defined prayer, at its deepest, as a special kind of listening. At all times there have been people—though not many—with a fine ear for those promptings that seem to pervade the world and inform the religious imagination. The Quaker faith, which has neither doctrine nor ritual in the ordinary sense, consists mainly of a welcoming attention and a generous openness to these whispered indices of the spirit. And now Penn was learning to listen.

Though he had not yet formally joined the Quakers, Penn

went to nearly all the secret Quaker Meetings near Cork. More and more he felt drawn not merely to the contemplative aspect of Quakerism but also to the practical side of religion.

Silent meditation—the mystic listening—was of course the central element in Quakerism. But unlike the mystics of medieval Europe and the gurus of the East, who sought illumination in solitude, the Quakers constantly emphasized the social character of faith. The Meeting—the human collectivity through which spirit takes form within life—was the basic instrument of Quakerism. Whatever religion might mean in regard to Heaven, in regard to Earth it meant the organization of communal purpose.

Traditionally, Christian churches imposed this purpose by authority and coercion. The Quakers, by contrast, allowed the purpose to form and assert itself spontaneously from within the community through open interchange in a Meeting of equals. No priest, no pastor presided with guiding power. No hierarchy of bishops issued directives. No altar or steeple claimed totemic status or demanded obedient submission of mind and soul. The Meeting was, in essence, each person's private pursuit of thought within a frame of reverence and an aura of mutuality. Sharing thus became possible, and the Meeting represented, in the strict literal sense, a Society of Friends.

Given the political situation of the Quakers under King Charles II, whose laws made every Quaker Meeting a crime, Penn was running risks. The predictable trouble finally caught up with him on September 3, 1667, when a ruffian soldier stumbled upon a Quaker Meeting in Cork. Knowing that the pacifist Quakers would harm nobody, the solitary soldier felt himself emboldened to a heroic act: Single-handed, he would rout the whole assembly. Bursting into the house and rudely harassing the terrified Quakers, the soldier suddenly found himself confronted by William Penn. Faced with a gentleman of rank, and noticing Penn's hand upon the hilt of his jeweled sword, the soldier faltered. Penn, by contrast, was quite certain of himself. He had often seen his father deal summarily with some recalcitrant wretch of a sailor, and he too had a natural air of command. Without further ado, Penn disarmed the soldier, grabbed him by the collar, and started pushing him toward the hallway. Horrified, the Quakers rushed toward Penn, begging him to abstain from his obvious intent of kicking the squirming soldier down the stairs. Penn, deferring to the Quakers' principles of nonviolence, released his hold and let the man go.

That was a mistake. Freed from Penn's grip, the soldier rushed out of the house, only to return minutes later with a posse of constables, who arrested everyone in sight. Arraigned before the Mayor's Court, Penn stood in the prisoners' dock with the rest of the Quakers. But the mayor, apparently knowing who had come before him, was still trying to find a way out of an awkward situation. The young gentleman, he announced from the bench, was obviously not a Quaker. Hence it was a case of false arrest. The gentleman was free to leave, with apologies of the court. All others were to be jailed.

Penn didn't have to make a decision. The decision had been made quietly and deep within him long before. Released from the prisoner's dock, he stepped before the bench, asking permission to correct an error. He should like to inform the court that he, William Penn of Kinsale, son of Admiral Sir William Penn, was indeed a Quaker.

In the unlikeliest of places and in defiance of circumstance, Penn had at last made his declaration. Now he had one more request to the court: He would like to be charged with the same crimes and offenses as the others. Moreover, as an Oxford scholar and lawyer of Lincoln's Inn, he would act as his own counsel and assume the defense of the others. And incidentally, he wanted to know on what charge they were detained.

The mayor was uncomfortable. He was not accustomed to

being challenged by prisoners. He had expected the usual contingent of docile Quakers in the dock. And now this eloquent young man with his assured manner had somehow managed to turn everything upside down, putting the judge on the defensive. What had started as a routine arraignment had been turned into a test case. An example had to be set. Gruffly the judge answered Penn: The charges were for tumult and riotous assembly. Moreover, unless Penn posted bond for his future good behavior, he too would be sent to prison.

Under what law did the court sustain the charge? Penn demanded.

"A proclamation in the year 1660, and new instructions to revive that dead and antiquated order," the reply came from the bench.

Penn knew this ordinance, having studied it during his legal training. That law, he pointed out, had been passed specifically against a group of radical religious revolutionaries known as the Fifth Monarchy Men, who some years before had attempted to overthrow the government to make room for the Kingdom of Christ. Penn argued that a law specifically passed against that group did not apply to the Quakers, who had no revolutionary intentions. This argument failed to impress the mayor, who ordered Penn and his friends locked up. But it was Penn who, in his own way, had the last word. With his sense of drama and symbolic gesture, Penn paused at the prison gate, unbuckled his magnificent sword, and handed it with a polite bow to a nonplussed bystander. Henceforth, he announced, he would walk unarmed in the world.

This sense of the grand gesture, so typical of Penn, also shaped the rhetoric of a letter he wrote from jail. Nothing in it betrays the shock and humiliation his first imprisonment must have caused him. Rather, it is a reasoned demand not merely for personal justice but for the whole concept of religious tolerance, which had hardly yet been voiced at that time. Writing to the Earl of Orrery, Lord President of the Province,

Penn declares: "Religion, which is at once my crime and my innocence, makes me a prisoner to the mayor's malice, but mine own free man. . . . Though to dissent from a national system imposed by authority renders men heretics, I dare believe your lordship is better read in reason and theology than to subscribe to a maxim so vulgar and untrue."

Again, authority is not merely legally challenged, but morally put on the defensive. The letter points out that, as a purely religious group, the Quakers had no manifest political intentions and should therefore not be subjected to restrictive laws aimed primarily at political control.

This was a radical doctrine. From prehistory to the present, no period had ever divorced belief from politics. On the contrary, politics is always—by psychological necessity—based on belief. Traditional churches as well as modern political ideologies regard the state as the concrete form of faith. That is why, in Penn's time, the suppression of dissident beliefs was considered essential to the security of government. Penn's letter challenged this basic principle of the governing power. In effect, he was advocating the separation of church and state— a principle not recognized until a century later, in the framing of the American Constitution.

It is doubtful that the Earl of Orrery, the recipient of the letter and himself one of the English oppressors of Ireland, was convinced by Penn's libertarian views. But it was shocking to the Earl that the son of Admiral Penn was a prisoner under his jurisdiction. He promptly ordered Penn's release. He also felt that the young man was getting a bit out of bounds and ought to be taken firmly in hand. He therefore sent a letter to the Admiral, informing him of his son's adventure.

By return mail, Penn received this letter from his father:

Navy Office, October 12, 1667

Son William:

I have writ several letters to you since I received any from you. By this I charge you strictly and command that you

come to me with all possible speed. In expectation of
your compliance, I remain,

Your affectionate father,
W. Penn

This style used to work wonders with subaltern officers in
the service. To the Admiral, this seemed the right tone for
getting quick action. But apparently it made little impression
on the Admiral's wayward son. The letter went unheeded.
Another soon followed:

Navy Office, October 22, 1667
Son William:
I hope this will find you in health. The cause of this writing is to charge you to repair to me with all possible speed,
presently after your receipt of it, and not to make any
stay there, or any other place upon your road, until it
pleases God you see me (unless for necessary rest and
refreshment).

Your affectionate father,
W. Penn

William suspected that the Admiral had learned of his
sojourn in jail and hardly looked forward to the apparently
unavoidable reunion. In fact, he was so distressed at the
prospect that he asked one of his new Quaker friends, Josiah
Coale, to come along for moral support. He was still young
enough to believe that a friend, or anyone else, could shield
him from the consequences of his own actions.

Penn's confrontation with his father was terrible, in the profound sense of that word. To the Admiral, William's conversion was a personal betrayal, a fall from grace. Two world
views collided. There was no middle ground, and the conflict
blazed in all its bitterness at the first encounter.

With the tactlessness of youth and the arrogance of a fresh
convert intoxicated with his new ideas, William did everything
to intensify the clash. Playing his new role as a Quaker with

his usual zest for self-dramatization, he refused to doff his hat and addressed the Admiral with "thee" and "thou"—then regarded as contemptuous forms of speech. The Admiral took this as a personal affront.

William explained that he now observed these Quaker customs "in obedience to God" and that no insult was intended. The Admiral suggested that common forms of social courtesy might be observed without compromising religious conviction. Not so, William insisted; for using the polite form of address— the plural "you"—and removing one's hat were forms of deference, a recognition of rank. Such courtesies were symbols of inequality. As a Quaker, he could not, by word or gesture, admit that any man stood higher than another, for all were graced by the spirit of God.

The Admiral pondered this awhile. He was not wholly impervious to moral reflection, and was capable of weighing the merit of such argument. But the horizons of his mind had been drawn by lifelong conditioning in the military and at court. To him, rank was a natural part of human reality. His ethical imagination worked within this frame and could not transcend it. The idea of human equality appeared simply contrary to fact, and therefore absurd. Other norms might well apply in God's eternal realm, but the Admiral was a man of this world, and his life had been shaped by mundane standards. He had wielded authority all his years, and had deferred to authority when it was expected of him. And now the Admiral looked upon his son, who was also giving and obeying commands. But they were so different from his. Unable to comprehend the absolute character of William's moral imperatives, the Admiral at last suggested a naive compromise. William could say "thee" and "thou" to whomever he pleased, except to three persons: the King, the Duke of York, and the Admiral himself. In the presence of these three, William would also have to take off his hat.

But William, long trained to think in categorical terms,

could not agree to such arbitrary distinctions. Both logic and faith demanded consistency and totality. His answer to the Admiral's peace offer was an unqualified no.

The Admiral suppressed his rage. With all the self-control he could muster, he kept his voice even. He ordered William to go to his room, adding only that he should prepare himself to go out early the next day.

The Admiral ordered his coach to be readied in the morning. The streets were still empty as the Admiral and his son drove from their house in Wanstead toward the city in the December dawn. William probably feared that his father was taking him to Whitehall, before the King. Instead, the coach veered into a wooded area and halted. Here the Admiral and William could be alone and unobserved. Together, they left the coach and walked into the wintry woodlands.

With untypical calm, the Admiral explained to William the political and personal implications of his stand. He was close enough to the court to sense the ruthlessness by which the King would pursue his campaign of religious repression. Still reacting with paranoid fury to the murder of his father, the King was resolved to stamp out every trace of the religious nonconformity that had fueled Cromwell's revolution. He saw the official Anglican Church as an agent of the state, and—except for such established and politically manageable creeds as the Catholic and Presbyterian—he would tolerate no other sects. Particularly such movements as Quakerism, whose libertarian precepts were basically subversive to the idea of royal absolutism, would be crushed by the King's cruel and implacable power. Not even the Admiral himself would be able to protect William from the consequences of dissent. William was not merely ruining his father's career; he was also risking his own life.

Once again the Admiral had misjudged his son. His reasonable warning made no impression on William. If anything, it merely added sacrificial ardor to his resolve. Idealists, after all,

by definition, prefer that which is not to that which is.. Hence
they disdain vulgar practicality. Besides, the impressionable
young don't scare easily. Often they are half in love with death,
perhaps because it still seems so far away. Combining such
romantic self-negation with a reasoned wish for what is not,
young idealists are rarely deterred by danger. Their heroism
comes easy, and the price of glory seems affordable.

William was still saying no. He and his father were speaking
quietly. But their arguments, like their hearts, were locked into
an impasse. They could no longer persuade, because they no
longer touched. They felt cold in the December morning, and
returned to their waiting coach.

The Admiral ordered the coachman to drive them to a tavern where they might shake off the chill with a glass of mulled
wine. On arrival, the Admiral told the innkeeper that he
wanted to be served upstairs in a private room. After the wine
had been brought, the Admiral locked the door. Remembering
his last quarrel with his father, William shielded his head with
his arms in expectation of the cane. But it seems that William
misjudged his father as grossly as his father misjudged him.
Far from doing violence to William, the Admiral knelt down,
placed his elbows on the table, and folded his hands together.
He would now pray, he said, and ask God to keep William
from becoming a Quaker.

Only one thought flashed through William's mind: This
must not happen. Such a prayer must not be uttered. His conscience left him no choice: He had to countermand his father's
prayer before God—to pray against his father. That was the
ultimate betrayal, and William felt incapable of it. It was a
conflict he could neither resolve nor live with. He tore open
the window, crying that he would jump to his death.

The Admiral leaped up. For a long moment, father and son
looked at each other in abject despair. They had come to the
end of all possible roads.

Had this scene been invented by a playwright, the only way

out at this point would have been to bring down the curtain. Real life has no dramatic curtains. Instead, it provides trivial interruptions. Somebody knocked at the door.

Quickly, the Admiral and William pulled themselves together for a show of nonchalance. The gentleman entering was a friend of the Admiral's from the Navy Office. He had recognized Penn's coach at the tavern entrance and had come to join him for a morning drink. Of course, he was delighted to meet young William, of whom he had already heard so much. They all settled down for another glass. The immediate crisis had passed.

But the basic conflict remained. William felt that he could no longer remain at his father's house, and spent the early part of 1668 visiting Quaker Meetings in London and its environs, staying mostly with Quaker families in various places. Predictably, he was arrested again, but, since the law is applied differently to gentlemen of rank than to common people, the magistrate did not imprison him. Instead he notified the Admiral of William's crimes.

Once again the Admiral summoned his son, but this time he no longer reasoned with him. In the presence of his silent wife, the Admiral ordered William to remove all his belongings from the house, and not to return. He added that he would dispose of his estate "to them that pleased him better."

At twenty-four, William was now on his own, but hardly alone. His Quaker friends opened their hearts and their houses to him, and moving from place to place, he helped organize Quaker enclaves. A cavalier among commoners, he had to cope with class differences in personal style and social norms. But in the atmosphere of affection that pervaded most Quaker households, these differences were not offensive either to Penn or to his hosts. Besides, the embittered class antagonism that kindles hatred from differences in speech and manner had not yet developed in Penn's time. Such enmity between social classes did not arise until modern industrialism debased and deformed the common man into the proletarian, bereft of human dignity. In Penn's era, people of all stations still possessed an adequate sense of self, and thus were able to accept each other simply for what they were, without rancor. Penn therefore never felt the necessity to adjust, and retained his aristocratic ways even among the lowborn.

Living among Quakers, Penn learned a great deal about the background of the movement. As a distinct religious group, the Quakers were younger than Penn himself. During Cromwell's reign, in the early 1650s, the Society of Friends, as they later officially called themselves, had formed around an itinerant preacher named George Fox.

The son of a Leicestershire weaver, Fox was an unlearned man endowed with moral genius. During his teens he had become isolated and meditative; he withdrew from his family and all company, and spent years in solitary thought. Saddled with appalling repressions by his stern Puritan parents, he felt tormented by the sensual promptings of adolescence and strove against the "whisperings of Satan in the night season." To him, all pleasure seemed frivolous, a danger to the spirit. Suffused with a Calvinist sense of sin, he could not see that true delight had its own profundity as a source of reverence. As a man of vibrant aliveness and inner fervor, he probably responded intensely to all forms of sensory beauty, but his divided self did not permit him to acknowledge and express such spontaneous joy. In his journal he relates a dream in which a woman, dressed in white, walked with him into a treasure vault, extending her hand. But he restrained her, saying, "Touch not the treasure." In these inner struggles and renunciations he built up that enormous pressure of Puritan guilt which later served as his spiritual motive force and enabled him to accept the hardship and physical abuse that he had to endure as founder of a dissident sect.

Other entries in Fox's journal give harrowing clues to the

climate of his mind: ". . . when it was day, I wished for night, and when it was night, I wished for day . . . I could not believe that I should ever overcome: my troubles, my sorrows, and my temptations were so great." He fasted often to mortify the flesh and "went and sat in hollow trees and lonesome places . . . and frequently in the night walked mournfully about by myself for I was a man of sorrows."

His whole youth was a long sojourn in anomie. In modern parlance it might be called a psychotic interlude. But for truly creative minds such episodes often act as the necessary catalyst for personal growth. At the age of twenty-three, Fox was at last able to reintegrate his enormous inner resources. In 1647 he had the liberating epiphany for which his whole life had prepared him: "I had forsaken the priests . . . and the separate preachers also; for I saw there was none among them that could speak to my condition. I had nothing outwardly to help me, nor tell me what to do. Then, oh then, I heard a voice which said, 'There is one, even Christ Jesus, that can speak to thy condition,' and when I heard it my heart did leap for joy."

But the Christianity that sprang from this experience had little to do with conventional forms of faith. "God who made the world did not dwell in temples made with hands," Fox wrote. Instead of joining a faith, he fashioned one of his own, based on intensely individual recognitions. He began to wander from town to town, preaching in the streets. Sometimes he entered into churches during religious services, challenging the ministers and their religions, urging the congregation to forsake all received doctrine and attune themselves to the Inner Voice. Needless to say, his visits to established houses of worship were hardly welcome, and on many such occasions he barely escaped with his life.

From his conviction and from his profound self-renunciation Fox had distilled such manifest force of character that few could encounter him with indifference. Everywhere he went, he inspired overwhelming personal response. He had an uncommon ability to sense the emotional state of anyone with whom he came into contact and to communicate at a level beyond language. His inner ecstasy, as well as his serenity, spoke through his eyes. He could disarm enemies with a mere look—a quality he needed often enough to keep himself from serious injury. Religious or political leaders who preach messages of hope and speak to the innermost needs of the soul are rarely welcomed. They require of their listeners more than cynicism, more than despair, more than resignation. And those who are unable to rise to that challenge feel threatened by the very promise of inner freedom. Often, they are driven to destroy that which they most deeply long for. On one occasion, as Fox lay kicked and beaten on the ground, a local butcher raised his meat ax to cleave Fox's skull. Brushing his blood-wet hair from his face, Fox fixed the man with his calm and luminous gaze. The ax never fell.

Like all true prophets, Fox embodied the essence of his own age along with new forms of thought and feeling yet to emerge. Cromwell's revolution had disrupted every phase of life. Politics, religion, commerce were in turmoil. The fabric of everyday life had been torn. Caught in the tumult of events, people could no longer fathom the meaning of their own experience. With Catholics, Anglicans, and Puritans flaying each other in pursuit of contradictory goals, people could not make sense of their own lives; they grew estranged from their society and hence from themselves.

In such periods of transition, the alienated personality almost instinctively tries to heal itself by groping toward new viewpoints, toward new constructions of meaning in religion and philosophy. Through these new ideas people try to recognize and define their own altered positions in relation to their changed surroundings. In this sense, the new religious sects springing up in Penn's time paralleled the function of modern psychotherapies. They enabled people to shift their perspectives and reinterpret their experience. For religion, in essence, is a reconciliation between man and his world.

Roaming through England, Fox constantly sensed the urgent need for such new reconciliations, and the need confirmed his purpose. Thousands of people, dislocated by the civil war, wandered about begging, stealing where possible and robbing where necessary, helpless at the mercy of circumstance. Even those who remained settled felt adrift in the stream of over-whelming uncertainty. The poet Rainer Maria Rilke has de-scribed the plight of those who find no home in this world because they are caught between a decaying past and a yet unformed future:

> Each torpid turn of the world has
> such disinherited children,
> to whom no longer what's been
> and not yet what's coming belongs.

Spawned by such perplexity, new religions sprouted in En-gland like mushrooms after rain. Seekers, Ranters, Antinomi-ans, Soul Sleepers, Adamites, and scores of others touted their separate insights, each offering explanations for the confused state of affairs, each trying to make comprehensible why and how things had gone wrong. Some proposed radical remedies. The Diggers and Levelers, two of the more influential sects, advocated the abolition of private land ownership in favor of Christian communism. Other groups, like the Family of Love, sought salvation through the orgiastic liberation of the senses. Few of these religious movements had any realistic grasp of the surrounding political and economic conditions, and few of their leaders were adequately informed. But that hardly mattered to their followers. Disdainful of rational theology and unconcerned with basic information, the adherents of these sects were mostly impulsive people who proclaimed spontane-ous feeling to be the only valid type of religious experience and expression. All they wanted was a peg of faith to sustain the possibility of hope.

Under Cromwell, these sects flourished freely. Having established himself against the earlier authority of the Anglican Church, Cromwell practiced religious tolerance even to the extent of admitting Jews, who had been barred from England since the year 1290. Only after Cromwell's death and the restoration of the monarchy did these sects encounter governmental opposition that tested their strength for survival, and many of these sects quickly faded in the repressive period that followed.

One reason why Fox's movement proved more resistant than others may be that Fox had formulated a religion far more modern than he himself realized. By emphasizing the Inner Voice as the central factor in religious experience, Fox went a step beyond Luther. The Protestant Reformation had made man's relation to God personal rather than institutional. It freed the individual conscience from the traditional church, which held it bound in an endless cycle of officially defined sin and officially imposed penance. But even in Lutheran or Calvinist Protestantism, the church was still the main instrument of contact with God. By abolishing the church's authority over the soul, Fox made the personal relation to God a truly private relation.

This may seem a rather subtle and abstract point. But in fact, it may have been just this elusive factor that gave the Quaker movement the stamina for survival. For in privatizing the relation with God, Fox got hold of a notion that was just then beginning to emerge as a powerful force in modern history: the concept of the individual as a person.

Of course, people had always existed as separate persons in the sense of having separate bodies. But during earlier periods of history they had had no clear idea of their own unique selfhood. They thought of themselves mainly as part of their tribe, their group, or their village. Their awareness of themselves was not fully individuated. Until the Reformation, individual consciousness remained partly submerged within the collective body of feudal society and the great engulfing fold of the Catholic Church. Within such a framework, the individual felt himself woven into the social fabric—he was not an independent agent, capable of acting on his own moral authority.

But the Reformation, reinforced by the Cromwellian revolution, had given ordinary Englishmen an emergent sense of personhood—that proud and private sense of Self which has ever since characterized English-speaking people. The Quaker doctrine of the Inner Voice fit perfectly with this emergent self-awareness. George Fox prevailed where others faltered because his central notion was carried forward upon a deep-running tide of history.

The doctrine of the Inner Light, the reliance on private moral inspiration rather than collective norms, was not original with Fox. Ever since the Greek Stoics the way has been open in Western thought to let the individual person be the judge and arbiter of his own actions. But the church, as an instrument of social control, had consistently opposed that idea. Dissenting movements within the church had at various times tried to assert the autonomy of the individual soul in the relation to God. But most of these movements were declared to be heresies and were stopped by stern methods of thought control. For example the Waldensians and Albigensians of the Middle Ages were silenced by the simple means of being herded into caves—women and children along with men—where the Christian soldiers of the Holy Church cut them to pieces. Such methods of spiritual control were considered quite compatible with Christianity. In fact, medieval church literature spells out in careful detail the methods of torture by which heretics could be assured sufficient penitential agony before they died.

Only in Holland, that traditionally liberal enclave amid European absolutism, did a small group exist which anticipated the philosophy and lifestyle of the Quakers. Around 1360, a sect known as Brethren of the Common Life established itself near Amsterdam, espousing a theologically unstructured Christianity based mainly on the ethics of free and open human interaction. But their experiment later succumbed to the punitive rigor of the Spanish domination over the Low Countries. After all, a life of gentle consideration could hardly endure under conquerors like the Duke of Alba, who announced, "I am resolved to leave no single creature alive. The knife shall be put to every throat."

After the Reformation, the tide toward spiritual latitude could no longer be stemmed. True, the Bishop of Vienna still burned Balthasar Hubmaier, the leader of the Anabaptists, and drowned his heroic wife in the Danube after making her witness her husband's death. But such terror was no longer really effective and could not stop Hubmaier's movement from introducing the idea of personal religion throughout Switzerland, Austria, and Germany.

It was mainly from the continental Anabaptists that the new English sects drew their model of personal religion combined with programs of political reform. They met truculent opposition from the established Church of England, which was committed to the defense of the *status quo*. In its effort to preserve the traditional order, the official church constantly looked the other way instead of facing social reality. Many of England's social problems resulted from the existing disposition of land and property. But these property relations were exactly what the official church had to defend. Despite the threatening chaos, the Church of England loudly proclaimed that all was well and couldn't be better. The Dean of Worcester resorted to smoothly circular logic: Social inequality, he said, "was necessary for the establishment of superiority and subjection in human society."

But superiority and subjection—the whole machinery of domination—were exactly what the new religions would no longer accept. For all their differences, they had a common spiritual base in stressing human equality. Most of them aimed at restoring to Christianity its basic human meaning. They wanted to strip doctrinal encrustation from essential faith, do away with such concepts as the Trinity, Marian worship, and transubstantiation. They envisioned Christianity in the simple, direct terms of the Sermon on the Mount. And some of these sects succeeded, at least temporarily, in establishing communities resembling those later formed by the Quakers.

With all this gone before, the preaching of Fox fell upon prepared ground and attracted a variety of followers, ranging from a lunatic fringe seeking salvation in terms of ecstatic sexuality (an odd following for the severely Puritan Fox) to serious and disciplined persons of considerable wealth who felt attracted by the liberal, humanist premises of Quakerism.

The first groups gathering around Fox called themselves the Publishers of Truth, which to modern ears sounds like the self-important motto of some provincial newspaper. But in its time that phrase flew like a banner. It is significant that the members of the sect did not call themselves the "bearers" or "witnesses" of truth. The emphasis lay clearly and intentionally on the idea of "publishing"—of making known.

The word "publishing" had not yet acquired its modern connotation of print. It simply meant the spreading of information by any means, chiefly by example and word of mouth. The name "Quakers" was applied to Fox's followers, probably by contemptuous detractors, because some of the group would tremble under psychic strain as they sought their inner illuminations. The name stuck, even though the Quakers themselves later preferred to call themselves the Society of Friends.

By the time Penn joined the Quakers, the more self-controlled faction of the movement had succeeded in shaking off the undisciplined fringe elements whose grotesque conduct had earned the early Quakers a somewhat doubtful reputation. No longer were young Quakers like the music teacher Solomon Eccles running naked through a session of Parliament to dramatize the concept of divine purity. Nor did the later Quakers tolerate eccentrics like James Naylor, who rode into Bristol on an ass imitating Christ's entry into Jerusalem, thereby throwing the more impressionable Quaker women into fits of dancing and hysterical adulation. By and large, the movement had taken on an aura of well-mannered and responsible spiritual concern.

Penn's entry into the ranks of Quakers signaled the next stage of their development. Up to that point, the Quaker movement had been linked rather loosely to a set of notions and sentiments articulated by Fox. As a religion, it lacked adequate self-definition for want of a body of literature. Its precepts had been spread mainly by the preaching of Fox and Loe, men of profound moral passion, shining intelligence, but meager education. Though compelling in speech, they were incapable of coherent writing. Without any firm record in the form of a written text, their notions were likely to become distorted and falsified by their followers. There was acute danger that the Quaker movement might lose its character and identity simply because of inadequate transmission of ideas. Spiritual movements rarely survive without some permanent formulation of their precepts. Christ's teachings might not have survived without the chronicles of the Gospels and the interpretive writings of St. Paul. What the Quakers lacked was somebody with a theoretical turn of mind and sufficient writing skill to set down their basic ideology.

So Penn perceived his mission: He would put his knowledge of theology, his legal learning, and his Oxonian style at the service of his new religion. Through the power of print, he would become the Quakers' spokesman and defender and their first theorist. He had found not only his faith but also his vocation. He would be, in the literal sense, a publisher of truth.

As the first Quaker theologian, Penn faced a new and profound challenge, for Quakerism was, in effect, the first existential faith. Not only did it have to justify the ways of God to men. Since it rested upon freedom of conscience, it also had to justify the ways of men to God. Man had entered into a questing and questioning dialogue with his Creator. The child of God had come of age, able to deal with Good and Evil on his own terms in shaping his destiny, at least in this world. By the conscious, self-reflecting insight of the individual person, the cause and agency of human history had been taken from the sky and put into man's heart.

Seven

───

ASPECTS OF LOVE

Penn's pamphlets had three immediate results: sudden fame, criminal prosecution, and the romantic acquaintance of Guli Springett.

Rolling off clandestine presses, Penn's writings circulated secretly among Quakers in a manner typical of underground publications. Before Penn's time only a few printing presses had operated in the country, and they could be easily supervised by the authorities. But thanks to the Cromwellian revolution, the number of presses had multiplied. Along with a general rise in literacy, the increased use of print allowed—for almost the first time in history—the efficient spread of dissenting opinion. Legally, of course, everything printed had to be approved by government censors, and unlicensed publishing carried stiff penalties. But the risk of prison failed to daunt the underground press.

After the appearance of Penn's first pamphlets, Quaker families throughout England eagerly invited the young author to their homes to discuss his writings. The Quaker faith was still in formative ferment, and every new expression of its precepts aroused intense response. The fabric of the new faith was woven by this interchange of fresh ideas. It was hardly surprising, therefore, that Penn found himself the guest of Isaac Penington, one of the wealthiest and most influential members of the Quaker movement. At first, Penn had planned merely an overnight stay at Penington's palatial manor, located at Chalfont St. Peter, in Buckinghamshire. But after seeing Guli Springett, Penington's stepdaughter, he managed to prolong his sojourn for five days.

Before his religious conversion—particularly in his Paris days—Penn had enjoyed ample opportunity to meet attractive young ladies, though he was too discreet to leave a record of such encounters. Very likely, most of them were conventionally fashionable girls, carefully maneuvered by their ambitious mothers to cross the path of such eligible bachelors as young Mr. Penn. Their acquaintance could hardly have prepared Penn for a person like Guli.

"In all respects a very Desirable Woman," Thomas Ellwood, one of her steadfast admirers, wrote of her. "Whether regard was had to her Outward Person, which wanted nothing to render her completely Comely, or to the Endowments of her Mind, which were in every way Extraordinary; or to her outward Fortune, which was fair, which with some hath not the last nor the least place in Consideration." In his catalog of her virtues, Ellwood goes on to describe Guli's habitual kindness "expressed in her innocently open, free and familiar Conversation, springing from the abundant Affability, Courtesy and Sweetness of her natural Temper."

Ellwood was the highly accomplished literary secretary to John Milton, who at that time lived in a cottage on the Penington estate. Ellwood had known Guli since childhood and, like many others, was lastingly if hopelessly smitten with her. But even less biased accounts picture Guli as "a comely personage of a temper not easily moved to Extreams." The biographer John Aubrey characterizes her as "virtuous, generous & wise" and notes that she had "importunity of many Suitors, but resisted their motions." Penn, who had an eye for quality, evidently saw ample reason to prolong his stay.

Guli was descended on both sides from Puritan aristocracy. Her father, Sir William Springett, had been one of Cromwell's

officers. When he was killed, in the civil war, he left his wife
Mary a widow at nineteen, about to give birth to his daughter.
Italian names for women were fashionable at the time, as witness many Shakespearean heroines. This was one of the many
influences of the Italian Renaissance on the English poetic
imagination, and when the little girl was born she was formi-
dably christened Gulielma. However, throughout her life, Guli
much preferred the shortened version.

When Guli was ten, her mother met Isaac Penington, scion
of a prominent London family, who had fallen into permanent
melancholy—apparently as the result of being unable to reconcile the demands of a fashionable social life with his penchant
for philosophic reflection. Like many intelligent women, Lady
Springett felt attracted to handsome men in psychological
quandaries. Besides, Isaac's melancholy matched her own
subdued mood after the death of her husband. At any rate, the
two people found both comfort and stimulation in each other.
By the time they were married, in 1654, Isaac and Mary had
lifted each other from their respective emotional depressions,
and little Guli at last had a home as rich in human affection as
in worldly abundance.

Shortly after their marriage the Peningtons came under the
influence of a Quaker family living on their land, and this
greatly changed "the language, fashion, and customs" of their
life. "The giving up of these things," writes Mary Penington
in a long autobiographic letter, "cost me many tears." But she
had caught sight of a moral ideal—so the price didn't matter.
"I minded not the cost of pain, but judged it well worth the
utmost cost and pain to witness in myself such a change as I
saw in [the Quakers]—such power over the evil in human
nature."

Despite these changes and the Puritan sentiment evident in
Mary's letter, little Guli's life was hardly one of austerity. She
had a nanny to look after her and her own footman to pull her

about the lawns of Chalfont in an exquisite child-size coach.

Isaac Penington, Guli's stepfather, was a man of considerable gifts. He wrote extensively on religion and philosophy, entitling a collection of his writings, with typical self-deprecation, *The Works of the Long-Mournful and Sorely-Distressed Isac Penington*. Such humility may be appropriate for many gentlemen writers publishing at their own expense. It certainly wasn't called for in Penington's case. He was an amateur in the best and noblest sense of that word. His writings remain, along with Penn's own, among the best expositions of early Quaker thought.

In his unconventional ways, Penington did not share the prevalent view that women were uneducable. Having fallen in love with his wife partly as the result of intellectual harmony, he did not suppress Guli's natural interest in books, which became evident in her teens. On the contrary, he gave her the run of his library and introduced her to the delights of shared reading. Of course, it was unthinkable for a woman to attend a university, but under her stepfather's tutelage, Guli acquired a range and depth of learning virtually unique among women of her day.

These bookish tendencies—so similar to those of her future husband—gave Guli at an early age an uncommon poise, a kind of rueful equanimity, and a diffidence toward men. At the age of fifteen, the slender and exceptionally graceful girl already attracted admirers. One of them, a visitor to the estate, describes Guli's typical reaction:

> For my Part, I sought and at length found Means to cast myself into the Company of the Daughter, whom I found gathering Flowers in the Garden, attended by her Maid, who was also a Quaker. I addressed myself to her after my accustomed manner, with Intention to engage her in some Discourse. . . . Though she

treated me with a courteous Mien, yet, young as she was, the Gravity of her Look struck such an Awe upon me that I found myself not so much Master of myself as to pursue any further Converse with her. Wherefore, asking Pardon for my Boldness in having intruded myself into her private Walks, I withdrew not without some Disorder of the mind.

Another man, perhaps intrigued by that very air of remoteness, was less easily abashed. At a wayside inn, on a journey, a drunken servant assaulted her. This experience no doubt deepened her shyness and may account for Guli's later unreceptiveness to suitors, even though she treated them with a genuine regard that strengthened both their feelings and their persistence.

But all her hesitancies seemed to vanish at the sight of Penn. Almost at once, William and Guli recognized in each other a kindredness that swept away the barriers each of them had inwardly erected against just such an encounter.

As the French writer André Maurois has so charmingly observed, "A good marriage is like a long conversation that always seems too short." By that definition, the marriage of William and Guli began during those five days. In their long walks together they discovered in each other the range and intimacy of rapport and the emotional linkage by which two people can penetrate to the essence of love: to build by the deep and unhindered exchange of thought and feeling, and by the confirmation of touch, a necessary and mutually sustaining private world.

It was inevitable that William and Guli fell in love. The ways in which each had formed his own character naturally converged with the other. Each could see in the other a living image of his own innermost aspiration, transfigured by eros. As lovers, William and Guli idealized each other. But there was nothing false in this idealization, for each embodied the other's own essential truth.

Not until four years later did William and Guli actually marry, and their long engagement endured painful separations and uncertainties. Part of the time William was in prison. For long periods he was traveling abroad as a missionary for his faith. But their love withstood all these trials, and the profound quality of their interaction seems all the more remarkable in the context of their times.

Every era has its own standard specifications for love—the popular paradigm to which the majority unconsciously aspire and conform. In the ribald period of the Restoration, the fashion was for a kind of practical lustfulness that left little room for romantic illusion and even less for tender longing. Traditional demands for premarital chastity or marital fidelity, never very popular ideals, were relaxed in many segments of society. The resultant sensual directness often bypassed all possibilities of deeper psychic relatedness between lovers. Besides, many women were so stunted in their subtler individuation by the anti-feminine cast of the times that few of them ever developed much capacity for genuinely human interchange. Women's lives were mostly confined within their assigned roles as sex objects and household items, with motherhood as almost the only available form of deep human relationship.

Besides, for most young men and women of the titled and propertied classes, marriage was rarely a free choice of partners. True, most of them had enough sense not to fall in love with anyone unsuitable, and the girls, at any rate, were sheltered even from the possibility of a doubtful acquaintance. But on the whole, wherever marriage entailed the transfer of titles or property, it was arranged by the families and regarded as a sort of business merger. The participants might play their assigned parts willingly and even with pleasure. But transcendent spontaneity—the natural element of love—rarely entered into such orderly arrangements. The romantic abandon of the Elizabethans had long receded into dim remembrance. The new age, weary of romantic daring after the emotional excess of revolution, looked skeptically upon all claims to transcendence, public or personal. Small wonder that the prevailing attitude toward love grew cynical and brittle.

Against this background, the relation between William and Guli stood out as a singular product of the creative strength and generosity of their souls. Each was to the other "an entire and constant friend," and their long engagement became a rich growing season for their love.

It is a pity that none of the love letters presumably passing between William and Guli during their early acquaintance has been preserved. Such letters have special value to historians as intimate clues to the whole structure of personal feeling and fantasy in distant times. As documents of private sentiment, they frequently offer truer insight into the past than can be obtained from literature, art, or other more formal cultural residues.

But even without such direct evidence, one senses how the emotional climate of early Quakerism was reflected in the way William and Guli shaped their feelings for each other. For the whole Quaker tradition posits love, in its broadest sense, as a formative agent in all human association. Both the romantic ideal and the mystery of desire are retained in this concept, but separated from the senses and projected onto the level of religion. Another factor in such affinities is that, for more sensitive persons, the character of love often changes in times of turmoil and stress, growing more somber and deep as men and women seek in each other shelter and reassurance. For William and Guli, caught amid perils and persecution, love became the instrument for transmuting outward stress into inner calm. Later, when Quakerism no longer meant continual personal danger, the tense spiritual acuteness of their love sub-

The Tower of London, the scene of Penn's early childhood
and later imprisonment, as it appeared at the time.

The main building and a classroom at Chigwell School in Wanstead, Essex, where Penn received his first formal education.

The house in Rickmansworth, Hertfordshire, the first home of William Penn and Guli.

Admiral Sir William Penn, shortly after being knighted
by Charles II upon the king's return from exile.

This drawing of a Quaker meeting shows Penn seated second from the left on the dais.

The FRAME of the

GOVERNMENT

OF THE

Province of Pennsilvania

IN

AMERICA:

Together with certain

LAWS

Agreed upon in England

BY THE

GOVERNOUR

AND

Divers FREE-MEN of the aforesaid
PROVINCE.

To be further Explained and Confirmed there by the first
Provincial Council and *General Assembly* that shall
be held, if they see meet.

Printed in the Year M DC LXXXII.

The title page of Penn's "Frame of Government"
as published in 1682.

sided into the warmth and steadiness of quiet affection. But at all times it was a dynamic source of strength enabling Penn to carry the enormous psychic cost of what he felt to be his calling.

Enlivened by his new-found feelings for Guli, Penn now applied himself to his work with fresh verve. Some of his religious writings had already made him notorious beyond Quaker circles, largely because of his journalistic sense for catchy titles and controversial topics. One of his earliest pamphlets, for example, bore the ringing headline *The Truth Exalted* and took as its target nothing less than the doctrine of the Holy Trinity.

The aim of Penn's essay was to prove that the concept of the Trinity was unnecessary to signify the unity of God, Man, and Spirit. No doubt Penn was correct in questioning the place of the doctrine in the Christian faith, assailing the notion of Trinity as a construct of Scholastic theologians, concocted almost a thousand years after Christ. But he scattered his charge in argumentative grapeshot, wasting his thrust in discursive attacks on "persecutors, false prophets, tithemongers, deniers of revelation, opposers of perfection, men-pleasers, time-servers, and unprofitable teachers." Continually indulging himself in clumsy invective, Penn refers to the Catholic Church as "the Whore of Babylon, the corrupter of nations, drunk with the blood of saints and martyrs, maintained by cruelty," and accuses the church of propagating "dirty trash and foul superstition."

The Puritans came off no better. Penn calls them "hypocrites and revilers of God . . . worse than the worst." After heaping abuse on all religions except his own, Penn somewhat incongruously declares the possibility of human perfection. In all, *The Truth Exalted* hardly justifies its title and exalts mainly Penn's own spiritual arrogance. At best, it is the work of a fresh convert carried by his fervor beyond reasoned judgment.

Penn's attack on the Trinity so incensed a Presbyterian minister named Thomas Vincent that he denounced Penn from his pulpit in language as vehement as Penn's own. Eager for publicity, and ignoring the danger of open exposure, Penn asked for a public debate with Vincent. Surprisingly, Vincent agreed. Penn and a fellow Quaker named Whitehead were invited to speak at Vincent's church on August 31, 1668.

By the time they arrived, Vincent had already inflamed his congregation against the visitors. Shouts of "Blasphemer!" and "Villain!" greeted them as they entered the church. Vincent would let neither Penn nor Whitehead present a summary of his views. Instead, the minister subjected them to a doctrinal inquisition on his own terms in front of the howlingly derisive crowd. Before the Quakers could make adequate reply to the barrage of leading questions, the minister simply walked out with an assured air of having vanquished his opponents.

Left alone with the hostile congregation, Penn and Whitehead still tried to speak. Penn protested their rude reception: "Would Socrates, Cato or Seneca, whom they call heathens, have treated us with such unseemly carriage?" But the audience jeered and doused the candles. In the darkness, the meeting broke up in turmoil.

Penn's outrage provided the springboard for his next major work. If the Presbyterians would not listen in person, at least he could set forth his opinions in print. The result was *The Sandy Foundation Shaken,* a treatise more temperate in tone, sounder in theology, and more cogent in argument than Penn's earlier writings. It is, in fact, the first systematic exposition of Quaker beliefs.

The most important section of Penn's essay takes issue with the central mystery of the Christian faith: the belief that Christ's death on the cross atoned for the sins of the world. It is contradictory, Penn contends, that mankind could be saved from God's wrath by inflicting its own wrath upon Christ, God's son. For Penn, the idea of Christ as scapegoat—atoning by his agony for the defects of man—was simply intolerable. A scapegoat must be innocent, as Christ certainly was, but what justice was there in innocent suffering? What was the moral gain in pinning either man or God to a cross? How did such an act, if seen as necessary atonement, accord with the notion of the Christian God as just, merciful, and loving?

Penn's argument, of course, does not encompass the broader range of Christian thought, and it may be faulted for by-passing the specific mystique of the Christian construct. Espousing a rational ethic, Penn excludes the tragic vision that relates Christ's suffering to His love. Seen in that perspective, the Christian cross represents the perennial notion—woven through Western thought from Plato to Freud—that Love becomes fully aware of itself only in its transcendent dialogue with Death. God, like the primal father, must be murdered by His children so that, through His expiation of the guilt of His murderers, Love can at last pervade the community of survivors.

But Penn's mind was not attuned to such dark cadences. The anguished longing for redemptive love, born of suffering and mortality, was not dominant in his religiosity. His religious imagination was practical rather than metaphysical. That haunted inner poetry of the spirit, which Hegel calls the "quenchless thirst," had no place in Penn's rational temper. To him, the cross was just a Roman instrument of torture. Without the tragic vision, Christ's agony is bereft of supernal significance, and Penn could not perceive it as an act and a source of love.

As Penn saw it, the suffering of Jesus as a man was simply an incident of an earthly life, lamentable but not extraordinary. After all, crucifixion was a fate shared by countless other criminals, and hardly seemed a symbol appropriate for worship. In essence, Penn was asking: Why must Christian hope and Christian morality be founded on the pain and horror of blood sacrifice?

This was a tremendous question. In opposing his rational ethic to the sacred and magical faith in the redemptive power of blood, Penn had—perhaps without realizing it—committed an enormity. He had struck at the very heart of the Christian theory of salvation.

This point was by no means lost on one of the more attentive readers of Penn's pamphlet—the Bishop of London. Penn's way of thinking wasn't new to the Bishop. A competent theologian, he was aware of the shift toward scientific attitudes which permeated Europe at the time and devalued the traditional symbols of piety. Ever since that Polish astronomer Copernicus had suggested that the earth was not the center of the universe, impious ideas had been rampant. There had been trouble in Italy with a man named Giordano Bruno, who had to be burned for insisting that the universe was an infinity of stars rather than the neat and comprehensible three-story home of heaven, earth, and hell. And despite the silencing of Galileo, the questioning attitude of these astronomers and scientists was apparently infecting even the minds of religious persons. Submissive acceptance of eternal mystery—of magic faith—was giving way to this rational questioning. That infernal Frenchman, Descartes, even wanted to test faith by reason in order to arrive at a rational faith—whatever that might mean. Obviously, this young chap Penn was one of those clever, sincere, but misguided men trying to put some new kind of ethical-rational religion in the place of sanctified doctrine. As a responsible authority of the church, he—the Bishop—had to stop this. Like all high church officials during the Restoration, the Bishop had the power to order the arrest of anyone guilty of improper thinking. Besides, Penn was technically guilty for not having obtained an official printing permission for his tract.

At the Bishop's order, Penn was dragged off to the Tower. There he was to be held captive indefinitely or until he publicly recanted his statements. Or else, the Bishop swore, Penn would "die in prison." Penn retorted that "the Tower was the worst argument in the world" and that the Bishop would have to come up with a more logical refutation to make him change his position.

Penn had long known the Tower from the outside. He had been born on Tower Hill, and much of his childhood had been spent in the shadow of the squat, square fort whose foundations dated back to Roman times. But now the familiar neighborhood landmark assumed new aspects for Penn. On the way to his cell, he passed the torture chambers, reminders of the rack and wheel as instruments of British justice. Here, too, *peine forte et dure* had been practiced as a method of eliciting testimony. In this procedure, the prisoner was sandwiched between wooden boards. Then heavy stones were piled on him, gradually, during his interrogation. If he remained recalcitrant, more weight would be added slowly, until it crushed his chest. In Penn's time, aids to questioning had become more restrained. But the conditions of his imprisonment were grim enough.

His cell was a tiny cubicle directly under the roof. It was poorly heated, and Penn suffered greatly from the cold after his arrest in December. He was allowed no recreation, no visitors, and almost no written contact with the outside world.

After weeks of solitary confinement, a message came from the Bishop: "Recant in Common Garden at an appointed time before all the City, or else be prisoner for life."

Penn weighed the matter. He was still young. Whatever life lay before him was now forfeit. His whole world had shrunk to a dingy cell. And he longed to see Guli. But he sent this reply to the Bishop: "My prison shall be my grave before I will budge a jot; for I owe my conscience to no mortal man."

Now Penn had but one thing in abundance: time to reflect upon his situation. He needed to understand his own motives and actions, to come to terms with his condemnation, his criminality.

"I owe my conscience to no mortal man," he had written to

the Bishop. That was the spiritual peg on which all circumstance hung. His faith had committed him to the supremacy of conscience. And through his vision of a religiously bonded community he was moving toward a politics of conscience. But here he came upon a paradox: Conscience as a political factor is in itself antithetical to politics. Since conscience cannot be governed or conscribed, it is inherently outside the structure of politics, outside law; therefore it is inherently criminal. It was this relation between conscience and criminality that now made Penn a prisoner. He might take comfort in the thought that Christ Himself was a criminal who had become involved in political matters, chastising moneylenders, rebuking the rich, and linking God's grace to a social ethic. Christ, too, had come into conflict with authorities of the state, who felt they had to do away with Him.

No doubt such reflections deepened Penn's commitment and made his captivity more bearable. On the whole, Penn accepted his fate with remarkable equanimity. Born long before the Romantic Age made self-dramatization the preferred way of understanding one's own experience, he apparently felt no inner need to assume a posture of outrage. He seemed to regard other people's malice and his own ill fortune as part of what Santayana later called "normal madness." His entire Quaker experience convinced him that the aim of law under the Restoration was not to punish the guilty but to crush the free. True enough, this incensed him. But along with his indignation, he had a kind of regretful understanding of the deep folly of human affairs, and this somber awareness saved him from becoming bitter.

Yet for all his apparent calm, Penn was far from resigned to a lifetime in prison. Impatiently, he demanded his release from Lord Arlington, the Principal Secretary of State. His imprisonment, Penn claimed, was illegal. He had not been brought to trial; he had not been heard in his own defense. Again, Penn's petition argues for freedom of conscience as a principle, claiming that it is unjust to punish people for their opinions: "Force," he writes, "may make hypocrites, but it can never make converts."

Even when writing from sheer wretchedness, Penn exhibits Cavalier flair. Not for a moment does he lose his self-assurance when addressing Lord Arlington: "I make no apology for my letter as a trouble—the usual style of suppliants; because I think the honor that will accrue to thee by being just and releasing the opprest, exceeds the advantage that can succeed to me."

It was one of the few occasions when Penn deliberately used the offensive "thee" in a letter to a high official. He expected to be on trial for heresy and would not weaken a principle involved by compromising on form—even at the risk of enraging an official on whose fairness he depended.

The government, however, had no wish to examine Penn in open court. His defense might have proved too persuasive, and embarrassing to the Church of England. Of course, it was also embarrassing to the government to keep Penn in jail without trial. He was constantly reminded that he held the key to his own release: All he had to do was recant. Thus the case stood at an impasse.

The matter got even murkier when "a paper full of rant and treason against his Majesty" was found in Lord Arlington's office among the files dealing with the Penn case. How the paper got there was never fully explained. One supposition was that it had been found on Penn on the day of his arrest.

If the authorship of that paper could have been traced to Penn, it would have meant the death penalty—a convenient way to dispose of the troublesome young man once and for all. But Penn vehemently denied any knowledge of the scurrilous document. Because of the gravity of the possible charges, Arlington ordered an investigation, which established that the document had not come from Penn.

The incident opens up questions that have never been answered. Was the document deliberately planted to incriminate Penn? If so, why and by whom? Had Lord Arlington been directed from higher up to exonerate Penn in any case, to save him from possible execution as a traitor? The latter is not unlikely in view of certain facts later come to light.

As it turned out, the Bishop of London was not the only person responsible for Penn's captivity. At the Bishop's behest, King Charles himself had signed the blasphemy warrant against Penn. The royal friend of the Penns had become William's jailer not from malice but, more likely, in the mistaken hope that the harrowing experience of solitary confinement would make Penn recant. Thus the King had perhaps hoped to save the promising young man from the misfortune of being a Quaker. Like most stratagems to punish people for their own good, the plan had misfired. Getting Penn into jail had been easy enough. But not even the King could now get him out. A summary pardon would not do. If Penn could just walk out, the Bishop would lose face; especially after his ringing demands for Penn's recantation. The Church of England itself would appear compromised. So public law and personal loyalty conflicted at the highest level, and even the King's hands were bound.

Months passed, but Penn, cut off from all human contact in his tiny cell, showed no sign of relenting. He had been given permission to keep writing materials, possibly in the hope that he might write a retraction of his views. Instead, he set to work on yet another theological essay. Again his title was inflammatory, waving above the issues like a flag: *No Cross, No Crown*.

Ortega y Gasset, the Spanish philosopher, once uttered the dark dictum that "the only true thoughts are those of the shipwrecked." Extreme adversity indeed tends to clarify one's thinking, and Penn's prison writings reveal a new depth. *No Cross, No Crown* is a thorough explication of the Quaker ideology for whose sake he was in prison. As the title implies, the essay rejects both spiritual and political domination of the human soul. Much of it deals with controversies of the time which are of little interest to later readers. But in crystallizing the basic assumptions of Quakerism, the work became one of the classics of Quaker literature.

Penn builds his case against religious dogma and dependence on received doctrine and authority. In their place, he offers a dramatically modern concept: an experimental religion based on actual life experience. Arguing almost like a twentieth-century existentialist, Penn drives home his central point: There can be no authority to establish Truth; but Truth, as manifest in human existence, is the sole authority.

The essay reflects Penn's range of erudition, tracing the development of the ideas he presents to such sources as Socrates, Plato, Aristotle, Polybius, Cicero, St. Augustine, St. Jerome, St. Ignatius, Luther, Calvin, Erasmus, Sir Philip Sidney, Grotius, John Donne, and Roger Bacon. In all, he cites sixty-eight authors, along with four hundred biblical passages. That a man of twenty-four should have amassed such stores of knowledge is in itself remarkable. Even more astounding is the fact that, writing in prison, Penn was able to work without access to source materials and cite his quotations from memory.

Penn's essay is notable for yet another reason. It was among the first religious treatises to employ the method of historical analysis. Most of Penn's contemporaries still wrote as if the pattern of human affairs and the nature of human knowledge were fixed for all time. They saw history merely as a string of happenings against an invariant background. Human nature was supposed to be unchanging, and human thought was supposed to be forever contained in the same inflexible frame of formal logic. This assumption was the heritage of the Middle Ages, and it so constrained the imagination that nobody could conceive of change and evolution. Humanity appeared motionless, frozen in the pose of eternity, at least until the Last Judgment.

In *No Cross, No Crown* Penn broke through this confining

mold. Tracing the idea of non-doctrinal religion from classical Greece to Spinoza, he was among the first to treat such a topic in terms of its development in time. Unlike earlier, static modes of thought, Penn's view of history as the flow and growth of human ideas allows for unlimited possibilities of change.

Certainly Penn was not the only scholar in his day to develop this historical viewpoint, but he was among the first to employ the principle of historicity—of perceiving dynamic change as a condition of human existence. Not until Hegel, more than a century later, was this principle fully recognized and elaborated.

While writing *No Cross, No Crown,* Penn kept petitioning for his release. "What if I differ from some religious apprehensions?" he wrote Lord Arlington. "Am I therefore incompatible with the being of human societies? Shall it not be remembered with what success kingdoms and commonwealths have lived under the balance of diverse parties?"

Again Penn reveals his striking modernity of thought. His rhetorical questions demand that his most advanced ideas be taken for granted. The basic assumption set forth in his letter to Lord Arlington is nothing less than the idea of democratic pluralism, foreshadowing the political philosophy of the future American republic.

His petition continues: "I think it's time, and I desire I may be ordered a release to follow my ordinary employments; but if it should yet be scrupled or denied upon the least dissatisfaction unremoved, I entreat the favor of access to the King, where I shall freely and justly answer to all such interrogatories as may concern my present case."

With characteristic self-assurance, Penn wanted to argue his case before the King himself. The King was apparently told of Penn's request. Though he would not consent to receive the prisoner in audience, he devised other ways of establishing negotiations with the isolated Penn. One of the royal chaplains, Dr. Edward Stillingfleete, was asked to visit Penn in the Tower.

Stillingfleete seems to have been a remarkably liberal theologian and a man of profound human sympathy. To Penn, his visits must have been a joyful surcease from the torments of enforced loneliness. After months of being cast entirely upon his own resources for inner sustenance, these visits were Penn's first encounter with another person of kindred sensibilities and concerns. With Stillingfleete, Penn could talk about the ideas that had come to occupy him with almost obsessive intensity during his imprisonment. The thoughts and theories he had developed during the writing of his tract he could now at last share with another person of competent intelligence. The tremendous psychic relief this meeting must have brought him probably contributed much to the rapport and mutual liking that soon sprang up between the royal chaplain and the young heretic.

At first, Stillingfleete hoped to prevail on Penn for the recantation demanded by the Bishop. But he soon sensed that Penn was not a man who would save his life by confessing to what he believed to be a lie. Stillingfleete therefore switched his approach. Perhaps the blasphemy charge resulted from a mere misunderstanding of Penn's remarks on the meaning of the cross. The Bishop had interpreted Penn's view of the crucifixion as a denial of Christ's divinity. Stillingfleete perceived that Penn had not intended such implications. Perhaps, Stillingfleete suggested, Penn could write another essay to explain that his earlier work did not in fact deny the divinity of the Saviour. That, presumably, would reassure the Bishop.

Penn promptly set to work on such a tract. Under the conciliatory if coy title of *Innocency with Her Open Face*, Penn wrote what is basically a commentary on the earlier essay that had attacked both the concept of the Trinity and the efficacy of the crucifixion as an instrument of salvation. The subtitle states specifically that the new tract was "presented by Way of Apology for the Book Entitled *The Sandy Foundation Shaken*."

But Penn's new work was far from an outright retraction.

In effect he restated his earlier assertions, but this time he carefully pointed out the limits of their implications. In the first place, he reminds the reader, his dispute was with the Presbyterians, not the Church of England. This was a clever political touch, for neither the King nor the Bishop had much sympathy for Presbyterians. Then, on more substantive grounds, Penn argues that his objections to sacrificial death do not *per se* impugn Christ's divinity. God as manifest in Christ, Penn suggests, is indeed eternal and infinite *just because* He is not a God of death and vengeance but the divinity of love and of the boundless compassion that encompasses all things, all creatures, and all time.

A theology of love is inherently radical; for love, like conscience, is autonomous and ungovernable. But in ultimate Christian terms, the theology of love is also the most conservative, since it rests upon the mystic core of the faith. Whether such theology is seen as radical or conservative depends upon the interpretation. Fortunately, Penn had a sympathetic interpreter in Dr. Stillingfleete, who was commissioned by the King's Privy Council to evaluate Penn's new essay. Stillingfleete's report exonerated Penn of blasphemous intent, and on July 28, 1669, at a meeting of the Council, the King himself officially expressed his approval of Stillingfleete's report and of Penn's manuscript. As the head of the Church and Defender of the Faith, the King of England carried sufficient spiritual authority to make his decision binding on the Bishop. Nothing now stood in the way of Penn's release. A royal order was dispatched to the Lieutenant of the Tower to set the prisoner free.

After eight months in prison, during which the twenty-four-year-old Penn had produced the vital texts that form the theoretical basis for the Quaker faith, he at last walked out into the summer sun.

Eight

ON TRIAL

> Unlike puppets, we have the possibility of stopping in
> our movements, looking up and perceiving the machin-
> ery by which we have been moved. In this act lies the
> first step toward freedom.
>
> —PETER BERGER

Penn's prison experience should have taught him some practical sense. At least his friends at court thought so. The King,
in particular, regarded the Tower of London as an educational
institution where one might learn caution as a civic virtue. But
that lesson was lost on Penn. He missed the whole point of
Dr. Stillingfleete's mission and the King's intervention. He
considered his release a matter of plain justice, not a royal
favor to be repaid by his acquiescence. The young man whom
captivity could not break, freedom could not bribe.

This need not have come as surprise to the King of England.
After all, Penn had quite adequately explained himself: "I
shall not budge . . . for I owe my conscience to no mortal
man." But the King, who owed *his* conscience to all the con-
tingencies of great power, could not know what Penn meant.

Penn had a rare quality that made him incomprehensible to
more accommodating men. He had courage. Cowardice is
understandable. Courage is not. It is a mystery whose sources,
like those of faith, are beyond reason. In fact, faith and cour-

age are so related that, in danger, faith is experienced as the protective shield that warrants courage. This may explain why religious martyrs and political prisoners under torture are sometimes able to endure pain with dignity. Here lies the ultimate proving ground for the power of ideas, and Penn would not shy away from it. The stage was thus set for continued conflict, and the span of Penn's freedom was predictably brief.

For some months after his release, Penn busied himself with estate matters in Ireland. The Admiral had grown too ill to attend to his properties and left his business affairs in the hands of his otherwise still estranged son. The elder Penn could no longer work at the Navy Office, which in any case would have held little joy for him, since the Dutch had virtually wrecked the English fleet in a belated but decisive victory. Even the *Royal Charles,* the Admiral's beloved flagship, had fallen prey to the enemy. Now he mostly sat home, "very ill of a dropsy-scurvy and jandies," as Lady Penn recounts. "He hath a very great belly and full of water and the fisick was to get out the water if possible, but the doctor had given over and had said that the first winter would carry him away. He seldom walks in the garden."

On his journeys between London and Ireland, Penn regularly stopped off to see Guli. His visits were almost the only happy moments in Guli's life now. Misfortune had befallen her family. Their great estates had been confiscated by the Crown because of their Quaker beliefs, and the Peningtons now lived in more modest circumstances at Bury Farm, not far from their former mansion at Chalfont. Isaac Penington himself had been suffering much abuse from vulgar and vituperative constables.

Measures against the Quakers were growing more stringent. Oddly enough, the reason for this increased persecution had little to do with Quakerism as such but was the byproduct of one of the strangest episodes in the whole dismal history of secret plots.

King Charles, born of a Catholic mother, had always had

secret leanings toward Catholicism. These were strengthened by his dislike of Puritanism in all its forms and by his sincerely felt need to obtain ready absolution from the venial sins of his rampant sexuality. Early in 1670, the King mixed international politics with these personal problems in an almost grotesque scheme. Ostensibly, England was just then forming an alliance with Sweden and Holland which promised two advantages: It would end the naval flare-ups between England and Holland, and it would allow the three allied Protestant countries to contain the colonial expansion of France. Secretly, however, King Charles was negotiating with France to bring Catholicism back to England as the official state religion. The upshot was the secret Treaty of Dover, which allied England and France against Holland and called for the King to confess publicly to the Roman religion and to accept French money and French troops to re-establish Catholicism in England.

The plan miscarried, but meanwhile the English Parliament, dominated by Anglicans, got wind of these schemes. Acting promptly to forestall the machinations of the King against his own country, they put sharp new teeth into the Conventicle Act, the law by which religious dissidence was to be rooted out. Specifically, the law was to provide "speedy remedies against the growing and dangerous practices of seditious sectaries and other disloyal persons, who, under pretence of tender consciences, have or may at their meetings contrive insurrections." In short, the law was broad enough to be used against all forms of unorthodoxy.

The Conventicle Act did little to quell Catholic insurgence, but it was wielded lustily as a club against the Quakers. Catholics, after all, could not be recklessly baited. They were too powerful. So the new law was like a weapon in search of a target. The Quakers, being helpless, were more inviting victims. Thousands were imprisoned, their goods forfeit, and many died in the dank and filthy jails.

Soon after the new law took effect, Penn returned to London

to confer with his Quaker friends about possible courses of action in this crisis. Penn's basic formula was simple: Always put justice above law, and when the law is unjust, challenge it directly.

This precept has become an attitude common to modern reformers like Mohandas Gandhi and Martin Luther King. But in Penn's time the approach was new. It reflected a mood and a style of political action that had sprung up in the age of Cromwell. In earlier, traditionally authoritarian times, the only thinkable attitude had been that the law must be obeyed simply because it is law. Obedience—more than poverty and chastity —was the chief Christian virtue of the feudal era. In rebelling against this absolutism of law, Penn was asserting another aspect of the Christian heritage: Christ's own dictum that the law was made for man, not man for the law.

From theory to practice was only a simple step. Since the Conventicle Act forbade public assembly for the expression of nonconformist views, the law could be challenged simply by calling such a meeting.

Penn decided to speak in the open street. He let it be known among Quakers that he would talk at a corner on Gracechurch Street on August 14, 1670. The authorities also knew of his plan. A company of soldiers awaited him when he appeared with William Meade, another Quaker, who had been a colonel in Cromwell's army and later became a linen merchant. As soon as Penn began to speak, the soldiers arrested both him and Meade. The warrant had been issued in advance by Sir Samuel Starling, the Lord Mayor of London, who in this capacity also acted as the highest municipal judge. Sir Samuel announced that he would personally try the case against Penn.

Sir Samuel sensed another chance of making political hay. When serving Cromwell, he had been a fierce prosecutor of Royalists. Now that he served the King, he seemed even more eager to prove true devotion to whoever was on top. Having Penn in court would give him opportunity to stage a show trial.

He was too blunt-minded to realize that such display for lawful zeal would only embarrass the King, who was already too deep in his secret troubles to intervene for Penn again. Sir Samuel also failed to foresee that publicity trials against sophisticated defendants sometimes carry greater risk for the judge than for the accused.

Starling emerges from the trial record as a man of sufficient narrowness to qualify as anybody's political tool. To him, the law was not the earthly arbiter of good and evil, but merely an extension of the policeman's club. Moreover, Sir Samuel lacked all concept of the creative function of a judge under English common law. Equipped with civic sense and humane vision, even a conservative judge can deal constructively with radical dissidence. For such a judge, the real issue is not to punish the dissenter but to make it clear why dissent is punished. In justifying the norms of society by the argument and logic of his decision, even a punitive judge can provide a creative dialectic between tradition and reform.

All this lay beyond Sir Samuel's grasp. But in the end he succeeded in his fondest ambition: He made legal history. His blatant incompetence made the Penn trial a landmark case that shaped the future of English and American justice.

One reason why courts dispense dubious entertainment more often than justice or wisdom is that law and life maintain only tenuous and ambivalent connections. As a code toward the realization of ideal human conduct, the law is supposedly majestic. As an abstract foil for concrete human action, the law is also absurd. These contrasting faces of the law acted like living characters in Penn's trial, making it a courtroom drama in a deeper sense. Not only the fate of the participants hinged on the outcome, but also the fate of the principles under which they were convened in court on September 1, 1670.

Even the setting was theatrical. No stage designer could have contrived anything more darkly ominous than the somber Gothic of Old Bailey. Leaded windows set deep into massive

stone walls admitted light in thin shafts. Like stage illumination, these bright but dusty beams pierced the vaulted dusk and
explored the carved woodwork on the paneled room coaxing a
kind of spectral animation from its curlicues. Indeed, the architecture of Old Bailey provided a suitable backdrop for the
eerie encounter between the abstractions of law and the illusions of life.

As Penn and Meade were led into the court, a bailiff stood
close behind the door, as if in ambush. As the accused passed
him, he grabbed them roughly from behind and pulled off their
hats. This maneuver had no doubt been planned to give Sir
Samuel a chance to demonstrate his brand of judicial fairness.
He ordered the bailiff to restore the hats to their owners and
replace them from where they had been snatched: that is, to
put them back on the heads of Penn and Meade. Thereupon
the judge brought down his gavel and fined each of the defendants forty marks—a considerable sum—declaring that the
wearing of hats constituted contempt of court.

The judiciary of Alice's wonderland or the domains of Franz
Kafka could hardly have bettered this procedure. Even before
the trial opened the defendants were under censure and correction. The atmosphere was now set.

At the outset of the proceedings, the prisoners identified
themselves. Sir Samuel interrupted this formality by remarking
that Penn ought to be whipped for being the son of Admiral
Penn, whom he accused of starving his sailors while embezzling
the money that should have bought their rations. It was probably one of the last occasions when the notion of inherited
guilt was aired by a judge in an English court. Penn answered
quietly: "I could very well hear severe expressions addressed
to me concerning myself, but I am sorry to hear abuses of my
father, who is not present [to defend himself]."

Penn's rebuke to the judge stirred approving murmurs in
the courtroom crowd. Admiral Penn was still a popular hero,

and the spectators were moved by his son's gallantry toward his estranged father.

The Crown now presented its case. The clerk droned out the indictment. Only at the end did he speak succinctly: "What say you, William Penn and William Meade? Are you guilty as you stand indicted, in manner and form as aforesaid, or not guilty?"

Penn protested: "It is impossible that we should be able to remember the indictment verbatim, and therefore we desire a copy of it, as is customary in like occasions."

John Howel, the Recorder of the Court, acting as public prosecutor, curtly refused this request: "You must first plead to the indictment before you can have a copy of it."

Deprived of exact knowledge of the charges brought against them, Penn and Meade took the course they had planned all along, which was now the only reasonable course open to them. They entered pleas of not guilty.

After the jury had been sworn in, the indictment was repeated for their benefit. It turned out that Penn and Meade stood accused of having caused "unlawful and tumultuous assembly . . . to the disturbance of the Peace of Lord and King . . . to the great terror and disturbance of many of his Liege people and Subjects, to the ill example of all others, against the Peace of said Lord and King, his Crown and his Dignity."

Significantly, the indictment did not refer specifically to the Conventicle Act Penn wanted to challenge. Apparently the government did not wish to endanger its chief instrument of religious and political control by exposing it to a test case. While this lack of specificity in the charge frustrated Penn's original intent, it also left him with considerable latitude for maneuvering.

The prosecution now called its first witness, who testified that he had indeed heard Penn "speak to a crowd of people in

Gracechurch Street." Leading his witness, the prosecutor tried to establish that Penn was not merely "speaking," but was in fact "preaching" with presumably seditious intent. But the witness replied: "There was such a great noise that I could not tell what he said." The content of Penn's speech was thus never established in court.

Pouncing on this flaw in the Crown's case, Penn moved to the counterattack. Not only did he claim innocence, he challenged the very ground of the indictment. In the name of religious freedom, he demanded the explicit right to speak or preach freely anywhere. It was Penn's strategic move. The accused indicted not only the law but the prior assumptions legitimated by the law. Speaking as much to the gallery as to the bench, he proclaimed:

> We confess ourselves to be so far from recanting, declining to vindicate the assembling of ourselves to preach, pray or worship the Eternal Holy Just God, that we declare to all the world that we do believe it to be our indispensable duty to meet incessantly for so good an account; nor shall all the powers upon earth be able to divert us from reverencing and adoring our God, who made us.

Richard Brown, one of the associate judges, broke in: "You are not here for worshipping God but for breaking the law."

Penn retorted: "I affirm I have broken no law, nor am I guilty of the indictment that is laid to my charge. . . . I desire you would let me know under what law you prosecute me and upon what law you ground my indictment."

The question had been directed to the recorder, the court's legal expert. The recorder answered: "The Common Law."

Penn asked for a specific citation of precedent.

The recorder refused: "You must not think that I am able to

run up so many years and so many adjudged cases, which we call the Common Law, just to answer your curiosity."

Penn: "This answer is very short of my question. For if the Law be Common, it should not be so hard to produce."

Recorder: "Sir, will you plead to the indictment?"

"Shall I plead to an indictment that hath no foundation in Law?" Penn demanded; and he went on to point out that even the jury could not bring a verdict unless it knew exactly on what grounds he was charged.

The courtroom crowd was beginning to enjoy itself. Here this handsome, twenty-six-year-old man was pulling the legal rug right from under the Lord Mayor of London. The recorder felt uneasy and tried to cut down Penn with a personal remark. "You're a fancy fellow," the recorder sneered at Penn.

But the insult merely set the stage for Penn. He was an experienced public speaker and knew when he had his audience with him. Sensing the sympathy of the spectators, he launched into the kind of grandstand play he had always loved: "I say, it is my place to speak to matter of law. I am arraigned a prisoner. My liberty, which is next to life itself, is now concerned. . . . I say again: unless you show me—*and the people*—the law you ground my indictment upon, I shall take it for granted that your proceedings are merely arbitrary."

In effect, Penn was challenging the court to cite the Conventicle Act he wanted to test. This was precisely what the court wanted to avoid. So, in a sense, Penn had the upper hand, and he made the most of it: "The question is not whether I am guilty of this indictment, but whether the indictment be legal. It is too general and imperfect an answer to say that it is the common law, unless we know both where and what it is. For where there is no law, there can be no transgression; and a law which is not in being is so far from common that it is no law at all."

Penn was merely saying that you can't break nonexistent

laws. Put off by such simple logic, the recorder preferred to stick to personal remarks: "You are an impertinent fellow! Will you teach the court what law is? It's *lex non scripta* [the unwritten law] which many have studied thirty or forty years. . . . And you would have me tell you in a moment!"

Penn merely observed that if the common law is so hard to understand it surely can't be very common. As soon as the snicker from the gallery subsided, he nailed down his quip with legal specifics. He cited certain paragraphs in Coke's *Institutes of Law,* the most reputable legal compendium of that period. If the recorder wished to enlighten himself on the definition and extent of common law in relation to common right and charter privileges, he could do so by consulting 9 Hen. 3.29, 25 Edw. 1.1, 2 Edw. 3.8 in Volume Two of the *Institutes,* on page thirty-six.

Not only did this young rebel know law; he could cite it from memory.

"You are a troublesome fellow!" the recorder bellowed. "It is not for the honor of the court to suffer you to go on!"

Penn: "I have asked you but one question, and you have not answered me, though the rights and privileges of every Englishman be concerned in it."

Recorder: "If I should suffer you to ask questions till to-morrow morning, you would never be the wiser."

Penn: "That depends upon the answers."

Recorder: "Take him away. [To the judge] My Lord, if you take not some course with this pestilent fellow to stop his mouth, we shall not be able to do any thing tonight."

Judge: "Take him away. Take him away. Turn him into the bail-dock."

The bailiffs approached with a portable cage, into which Penn was to be locked like a giant bird. But before they could pull him down and shove him in, Penn wheeled about. With the bailiffs already holding his arms, he shouted to the gallery:

Is this justice or true judgment? Must I therefore be taken away because I plead for the fundamental laws of England? However, this I leave upon the consciences of you who are the jury and my sole judges: that if these ancient and fundamental laws, which relate to liberty and property, and which are not limited to particular persuasions in matters of religion, must not be indispensably maintained and observed, who then can say that he has a right to the coat upon his back? Certainly our liberties are to be openly invaded, our wives to be ravished, our children slaved, our families ruined, and our estates led away in triumph by every sturdy beggar and malicious informer—as *their* trophies but *our* forfeits for conscience's sake. The Lord of heaven and earth will be judge between us in this matter.

Recorder: "Be silent there!"

Penn: "I am not to be silent in a case where I am so much concerned, and not only myself, but many ten thousand families besides."

At a sign from the bench, the bailiffs now forced Penn into the cage. He offered no resistance. Like a captured animal, he was carried to a distant corner, where he and his cage were dumped behind a high partition.

The court then called Meade into the prisoner's dock, hoping perhaps to find him more docile. But Penn had coached Meade on points of law and style of argument, and Meade proved as intractable as Penn himself. The judge promptly ordered Meade to be caged together with Penn, behind the partition. Then he presented his charge to the jury in the absence of the accused.

This was illegal, and the prisoners knew it. Penn succeeded in clambering up inside the cage. Raising his head above the partition, he shouted to the jury that not only his rights but their rights also had been violated. Not only had the charge been read in his absence, but the jury had been ordered to bring in a verdict without hearing the defense. "Take notice," Penn warned, "ye cannot legally depart the court before I have been fully heard, having at least ten or twelve material points to offer in order to invalidate the indictment."

But the court was in no mood to hear arguments. The judge answered Penn's plea by ordering both prisoners to the "Hole." This was a special place of detention on the premises of Old Bailey. Penn describes it as "a stinking and noisome place, which the Mayor himself would have thought unfit for his swine."

After an hour and a half, Penn and Meade were released from this dungeon and brought back into the court to hear the jury return the verdict. Edward Bushel, the foreman of the jury, pronounced Penn guilty of "speaking in Gracechurch Street." For all practical purposes, this was a verdict for acquittal, speaking was no crime, not even under the noxious statutes of the Conventicle Act.

"Is that all?" Sir Samuel asked.

"That is all I have in commission," replied Bushel.

Furious at seeing the case dissolve, the judge prompted the jury foreman: "Was it not unlawful assembly? You meant he was speaking to a tumult of people there."

Bushel shook his head; he repeated his original verdict.

Enraged, Sir Samuel berated Bushel and the jury and threatened to have Bushel branded.

When Sir Samuel had exhausted his stock of invective, the recorder's voice rasped out: "The Law of England will not allow you to depart till you have given your verdict."

Bushel quietly replied: "We have given our verdict and we can give no other." Then Bushel went a step further in his defiance of the court. Suspecting that the judge and the recorder might somehow pervert the finding of the jury, Bushel asked for paper, pen, and ink. He formally wrote out the verdict and had it signed by all the members of the jury:

Thomas Veer, John Hammond, Henry Henley, Henry Michel, John Brightman, Charles Milson, Gregory Walker, John Baily, William Lever, James Damask, William Plumsted. After they had all signed, Bushel affixed his own name and handed the written verdict to the court.

Sir Samuel's reaction, as Penn mildly describes it, "exceeded the bounds of reason and civility." After calming down, the judge had a suggestion. Perhaps the jury could pick another foreman to guide them to a more obliging opinion. "What will you be led by such a silly fellow as Bushel?" Sir Samuel asked the jurors. "An impudent, canting fellow!"

But the jurors declared their confidence in Bushel. He must have been a remarkable man. Apparently, he understood the issues at stake, valued his own integrity, and was able to make the jurors value theirs. Unanimously, the jury announced that they would stick with both Bushel and their verdict.

By rights, the judge would now have to acquit the defendants. But after hasty consultation with the recorder, he announced a new strategy: "Gentlemen, you shall not be dismissed till we have a verdict the court will accept; and you shall be locked up without meat, drink, fire, and tobacco. You shall not think thus to abuse the court; we will have a verdict, by the help of God, or you shall starve for it."

Penn leaped up, shouting: "My jury, who are my judges, ought not to be so menaced!"

Recorder: "Stop that fellow's mouth!"

The bailiff produced a gag. But before it could be applied, Penn broke free long enough to shout: "The agreement of twelve men is a verdict in law, and such a one being given by the jury, *I require the Clerk of the Court to record it, as he will answer it at his peril.* And if they bring another verdict contrary to this, I affirm they are perjured men in law!"

Dragged off by the bailiffs, Penn managed to fix his eyes on the jury and utter his final challenge: "You are Englishmen. Mind your privilege: Give not away your right!"

The court was not adjourned. It simply broke up, as the bailiffs moved in on both the prisoners and the jury.

The jury had a rough night. Crowded into a cell barely large enough to hold them, they were left, as Penn reports, "without meat, drink, or fire or any accommodation; they had not so much as a chamber-pot, though desired."

At seven the next morning, the ill-slept and unwashed prisoners and jurors were again taken into court. Bushel's attempt to protest the treatment of the jury was silenced by threat of imprisonment. Sir Samuel then formally questioned the jury: "Are you agreed upon your verdict?" The jurors nodded.

"Who shall speak for you?" Sir Samuel asked.

Again the jurors indicated Bushel. Again Bushel repeated the earlier verdict: William Penn was guilty of speaking in Gracechurch Street.

Judge: "Not unlawful assembly?"

Bushel: "No, my Lord. We give no other verdict than we gave last night. We have no other verdict to give."

Judge and jury were again locked in conflict, as on the day before. Sir Samuel's patience was wearing thin. Angrily he turned on Bushel: "You are a factious fellow. I'll take a course with you!"

Bushel: "I have done according to my conscience."

The judge then threatened to have Bushel's throat cut.

Sir Samuel's jurisprudence was even more frustrated in the case against Meade. Since Meade had never even spoken at the meeting in Gracechurch Street, the jury found him not guilty on all counts. Penn took this finding to raise another legal point: "I desire to ask the Recorder a question: Do you allow the verdict given of William Meade?"

Recorder: "It cannot be a verdict, because you are indicted for a conspiracy; one being found guilty and not the other could not be a verdict [on a conspiracy charge]."

Meade: "How! Is Not Guilty not a verdict?"

Recorder: "It is no verdict."

Penn: "I affirm that the consent of a jury is a verdict in law; and if William Meade be not guilty, it consequently follows that I am clear, since you have indicted us on a conspiracy, and I could not possibly conspire alone."

Penn's logic was not convenient for Sir Samuel, and he answered by saying that he would cut off Bushel's nose. Penn stuck to more pertinent points: "What hope is there of ever having justice done when juries are threatened? Unhappy are those juries who are threatened to be fined, starved, and ruined if they give not verdicts contrary to their consciences."

Again, the recorder felt uneasy about Penn raising questions of principle. He turned to the judge: "My Lord, you must take a course with this fellow." Sir Samuel obliged. Pointing to Penn, he ordered: "Stop his mouth! Bring fetters! Stake him to the ground!"

Penn: "Do your pleasure. I matter not your fetters."

The recorder finally explained a little of his own legal philosophy: "Till now I never understood the policy and prudence of the Spaniards in allowing the Inquisition," he confessed. But Penn apparently had convinced the recorder of the need for inquisitorial methods. "It will never be well with us," the recorder announced, "till something like the Spanish Inquisition be in England."

The recorder seemed unaware that, by invoking the Inquisition, he had denied and defamed the very spirit of English law, which he was sworn to uphold. By positing law to be the hangman of freedom, he unwittingly underlined a basic contention made earlier by Penn: that law subverts its own cause as an instrument of justice unless it is based on the "natural law" of essential and irreducible human liberties. Penn had cited the Magna Charta in support of his reference to the natural law, but the court ignored his allusion to the very cornerstone of English jurisprudence.

The trial now stood at an impasse. The court would not ac-

cept the jury's verdict. The jury would render no other. Sir
Samuel resolved this perplexity, at least for the moment, by an
old and reliable judicial device: lock up everybody. The prisoners were returned to their hold. But the jury refused to
budge. Not until the bailiffs threatened force and injury did the
twelve men again descend to their miserable quarters, for
another night of hunger and discomfort.

The third day began like the obsessive replay of a familiar
nightmare. Again the judge demanded a verdict from Bushel.
Again Bushel replied that the verdict had already been given.
The judge insisted on a new verdict. This time Bushel obliged
and amended the original finding. Explicitly he declared both
Penn and Meade not guilty.

Sir Samuel seemed stunned. He then took a remarkable step:
He pronounced sentence upon the jury. He fined each jury
member forty marks—a sum about equivalent to the yearly
wage of an average workman—and ordered their imprisonment until payment of the fine.

Penn, who had been released from his fetters to hear the
verdict, now strode up to the bench. He reminded the judge
that the jury had found him innocent. "I demand my liberty,
being freed by the jury!"

But Sir Samuel had prepared a surprise for Penn and Meade.
Had they forgotten their fine for wearing hats in court? Until
that fine was paid, they too would remain imprisoned.

Meade remarked that it was the judge himself who had ordered the hats to be placed on the prisoners' heads. Consequently, Meade argued, the judge should pay the fine. This
argument found favor with the spectators, if not with the court.
Penn then offered another technical point for consideration.
The fine had been summarily imposed. But as a freeman under
English law, Penn claimed, he could not be fined except on
judgment by a jury of his peers. And the matter about the hats
had never been submitted to the jury.

The recorder motioned to the bailiffs: "Take him away!"

But Penn managed a last word as the bailiffs dragged him off: "I can never urge the fundamental laws of England but you cry: 'Take him away!' 'Tis no wonder, since the Spanish Inquisition hath so great a place in the Recorder's heart!"

Penn, Meade, and the jury were now carted off to Newgate, perhaps the most loathsome prison in all England. One contemporary account describes it as so crowded that "the breath and steam that came from so many so close together was enough to cause sickness." Depraved criminals played with "the quartered bodies of men who had been executed." The heads of the dead were boiled in the prison yard to keep them from rotting too soon, for they were intended for purposes of public education. Impaled on poles, the heads were displayed on the squares and bridges of the city as a deterrent to criminality. But before they went on public exhibition the heads served for the entertainment of the inmates at Newgate. "The hangman fetched them in a dirty basket, and setting them down amongst the felons, he and they made sport with them. They took them by the hair, flouting, jeering and laughing at them, and boxed their ears and cheeks." Such were the surroundings in which Penn, Meade, and their imprisoned jury now found themselves.

What weighed most heavily upon Penn during his imprisonment was the knowledge that his father's illness had worsened. The son was anxious for a reconciliation before the Admiral's impending death. He wrote his father from prison: "Because I cannot come, I write. I am very well and have no trouble upon my spirits. I am more concerned at thy distemper and the pains that attend it than my own imprisonment. . . . Solace thy mind in thoughts of better things, dear father. Let not this wicked world disturb thy mind."

The dying man was greatly moved by this expression of his son's regard after so long and so bitter a separation. If there was anything he wanted in this world, it was to see William once more and make peace with him.

William suspected that his father planned to free him by paying his fine. "I intreat thee not to purchase my liberty," he wrote to the Admiral. To pay the fine would be to admit guilt. William was unwilling to make this concession. He planned to sue for illegal imprisonment. That, he felt, was the only way to affirm principle. But Admiral Penn knew that he had no time for such legal maneuvers. A messenger, presumably sent by the Admiral, appeared at the prison office to pay the fines for both Penn and Meade. They were immediately set free.

The Admiral had only six days left to live when Penn reached the house at Wanstead, on September 9. But in this brief time father and son achieved a full reconciliation. The Admiral had never understood his son's beliefs, but during William's trials and imprisonments he had gained a deep if somewhat grudging respect for William's integrity and strength of character. In the isolation imposed on him by his illness, the Admiral himself had reflected much on the shifting of values and vanities. The world looked much different from his sickbed than it had once looked from the bridge of his command ship. At last he was able to give his son a token of the parental support William had always longed for. The Admiral said to William: "Let nothing in this world tempt you to wrong your conscience."

As a military man, the Admiral had known how to calculate risks and he knew that William lacked this talent for caution. The younger Penn would be crushed by his own audacity unless he could rely on high political protection. So, as his last official act, the Admiral sent a note to an old friend, the Duke of York. As the King's brother, the Duke stood next in the line of royal succession and next in influence to the King himself. To him the Admiral commended his wayward son.

Neither the Duke nor the King had forgotten what England owed the Admiral. Within hours after receipt of the letter they dispatched a joint reply under the royal seal. The King and the

Duke assured the Admiral that, as far as possible, his erratic son would enjoy the good will and protection of the Crown.

The Admiral's last move and the King's response formed a turning point in Penn's career. It cast him in a dual role: He would be counsellor to the King while at the same time serving as leader of the dissident Quakers. This dual role eventually culminated in Penn's greatest achievement: the founding of his colony in America.

The King's assurance about William seemed to relieve the Admiral of all remaining tension. Soon after, he subsided into intermittent coma. His last coherent words were an acceptance: "The snares of life are greater than the fears of death. I am weary of the world. I would not live over my days if I could command them with a wish."

A few days later, England paid its hero the last honor. Six horses drew the Admiral's hearse, four companies of soldiers formed his cortege, and the flags of his squadron flew over his grave.

In her grief, Margaret Penn could not find words for her husband's epitaph. William found them for her:

> He withdrew, prepared and made for his end; and with a gentle and even gale, in much peace, arrived and anchored in his last and best port, at Wanstead in the County of Essex, the 16th of September, 1670, being then but forty-nine and four months old. To his name and memory his surviving lady hath erected this remembrance.

Eight of the jurors at Penn's trial bought their freedom by paying their fines. But Edward Bushel and three others—John Hammond, Charles Milson, and John Baily—were too embittered to traffic in such compromise. After two months of persistent effort, while still captive at Newgate, they at last succeeded in bringing the irregularities of their trial to the

Court of Common Pleas. This appeals court issued a writ of habeas corpus to get the four men out of Newgate. As soon as they were free, they filed suit for false arrest against Sir Samuel and against John Howel, the recorder.

It was an awkward case, full of political byplay, and few judges cared to have it in their jurisdiction. Tossed from court to court, the case finally came before Sir John Vaughan, Lord Chief Justice of England. He and his eleven associate justices decided unanimously that juries must be free to render verdicts according to their own reason upon the evidence presented. No jury could be coerced. As Sir John wrote in his searching opinion, the judge "may try to open the eyes of the jurors, but not lead them by the nose." The Penn case thus formally established the principle that no jury can be punished for its verdict.

To what degree this decision advanced the cause of justice may be debated by legal theorists. All human judgment is fallible, and collective judgments—even if free from distortive passion—are often more guided by unspoken assumptions and unconscious solidarities than by judicial reason. The freedom of the jury is no guarantee of justice. But in rendering the jury independent of the judge the Penn case provided a lasting bulwark against the most ominous of modern tyrannies: the tyranny of law.

Nine

TRANSITIONS

The death of the Admiral changed Penn's position in the eyes of his contemporaries. No longer was he the son rebelling against his famous father. Now he stood alone, himself famous, an autonomous figure defined solely by his own action.

He had become independent in other ways also. In spite of earlier threats, the Admiral had not disinherited William, and the income from his estates now made William a rich man. He shared the Quaker principle of austerity more in theory than in practice, and now at last he was able to indulge his yearning for fine things. He still dressed in Cavalier costume with its exuberant colors and frills, and wore somber Quaker garb only reluctantly when the occasion required it. Even then, he often sported silver buckles on his shoes and stylishly complemented the Quaker brown with a sky-blue vest of satin. As for his taste in horses, carriages, and furniture, it was lucky that he had such ample means.

For a while, however, Penn was unable to enjoy the comforts of his new financial status. Newgate Prison claimed him once again. Sir Samuel had been laying traps for Penn. Smarting from juridical humiliation ever since his trial procedure had been repudiated in the appeals courts, the vengeful magistrate had kept his police spies on Penn. Catching him in a technical violation of an assembly statute, Sir Samuel summarily sentenced Penn to the maximum term of six months. It was a clear-cut case without recourse.

Sir Samuel wasn't the only one pleased to see Penn in jail. Even some of the Cavalier friends of Penn's family felt that William had been justly punished. In their eyes, Penn's offense was far graver than any of the charges brought against him.

What was this guilt that drew upon him the vindictive resentment of both his judges and his peers? The real issue remained unspoken deep within the unconscious of his persecutors. Had he been just another shiftless rebel like so many religious dissenters in his day he might have been treated with casual indifference, perhaps even with a glimmer of compassion. Penn's transgression was that—rich, educated, and eminently capable—he had engaged himself in a cause basically directed against the establishment that had produced him.

Only once did this hidden resentment break through into the open. Sir John Robinson who, as Lieutenant of the Tower, had had charge of Penn's earlier imprisonment, explicitly reproached Penn for stepping across class barriers in his association with the Quakers: "I vow, Mr. Penn, I am sorry for you," Sir John commiserated. "You are an ingenious gentleman—all the world must allow that. And you have a plentiful estate. Why should you render yourself unhappy by associating with such vulgar people?"

On the surface, of course, the issues involved in Penn's "misconduct" were religious rather than economic. But at a deeper level economic implications were decisive, if unacknowledged. Since the suppressed sects, including the Quakers, drew their membership mostly from among the poor, what was really at stake was a social movement. If free assembly were granted to these sects, the non-propertied classes might more effectively formulate their interests and assert their demands in the political arena. This development was precisely what both the Crown and the Established Church of England sought to prevent. The official attitude toward the poor rested on a traditional double standard: To treat the poor with charity was a Christian duty; to treat them as human equals was a political crime. Penn's real offense was his failure to make this distinction.

Still haunted by the hopes and fears instilled by Cromwell's revolution, England could not take a rational view of social change. Rather than face the problems, the Government tried to hide them under a patchwork of inadequate compromise. The aim was to preserve aristocratic privilege while giving the middle and lower classes just enough economic opportunity to head off violent unrest. What the Cavalier Government did not understand was that such a policy was entirely impractical under the new conditions of beginning industrialism and expanding trade. Under the new economic system, the lower classes had to be drawn more fully into the production process to speed the growth of enterprise. But this is precisely what the Cavaliers with their ingrained class bias could not conceive.

Lacking reasoned comprehension of their own policies, the Cavaliers and the Established Church felt vulnerable, and this was the real cause of their resentment of Penn. For Penn, instead of supporting the class to which he belonged, had recklessly meddled with the machinery of their compromises.

The establishment didn't fear the dull, unfocused discontent always latent in the lower classes. As long as these segments of the population lacked organizational and administrative skills, they presented no real danger, no matter how deep their despair. But the English had learned one thing from Cromwell: Discontent explodes when given leadership that is both competent and charismatic. Penn, it was clear, might develop into just such a leader. Consequently, he was a dangerous man.

Penn himself would have been shocked at this thought. Despite his religious dissent, he was no revolutionary. His principles were liberal, but his method was orderly and, if anything, scrupulously legalistic. It would never have occurred to him that he was in jail for having become an unwitting instrument of class conflict.

As usual, Penn used his prison time for writing, completing

two essays during his six-month term. The titles indicate both subject and mood: *The Great Case of Liberty of Conscience* and *Truth Rescued from the Imposture or A Brief Reply to a Mere Rhapsody of Lies, Folly and Slander.*

The first of these essays, pleading for freedom of thought and expression, develops an argument given in Milton's *Areopagitica,* one of the great political tracts of Penn's time. But Penn's essay also strikingly anticipates the position presented nearly two centuries later by John Stuart Mill in his famous essay *On Liberty.* Even error must be allowed free expression in order to test the truth. True recognitions result from open discourse. Hence, if truth is to be sought and served, there can be no orthodoxy. Like Mill, Penn maintains that those who attempt to limit the permissible range of thought ultimately destroy their own freedom. Any freedom that must be guarded by the suppression of thought is in fact not freedom but domination, and in itself a form of bondage. To suppress a person's opinion doesn't merely harm that person: it causes public damage, because the public is denied the chance to examine that opinion for whatever it may be worth.

Penn developed these premises mainly in regard to religious toleration. That, after all, was the immediate issue. But the argument extends logically beyond religious tolerance to every aspect of social and political thought. *The Great Case of Liberty of Conscience* thus becomes part of a tragic yet profoundly hopeful literature: prison writings about freedom.

These essays were not the only kind of writing Penn did in prison. Much of the time his mind was on Guli, and he managed to send her several poems from Newgate. A fragment of a prison manuscript entitled *Right Marriage as It Stands in the Light and Council of the Lord God* also survives. Its agonized crossings-out and arduous corrections bear witness to the pain and earnestness with which Penn tried to fit his erotic passions into a religious philosophy of love. Amid the horrors and privations of Newgate, Penn struggled with these private longings and his need to encompass them within his religious framework. This was no easy task for a man of his Puritan proclivities, and only a few tormented pages remain witness to his burden.

Immediately on his release, in August, 1671, Penn rushed to visit Guli at Bury Farm. They had had so little time together. Their engagement had been mostly a series of separations occasioned by Penn's imprisonments. Even now their reunion was to be brief. Having immersed himself in theology and religious polemics while writing his prison essays, Penn now felt the need to do active missionary work on behalf of the Quakers. But the clandestine, conspiratorial atmosphere of Quakerism in England would not permit the open evangelism Penn envisioned. For that he would have to go abroad. After barely more than a week with Guli, Penn set off for Holland.

Holland was the logical place for Penn's project. Ever since they had shaken off Spanish domination, the Dutch had made their new republic a meeting ground for new ideas. Their country thus became a pivot for the historic turn toward what is now called the modern age.

Holland was the first country to develop an essentially modern power structure. With public power democratically diffused in the rising merchant class rather than concentrated in the hands of kings and bishops, Holland became the first center of liberal capitalism. As a result, the possibilities of life expanded enormously. The Dutch merchants and their newly invented stock companies needed a new kind of freedom—the freedom to make money. From this sprang other freedoms and a new set of values quite different from those of the hereditary aristocracies that still dominated the rest of Europe. The idea of free enterprise, going far beyond economics, spilled over into other areas, preparing the ground for the new ideal of unfettered individualism. Each man was free to pursue his own ends, not only in business but also in the realms of art and intellect.

Dutch painting rose to new heights, with Rembrandt, Hals, and Vermeer imparting the humanist vision to canvas. Philosophy, embattled elsewhere, found a home in Holland. Descartes had taken refuge there, as had Hobbes and Locke, and at the time of Penn's visit Spinoza had just finished his *Ethica,* a work reflecting the main currents of the time by linking reason with piety and reconciling the new mathematical concept of nature with the contemplation of God. Scientific invention took great strides, particularly in the refinement of optical instruments. Manufacture became increasingly mechanized, and vast resources and energies went into the prodigious task of reclaiming land from the sea, building dikes, and draining fields. The flat horizons were dotted with windmills that drove the pumps, and the very air that moved them seemed the breath of the future.

After the cramped atmosphere of England, Penn felt invigorated by Holland's freedom and the palpable expression of hope in all these endeavors. It was his first experience of an open society, a model that later influenced his plans for Pennsylvania.

Most of all, Penn admired the religious tolerance that accompanied these liberalizing trends of early capitalism. Yet Holland's hospitality to creeds of all kinds wasn't altogether based on liberal principle. In part, religious freedom simply reflected the religious indifference of the new bourgeois class. As historian Kenneth Clark puts it, the paramount concern in the new mercantile society was no longer "Is it God's will?" The basic questions now were: "Will it work?" and "Does it pay?"

The character of ordinary life had been changed by this shift. Vital institutions were redefined in a new perspective. Bourgeois capitalism had secularized the state. The government now represented the community—not God. Religion had become a private matter.

Penn found this pattern congenial. Quakerism, by stressing the individual nature of the religious experience, accorded with the Dutch idea of personal religion. As for the communal aspect of faith, Penn believed that religious organization should be separate from the administrative and coercive power of the state.

With two companions, Thomas Rudyard and Benjamin Furly, Penn proceeded northward from Rotterdam, speaking to religious assemblies in the towns along the way. Furly, an Englishman who had been living in Holland for years, provided local contacts and acted as translator. It is not known whether Penn succeeded in establishing permanent Quaker assemblies in these communities. No detailed records of this journey exist. But it seems likely that he enjoyed a sympathetic reception in most places. Thanks to the prevailing tolerance, religiously inclined people had become used to hearing different viewpoints and exploring spiritual alternatives. They viewed diversity of religious opinion as a possible enrichment rather than as a threat to their own ideas.

Traveling mostly on horseback, Penn and his companions rode across landscapes that still looked just as Ruisdael and Hobbema had painted them. Thatched cottages, built low to the ground, stood in the shade of large elms that made the houses almost invisible. From a distance, a village looked like a tree grove among the open fields. With water abundant in all of Holland, a pond usually formed the center of the village. Here women washed clothes, exchanged gossip, and tried to sort out their own ducks and geese from those of their neighbors. Cobblers, coopers, and other craftsmen also would often take their work out into the open during the warm months so that the banks of those village ponds often seemed as lively as any scene painted by Brueghel.

On approaching larger settlements, Penn and his friends could usually recognize their destination from afar. A belfry rising from the horizon would serve as a distinctive landmark for each town. Hung with tiered ranks of bells which pealed each hour with clangorous anthems, these towers were the pride of their cities. The art of bell-ringing was then at its peak and expert carillonneurs knew how to tug at the bell-ropes with almost orchestral precision. Even Penn, with his doctrinal disdain for bells and towers, must have been charmed by the melodies floating out over the land.

In September, 1671, Penn and his friends reached Amsterdam, probably passing into the walled city by barge through one of the massive water gates regulating the tidal flow in the tree-shaded canals. With his strong sense for urban design, Penn was surely delighted by the toylike houses with their tile decorations, and their stepped gables mirrored in the water of the *grachten.*

From Holland, Penn turned southward toward Germany, hoping to make contact with some of the groups springing from German tradition of mystical Christianity. Like the Quakers, some of these groups were guided by belief in the Inner Light, a concept first formalized by the German mystic Hans Denck. In some ways, Denck had anticipated the Quakers. Since the Inner Light illuminates each soul, he argued, fundamental individualism and spiritual freedom are necessary to let these faculties unfold. "God has given free will to man," he wrote, "in order that he may choose for himself either the good or the evil. God compels nobody, for he will have no-one saved by compulsion." For a while, Denck was connected with the Anabaptist movement, which rejected such Lutheran and Calvinist precepts as original sin, predestination, election, and eternal damnation. It also rejected the dual ethic of the traditional churches, which proclaimed one standard of justice in heaven, another on earth. To Denck, this duality seemed hypocritical, a bold sham for protecting privilege, and an abridgment of human hope throughout the sphere of earthly life.

German sects springing from Denck's liberal theology reacted against the darker aspects of pietistic Protestantism, mainly against the obsessive interest in the subject of damnation, which has always been tinged with a kind of death-worship. To orthodox Protestants at that time, life was but the yearning of the soul for union with Christ, a kind of mystic love affair to be consummated in another world.

Such theological death fantasies fitted the somber mood after the Thirty Years' War, which shortly before had devastated Germany and reduced its population by a third. But as time passed some survivors felt that they had had quite enough of death and didn't want their churches constantly to remind them of their grief and terror. Searching for life-affirming alternatives, they found them in the spontaneity and freedom of the Inner Light doctrine of Denck. A cluster of semi-mystic sects thus sprang up in northern Germany to challenge both the Lutheran and the Calvinist orthodoxies.

These were the groups Penn wanted to visit. Their precepts were so similar to his own that he hoped either to convert these sects to Quakerism or to draw them into some kind of coalition. But Penn's ecumenical efforts were not successful. True, he was cordially received by Princess Elizabeth of the Palatine, one of the most important spiritual leaders of the German mystic movement, who was also Abbess of the Protestant Convent of Herford. The Princess was one of the remarkable women of her day. Spiritually vital and intellectually competent, she was learned in philosophy and theology, spoke many languages, and was also a talented artist, whose paintings and engravings had made her famous. In her younger years she had maintained a close friendship and steady correspondence with Descartes. After the philosopher's death, the Princess had become rather isolated, her provincial surroundings offering little company or conversation suited to her interests.

Penn's visit provided a rare and welcome opportunity for her to talk about her various philosophic concerns. But the Princess was more interested in the pleasure of discussion than in any practical organizational approach between the Quakers and the Labadists, her own sectarian group.

From the leader of the sect, Jean de Labadie, Penn met with stinging rebuff. A renegade Jesuit, de Labadie had left the Catholic Church and his native France to establish a mystic cult that practiced Christian communism, not only sharing material possessions but also raising children communally. The Labadists stressed spontaneity as a divine manifestation, and engaged in ecstatic dances and what one author describes as "exuberant revelry." Quite understandably, de Labadie feared that the English Quakers might not approve such unrestrained expressions of the Inner Light, and he took care to keep Penn at a distance. The Labadists were constantly in trouble with the civil authorities and had learned by bitter experience that it was better to keep outsiders out. When Penn and his companions arrived at the Labadist colony, they found all the doors locked and were left standing outside in a pelting rain. Discouraged by this experience, he abandoned further ecumenical efforts and felt anxious to get back home. He wanted to take care of certain matters there that had been delayed entirely too long.

On February 7, 1672, an announcement was posted at the Quaker Monthly Meeting at the village of Jordans:

> William Penn of Walthamstow in the County of Essex and Gulielma Maria Springett of Tiler's End Green in the County of Bucks propose their intention of taking each other in marriage.

Nearly four years had passed since those luminous days at Chalfont when William and Guli had first discovered each other—four years of troubled longing. The quality and endurance of their love had been tested beyond doubt, and when the wedding at last took place, on April 4, it seemed less a venture into a new life than the confirmation of a proven bond.

The ceremony took place in a small house at Chorleywood, believed to have once served as a hunting lodge for King John. Only a few friends gathered in the small, low-ceilinged room, where an open fireplace cast its warm light on William and Guli as they sat silently side by side. When their thoughts had gathered in the stillness, they took each other's hands and stood up. In simple words they declared their love and pledged their lives to each other. There was nothing more—no rings, no flowers, no promise of obedience. Then they sat down again in silent meditation.

Afterward they went to an adjoining house, where forty-six friends awaited them for a celebration. Thomas Ellwood, John Milton's secretary, who himself had so ardently courted Guli, found yet another way to express his devotion. As Clerk of the Meeting, he drew up the certificate of marriage and passed the document among the guests to be signed and witnessed by everyone present. Soon after, William and Guli entered the splendid new coach that Penn had had built specially for the occasion and drove off to the village of Rickmansworth, which was to be their first home. The little town was close enough to London to allow William to be near the center of events, but Penn's house stood in the open countryside amid lawns and gardens to provide Guli with the bucolic atmosphere she preferred.

Penn's life now flowed at a quieter pace. It was as if he were replenishing his strength after years of struggle. Ever since he had first arrived at Oxford, as a sixteen-year-old boy, he had been constantly wrestling with challenges set by his genius. He had pitted himself against his family, against his social surroundings, and—most painfully—against the doubts and hindrances to be overcome in his own mind. Impelled by an almost demonic sense of calling, as real to him as his own flesh and brains, he must often have thought the world was like a fortress wall studded with spikes against which he constantly flung himself. Now he needed respite. He needed time for himself and for Guli. He had to learn to take another person into his life.

He curtailed public activity. He would now serve the Quaker cause mainly through his writings, while cultivating a new taste for domesticity. Little is known of Penn's private life, but it seems that he and Guli enjoyed the kind of marriage that deepens with time.

Never having been a very practical person, Guli was not adept at managing a household. Throughout her life, she had relied on servants to look after ordinary things, and Penn saw to it that this pattern was maintained for her when they moved to a larger home at Worminghurst, a hilltop estate some fifteen miles from Brighton with a commanding view toward the coast. The house was fully staffed, so Guli could devote herself to reading, conversation with friends, and constant participation in her husband's interests. Their happiness was marred only by Guli's poor health. Always frail, she was further weakened by a succession of pregnancies, which official medical science at that time knew neither how to prevent nor how to render successful. Of her seven children, four were to die at birth or in early infancy. To fond parents the death of a young child must always be a sorrow beyond comprehension. Guli and William bore their shared grief in resignation to God's will.

To spend as much time as possible with Guli, Penn stuck close to his desk, pouring out political tracts in defense of the Quakers. A recurrent topic was the Quakers' refusal to swear oaths, one of the chief causes of their legal difficulties.

Like many later governments wishing to compel conformity, the authorities of England required loyalty oaths from almost everyone engaged in trade or the professions. Often such oaths were arbitrarily demanded, as a form of harassment, of persons with dissident beliefs. Unwilling to comply with this demand, Quakers were jailed by the thousands, and their goods were forfeited through confiscation. In his writings, Penn argued that the Quaker refusal to swear oaths had nothing to do with loyalty. The refusal, he pointed out, derived from Jesus' admonition, "But I say unto you, swear not at all." It was presumptuous, Penn maintained, to summon God as witness.

In his usual way, Penn presented an exhaustive survey of oath-taking, beginning with the Scythians and Persians, quoting dozens of Greek and Roman writers, and gradually following the historical path to oaths taken on the Bible. The following examples typify his historical method of presenting evidence:

> Xenocrates was so renowned at Athens for his virtuous life and great integrity that, being called to give his evidence by oath, the judges stood up and forbade the tender, because they would not have it thought that truth depended more upon an oath than the word of an honest man.

> Menander, the Greek poet, saith, "Flee an oath though thou shouldst swear justly" . . . and Epictetus, a famous and grave Stoic, counselled to refuse an oath altogether. . . . Quintilian saith that in time past it was a kind of infamy for grave and approved men to swear.

But Penn was too much attuned to live issues to argue entirely from precedent. Switching from historical to substantive grounds, he ends his plea with a plain and practical observation: Oath-taking is simply beside the point. Since liars aren't squeamish about perjury, an oath provides no assurance of truth.

Incessantly, Penn poured out polemics of this kind. His production was enormous. From the time he began writing, at the age of twenty-four, until his final illness paralyzed him, he averaged four treatises per year, totalling one and a half million words. No less than 157 separate titles found their way into print, and many of them were translated during Penn's lifetime, into German, French, Dutch, Danish, and Welsh.

But aside from his major theological essays and his important work in political theory, most of his writing was journalistic, concerned with timely topics and no lasting interest. Despite the synoptic cast of his mind, Penn never achieved a coherent corpus of literary work. Moreover, his writing often shows signs of haste, both in thought and style. He could formulate a trenchant idea or strike a ringing phrase, but too often they are buried in what one critic has called "turgid masses of inchoate authority." He simply didn't take time to polish his paragraphs. His manuscripts are mostly first drafts with hardly any corrections. His style grew even cloudier after he abandoned his desk and developed the habit of dictating to a secretary. Pacing about the room, he rambled on in endless sentences, indicating the punctuation by tapping his cane.

Another reason for the virtual unreadability of much of his output is his obsessive long-windedness. He simply couldn't make a point and let it go at that. Every idea was buttressed by elaboration, until the central thought was buried under supportive argument. His sentences and his readers were piled with documentation till they sank under the weight.

Why did Penn in his writing forsake the critical self-discipline so characteristic of him in every other way? One suspects that Penn was unduly proud of his erudition and let no opportunity pass to display it. If he was guilty of any sin, it was academic pride—possibly the compensatory result of his having been expelled from Oxford.

This stifling show of learning hardly endeared him to the

more simple-minded and plain-spoken members of the Quaker movement, who resented his conspicuous scholarship as much as his Cavalier manner. But ultimately Penn's scholarly approach benefited the Quakers in ways they could not have foreseen. His writings secured recognition for the Quakers as a serious and theologically well-grounded religious movement—a recognition attained by none of the other contemporary semi-mystic sects.

In effect, Penn had taken over the systematic exposition of Quaker tenets, a development not altogether appreciated by George Fox, who had founded the movement on a less intellectually structured and more intuitive basis. No open schism developed, and the personal friendship between Fox and Penn endured until the older man's death. Yet considerable tension developed within Quaker circles between those favoring the primitive piety of Fox and the adherents of Penn's more analytic formulations of faith.

If Penn's approach prevailed, it was because his kind of conceptual synthesis accorded with the mood of the times. The world of the seventeenth century was changing so fast that simple, traditional faith no longer satisfied the need for understanding that lies at the base of all theology. Faith now had to be combined with reasoned explanation, and Penn was the man who could do that.

The need for new explanatory schemes grew from a changed vision of the world. The discoveries of Copernicus, Kepler, and Galileo had become known to a growing circle of educated people. Now the earth was no longer the center of God's world. Drawing obvious inferences, perceptive minds immediately sensed that the new astronomy had not only reordered the heavens; it also cast doubt on the prevailing order among men. John Donne, combining the vision of the poet with that of the theologian, clearly saw the disturbing connection between heaven and earth:

The new philosophy calls all in doubt . . .
The sun is lost, and th'earth, and no man's wit
Can well direct him where to look for it.

.   .   .   .   .

'Tis all in pieces, all coherence gone;
All just supply and all relation.
Prince, subject, father, son are things forgot,
For every man alone thinks he has got
To be a Phoenix, and that then can be
None of that kind of which he is but he.

As the stars had been released from the rigid crystal spheres of Ptolemy, so men were now beginning to free themselves from the restraints of the feudal order. The individual emerges "that then can be none of that kind of which he is but he."

As Dean of St. Paul's, John Donne saw in this freedom the threat of chaos. But his contemporary, Sir John Eliot, already saw this change as the promise of a richer life. Even in prison, Eliot envisioned free inquiry as the key to human self-determination guided by critical intelligence: "All things are subject to the Mind. . . . It measures in one thought the whole circumference of heaven. And in this liberty and excellence of the mind is the perfection of man. . . . Man is an absolute master of himself; his own safety and tranquillity by God are made dependent on himself."

In the conflicts arising within these new horizons, both religion and politics lost their traditional moorings. Hobbes and Locke tried to construct frameworks to contain these new recognitions. Within a smaller scope, Penn addressed himself to a similar task. In his writings he created a synthesis in which faith, reason, and politics penetrated each other in a new way. Like others in his time, he had faith in reason. Hence he reasoned his faith. In doing so, he made Quakerism vital and viable, both as a religious movement and as a social force.

* * *

During his early thirties, Penn's life continued in a calm domestic manner. Occasionally he visited Quaker Meetings in various parts of England and engaged in debate with clerics and theologians. But these excursions were brief. Three children had so far been born to him and Guli, but none had survived. He felt that Guli needed his company after these bereavements, and he avoided long absences from home. But their fourth child, a boy named Springett, born in 1675, seemed strong and healthy. With Guli rejoicing in the child, Penn felt that she would not be distraught if he went abroad for a while to resume his missionary work. As always, Guli encouraged his plans, and in 1677 Penn set off once more for Holland and Germany.

Retracing his former route, he again visited Princess Elizabeth of the Palatine, who had become even more intensely absorbed in her speculative pursuits. The contemplative wealth she had gathered within herself now unfolded in daylong conversations with Penn. Even the Labadists, their eccentric founder having meanwhile died, readily received him, but there is no detailed record of what must have been a strange encounter between these sensuous seekers of divine ecstasy and the somber Britannic Penn.

From Westphalia, Penn ventured farther south than on his earlier mission. Coblenz, Cologne, and Duisburg were among the stops of his journey—cities just reborn after the ravages of the Thirty Years' War, rising in Baroque exuberance. Other Quaker missionaries had meanwhile visited these parts, and several Quaker communities had been established in the Rhineland. Penn's visit greatly strengthened these Quaker outposts, and prepared the ground for the later settlement of German Quakers in America.

The free growth of dissident religious communities in Holland and parts of Germany made a deep impression on Penn. How different, how much wider and more generous were the possibilities of life in an atmosphere of spiritual tolerance than in the oppressive climate of England. On returning home, he therefore resolved to carry his struggle for religious tolerance to the very center of power—the royal court. For years he had been neglecting the connections so carefully prepared for him by his father during his final illness. Now was the time to renew these ties to the royal House of Stuart.

King Charles and his brother James, the Duke of York, received Penn at Whitehall. The first visit was merely a formal courtesy. But as their acquaintance grew, both Charles and the Duke became personally fond of Penn, who refreshed the air of the royal chambers by his personal directness and an honesty of discourse rare to the ear of kings.

Hoping to win favor for the Quakers, Penn again brought up the issue of compulsory oaths. With the King's tacit approval, Penn took his case before the House of Commons, where he proposed that Quakers should be permitted to make legal affirmations by giving their solemn word of honor without invoking the divinity. But Parliament was in no mood for such concessions. Still paranoid with fear of a Catholic coup, Parliament consistently, if illogically, resisted every move toward toleration. To staunch Anglicans all forms of religious deviance seemed part of some sinister Papist plot. Penn himself was absurdly reviled as a Papist sympathizer.

The King himself was far more receptive. After all, Charles II was in a spiritual quandary. As Britain's ruler, he was head of the Anglican Church, the Defender of the Faith. Yet his private convictions had led him to become secretly a Catholic. A man so torn for the sake of his beliefs—no matter what his moral frailties—could understand the Quaker dilemma of being caught between the spirit and the law.

Sensing the King's sympathy, Penn proposed a bold plan. Since religious tolerance was politically unattainable in England, perhaps the Quaker problem could be solved by organized mass emigration. America, like a waiting promise across the sea, seemed the site of possible freedom.

As early as 1661, some Quaker leaders, notably Josiah Cale, had spoken of buying land from the Susquehanna Indians for a Quaker settlement, and by 1675 a number of small Quaker communities had been established along the Delaware River. George Fox himself had made a journey to America to consolidate and expand these Quaker outposts. His description of the new continent inspired Penn with the idea of a large-scale, planned community across the Atlantic. As a first step toward the realization of such hopes, Penn submitted to the King a petition for a land grant between the regions of Maryland and New Jersey.

The King's response was staggering in its generosity. He granted Penn a charter to territory roughly corresponding to the present state of Pennsylvania. The whole region was to be, in effect, Penn's personal domain. As proprietor, holding free title, Penn would be accountable only to the King. By the King's decree, "all persons settled or inhabiting within the said province do yield all due obedience to the said William Penn." In short, Penn was to be virtually a sovereign ruler.

The charter stipulated that Penn had to pay the King "two beaver skins to be delivered at our Castle at Windsor on the first day of January in every year" along with one-fifth of all the gold and silver mined in the province. In return, Penn received the right "to divide the land into towns and counties, to establish laws, create harbors, and rent and sell the land." Only one restriction kept Penn from full autonomy. He was denied the power to declare war, a proviso hardly troublesome to a pacifist.

What prompted King Charles to such lavishness was never fully clarified. Ostensibly, the grant was made in lieu of back pay owed to the Admiral. But this explanation would not convince any accountant. The Crown owed the Admiral about

£16,000—a sizable amount, to be sure, but hardly commensurate with the value of the King's gift, which made Penn the world's largest private landowner. Besides, Charles was not usually so eager to pay his debts. His creditors rarely even stood a chance of having their claims recognized. It was understood that loans extended to the King were actually bribes for royal favor.

Penn himself believed that the King was simply availing himself of the chance to ship a group of obstinate troublemakers out of the country. After all, the grant cost the King nothing, and, as Penn later put it, "the government at home was glad to be rid of us at so cheap a rate as a little parchment to be practiced in a desert 3,000 miles off."

The King's reasoning along these lines may well have gone beyond the immediate issue of Quaker resettlement. A party opposing many royal policies, the later Whig faction, was beginning to form in Parliament. Charles, though sometimes lenient in religious matters, still believed in the divine right of kings. He was therefore in principle incapable of coming to terms with Parliamentary opposition. In the back of his absolutist mind he probably envisioned the Quakers preparing a kind of penal colony where he might later deport all his political enemies. Penn and his followers might see America as their land of freedom. But as far as the King was concerned, the Quakers would be constructing the world's largest concentration camp.

A less jaundiced view of the King's motives simply assumes that Charles was once again trying to keep Penn out of trouble. In the emergent conflict between the Crown and Parliament, the King supposed, Penn would be right in the middle. Charles was prepared to crush any serious threat to his sovereignty. He also knew that Penn's liberal nonconformism would probably lead him to oppose the Crown. In that case, the King would have to hand his friend over to the hangman. He might sidestep this embarrassment if he could tempt Penn to go somewhere else, and America seemed far enough away.

All through the winter, the clerks at Whitehall worked on the details of the charter, trying to set the boundaries of the unknown region against the adjoining realms of Lord Baltimore and the Duke of York. At one point, a dispute arose about the name of the proposed province. The King proposed "Pennsylvania"—the Forests of Penn. Penn thought it would be immodest to have his own name attached to the land. But the King insisted. The new province was to be named in honor of Penn's father, the late Admiral. This was a gesture of royal gratitude to which Penn could not gracefully object.

On March 4, 1681, the charter received the signature of the King, was certified by the Lord Privy Seal and deposited in the Office of the Lord Chancellor. The next day, Penn jubilantly wrote to his friend Robert Turner: "It is a clear and just thing, and my God who has given it me through many difficulties, will, I believe, bless and make it the seed of a nation."

Ten

BLUEPRINT FOR UTOPIA

> Freedom is nothing abstract. It is the right of certain
> men to do certain things. Unless freedom is universal,
> it is only extended privilege.
>
> —CHRISTOPHER HILL

Having a country of his own forced a sudden change in Penn's
life. He had little time now for contemplation and scholarship. The American venture, the "Holy Experiment," as he
called it, imposed new and different demands. The religious
philosopher had to turn into a real-estate promoter; the social
theorist had to become a practical politician.

Penn took the transition in stride. In fact, he hardly seemed
aware of it. For him, there was no boundary between World
and Spirit. Being at home in both realms, he regarded one as
the natural and necessary extension of the other. If the spiritual
and material worlds ever seemed apart or at odds, Penn saw
it as his mission to build bridges between the two. That,
ultimately, was the purpose of the Holy Experiment.

His very choice of words—"Holy Experiment"—shows
how he conceived his task. The word "holy" points backward
to the time when all theoretical thought rested on a foundation of divine mystery and all truth was held to be revealed.
The word "experiment" looks forward to the scientific era in
which theory is liable to validation by evidence and truth is

actively discovered by controlled inquiry. Penn stood between these two frames of reference. As a man of faith who was also a practical social planner, Penn combined both approaches.

Barely a month after receiving his charter, Penn dispatched his cousin, William Markham, to be deputy governor of his province. Roughly a thousand settlers of various nationalities —mostly Swedish, Dutch, and English—already lived in the territory. Markham's first mission was to reassure them about their future and dispel any fear they might have about their status under the new authority. On arrival, Markham read Penn's first proclamation to his "subjects:"

> My friends: I hope you will not be troubled with your change. You are now fixed at the mercy of no governor that comes to make his fortune great. You shall be governed by laws of your own making, and live a free, and if you will, a sober and industrious people. I shall not usurp the right of any or oppress his person. . . . God has furnished me with a better resolution and has given me the grace to keep it.

To turn his utopian dream into a workable reality, Penn had to find more people willing to settle in the American wilderness. Though they suffered persecution in England, not many Quakers were ready to take the drastic step of uprooting themselves from their homes and villages to face the perils of the sea and the hardship of a land that offered little more than a vast expanse of virgin forest. To recruit settlers, Penn wrote a prospectus for his new country. The title clearly stated the purpose: *Some Account of the Province of Pennsilvania in America, Lately Granted under the Great Seal of England to William Penn, Made Publick for the Information of such as are or may be disposed to Transport themselves or Servants into those Parts.*

Of course, Penn himself had never been to America. But

the accuracy of his description shows how carefully he had researched the limited sources then available about those far-away regions that were now his own. In a letter of April 12, 1681, he notes that he checked his manuscript with "Traders, Planters and Shipmasters that know those Parts," adding, "I have foreborne allurement and writt truth."

Some Account indeed stands as a model of honest real-estate promotion. It gives a realistic picture of the land, of economic opportunities and required skills for prospective settlers, and sets forth the terms of land purchase, rents, and rights of occupancy. The prices were inviting. An acre rented for a penny per year, and an estate of five thousand acres could be bought for one hundred pounds.

Even at these rates, Penn stood to make a fortune from land sales, given the vast size of his domain. Yet, characteristically, he was more concerned with the welfare of his settlers than with clinching fast deals. One section of the pamphlet specifically warns against impulsive buying, and urges "who may be influenced to go into those parts to consider seriously the premises, as well as the inconveniency . . . so none may move rashly."

Despite these proper cautions, Penn's utopian hopes shine through the text. He dwells on the social evils of England, in comparison to which the American wilderness would seem almost paradisiacal. He even suggests that couples will prove more fertile in America and that everyone will live longer there: "The great Debauchery in this Kingdom has not only rendered many unfruitful when married, but they live out not half their lives." He speaks of the dislocation of farm populations through increasing urbanization, and concludes, not inaccurately, that solitary poverty and vagrancy await the dislocated. In America, by contrast, "such as could not marry here, but hardly live and allow themselves Cloaths, do marry there and bestow thrice more in All Necessaries and Conveniences (and not a little in Ornamental things too) for themselves, their Wives and Children, both as to Apparel and Household-stuff."

Whatever Penn's own idealistic visions may have been, he knew that the majority would be drawn to the New World by more tangible attractions. Thus, paradoxically, the great apostle of the spirit became the first to describe America as the land of material plenty.

The pamphlet was printed and distributed in April, 1681, by Benjamin Clark, a bookseller in Lombard Street, whose shop also served as a kind of information center for the Pennsylvania project. Penn's promotional effort proved immediately successful. Within six months he had disposed of more than 300,000 acres of land, much of it unsurveyed and unlocated, parceled out in lots ranging from 250 to 10,000 acres, to more than 250 prospective settlers. Most of them were fairly wealthy Quakers from London and Bristol, eager to secure a refuge in America if life became intolerable for them at home. The general terms of these contracts were set forth in more detail in a brochure entitled *Conditions and Concessions,* which Penn published on July 11, 1681. In October of that year, a party of settlers calling themselves First Adventurers sailed for America from London on a ship called *John and Sarah,* and another party set off soon afterward on the ship *Factor* from Bristol. Meanwhile, Penn's pamphlet was also translated into Dutch and German and circulated in the areas of Holland and Germany Penn had visited on his travels, where it set off a later wave of German and Dutch immigrants to Pennsylvania.

After completing *Some Account,* Penn turned his attention to the thornier task of providing a legal framework for his country. Ever since, as a student, he had first immersed himself in Plato, he had—perhaps unconsciously—modeled his own life on the concept of the philosopher-statesman; being aware, of course, that few philosophers ever held power and few statesmen had been notably philosophical. Now, by a rare quirk of fate, Penn was called upon to unite in himself the functions of thinker and ruler. Here was his chance to fill the usual gap between theory and practice in the conduct of human affairs and attempt a new reconciliation between private liberty and public order.

Penn had no illusions about his task. As a student of Machiavelli, whom he recommended as useful reading, he had been cautioned about practical politics. Machiavelli insisted that, to exercise power, a man must be prepared to imperil his soul. Penn resolved to turn Machiavelli upside down. He refused to concede that a politician must surrender his personal ethics to achieve the public good. Ethics, he insisted, were indivisible. His government was to be ethical in means as well as ends.

To resolve the Machiavellian conflict between public and private ethics, Penn postulated a community bound together not by imposed power but by moral consensus. The instrument for attaining this base of shared values was to be the Quaker Meeting. As an open forum for the exchange of ideas and beliefs, the Meeting would establish the cohesion necessary for such a community.

It was mainly for this reason that Penn kept stressing freedom of expression. He sensed what modern sociology has since codified: that people structure their private lives as well as their political communities largely according to the symbolic meanings that make up their world view. If there could be free symbolic exchange—open dialogue without official distortions imposed by the governing authority—then, he felt, people might attain creative self-recognition. They might become more clearly aware of their own and each other's value structures. From this, a communal consciousness might spontaneously emerge.

Such a community could accomplish what England, in Penn's time, had so tragically failed to achieve: room for change without destructive conflict.

The bold significance of this radically new approach to authority becomes fully understandable only through the most recent perspectives on the nature of governmental and political power. In their profound and provocative book *The Politics of Communication,* Claus Mueller and Carol Coe Conway analyze the formative interaction between authority and the structure of public discourse. According to their criteria, an open democratic society depends on the ability of all its members to recognize and articulate their needs rather than having their needs pre-defined and their rewards limited by the prevailing orthodoxy embedded in government. Aside from the absence of official or unconscious restraint on thought and expression, one main prerequisite for such "open" politics is approximately equal communicative competence of all members of the community. As Mueller and Conway put it:

> . . . the communicative partners, be they individuals, groups, or classes, would share a similar stock of semantic, syntactic, and lexical knowledge. The ability of all participants to analyze and synthesize would be more or less equal, and there would not be too great a difference in cognitive faculties. . . . Those engaging in communication would not be separated by attitudes which create social distance, and they would be sharing similar or mutually comprehensible expectations and values.

The Quakers of early Pennsylvania, sharing patterns of language and conceptualization as well as basic assumptions, approached these ideal conditions of discourse closer perhaps than any other society since.

Even so, Penn realized that this was a utopian vision. But he did his utmost to formulate a constitutional basis to permit at least a partial approach to the ideal of a society founded on the primacy of spirit.

It didn't come easy. No less than twenty drafts of Penn's *Frame of Government* repose at the Historical Society of Pennsylvania. His legislative concepts took many tortuous detours before they crystallized in their final form. In these successive drafts Penn evolved a political structure that established open discourse as the main principle of public direction.

At a time when the accepted authoritarian opinion held that "cogs are not meant to discourse on the operation of the wheel," Penn's politics seemed daringly original. Yet Penn's *Frame of Government* reflects ideas shared by other advanced thinkers of the period. John Locke, the most eminent of these, had proposed a similar constitution for Carolina, and in his *Treatise on Civil Government* Locke later epitomized his assumptions: "Man being born . . . with a title to perfect freedom and uncontrolled enjoyment of all the rights and privileges of the law of nature . . . no one can be put out of his estate and subjected to the political view of another, without his own consent." Nearly a century before Thomas Jefferson distilled his noble phrases about self-evident truths, inalienable rights, and the pursuit of happiness from Locke's doctrine, Penn took the same premise as the key to his own legal code.

To what extent Penn was acquainted with Locke's writings is a matter of scholarly dispute. At any rate, Penn's set of laws was truly innovative in one essential aspect. It was the first constitution that specified a method for its own amendment.

This was an altogether new idea. Not even Locke, in writing the basic law for Carolina, had made any provision for possible alteration. Locke regarded his Carolina constitution as a permanent model. For all his liberalism, he had not yet apprehended the principle of evolutionary change. By contrast, Penn's deep sense of history enabled him to recognize change as a social reality. The result was an open-ended constitution

that left the necessary legal space for change without violence
or revolution.

As a Quaker and a pacifist, Penn was particularly concerned with the problem of violence in statecraft. He was
realist enough to know that every previously known form of
government ultimately rested on force. He knew that when
reason, sentiment, and especially religion are invoked by the
state, it is often merely to hide the ready sword. Like other
political theorists of the time, notably Hobbes, Penn regarded
the state as a contract between rulers and ruled. But even if
the rule was democratic self-rule, the power of the government lay ultimately in its ability to punish, in extreme cases
by the selective killing of disruptive persons. As Hobbes put
it, "Covenants without swords are but words." How, then,
could governance be reconciled with the Quaker ideal of nonviolence?

Penn realized that this was a basically insoluble problem.
The best he could do was to draw up a legal code designed
to forestall extreme internal stress. In the narrow sense, this
meant finding a way to accommodate dissent within the law.
In a broader sense, it meant that Penn had to create a social
climate to liberate the moral potential of man so that the
freely given word would become a sufficient instrument of
contract, rendering the sword needless. Personal enmity, of
course, might still occur, but not class or group hatred. He
believed his *Frame of Government* was the best available
blueprint for such a society.

The state projected by Penn was a true "civil" society, in
marked contrast to the rigid theocracies established by the
Puritans in New England. The Puritans formulated their legal
codes on ancient biblical concepts. Their community was
conceived as a fixed structure, an unalterable covenant with
God in the old Hebrew sense. Because the Quakers were free
of that ancient Near Eastern and essentially despotic notion

of the divine covenant, it was possible for Penn to establish the first legal framework for a fluid democratic society, open to the development of new social norms. This surely ranks among Penn's most profound achievements.

The first to recognize the importance of Penn's political theories was Voltaire, almost a century after the fact. In his *Lettres philosophiques,* he credits Penn with creating "that golden age of which men talk and which probably has never existed anywhere except in Pennsylvania." Clearly, this is hyperbole. But Voltaire was writing under stress. Struggling in exile against French absolutism, he saw in Penn's liberal constitution indeed the token of a golden age. A later historian, Brent Barksdale, confirms Voltaire's judgment and declares flatly: "The government that William Penn established in 1682 was far more liberal and responsible to the people than any antecedent or contemporary form on earth. In the wilds of Pennsylvania he set up the only government in the known world that did not maintain a military defense against foreign invasion or internal uprising."

Internal evidence in Penn's twenty legal drafts shows that he probably consulted many people about his ideas and kept revising his text in keeping with their suggestions. Some apparently scoffed at his hope of maintaining a state without the use of force, and predicted the imminent collapse of a community so conceived. Penn met their objections in the preface to the *Frame of Government:* "They weakly err, that think there is no other use of government than correction, which is the coarsest part of it; daily experience tells us that the care and regulation of many other affairs more soft and daily necessary make up much the greatest part of government." The implication is that "the coarsest part" could perhaps altogether be dispensed with.

Force simply didn't fit into Penn's scheme, and a letter to his friend Dr. Tillotson expressed the same attitude in regard to religious tolerance: "I abhor two principles in religion, and pity those that own them. The first is obedience upon authority without conviction; and the other the destroying of them that differ from me for God's sake."

Curtailment of power was the single most important theme running through Penn's theory of government. Most remarkable, from a psychological viewpoint, was Penn's deliberate limitation of his own power. He himself realized how unusual this was. "I propose that which is extraordinary," he wrote in a letter to friends in Ireland, ". . . to leave myself and my successors no power of doing mischief, that the will of one man may not hinder the good of the whole country."

By the drastic limitation of his own power, Penn resolved a personal dilemma. Being himself the governing authority, Penn had to insist on obedience to the law. This put him in conflict with his own past; for, as a rebel, Penn had often acted on the belief that the law must be broken to keep the government from being lawless, that disobedience is necessary to renew and affirm the true function of law as an instrument of liberty. Caught in the paradox, Penn renounced his own power. His action recalls an observation by Karl Jaspers in his searching book *The Origin and Goal of History:*

> Self-limitation of power, not only from considerations of advantage but also from the recognition of justice, has been as perennial a feature of history as the urge to force. The greatest proclivity for such an attitude was perhaps to be found in aristocratic, moderate, inwardly cultured men; less in the average man, who is always disposed to consider himself right and the other wrong; none whatever in men of violence, who are not prepared to come to terms at all.

Though Penn took every possible precaution to reduce the personal element in government and to deny himself and his successors "the power of doing mischief," he realized that all government is personal—that it is human character rather than impersonal law that is the ultimate arbiter: "Wherefore governments rather depend upon men, than men upon governments. Let men be good, and the government cannot be bad; if it be ill, they will cure it. But if men be bad, let the government be ever so good, and they will endeavor to warp and spoil it to their turn."

In its particulars, the *Frame of Government* provided for two legislative chambers, the Council and the General Assembly, which amounted to an upper and a lower House. Members of both houses were to be elected yearly by the landowners and tenants of the province, and the Council, jointly with the governor, was to perform the executive functions. Public-office holders had to "confess and acknowledge the one Almighty and eternal God," which was presumed to make them Christians. No other religious requirement was imposed. No one was to be "molested or prejudiced for their religious persuasion or practice in matters of faith and worship, nor shall they be compelled at any time to frequent or maintain any religious worship, place or ministry, whatsoever."

The principles formulated by Penn contrasted sharply with the existing absolute monarchies of Europe, which maintained legal inequality between men through systems of privilege and hierarchy. Penn's liberalism went beyond the idea of freedom of religion and established other specific forms of freedom in opposition to the old system. First, there was individual freedom, such as the right to free enterprise without undue government intervention through monopoly, privilege, and similar restraints upon economic activity. Second, there was the right to private property and the accumulation of private capital, as opposed to the traditional forms of feudal ownership, which still persisted in Europe to a marked degree. Third, there were social freedoms, such as the right to education and free association, as well as political freedom assured through broad franchise and representative government.

As for criminal law, a simple comparison of figures shows how far Penn had departed from the British model. In England, a man could be hanged for any of more than two hundred offenses, including petty theft and "abduction with intent to wed." Penn recognized only two capital crimes—murder and treason—and there is evidence suggesting that he included the latter only at the insistence of his advisors. Moreover, prisons were conceived as corrective rather than punitive, all cases were to be tried before a jury, and all trials were to be public. The man who had so gravely suffered from the caprice of law took care to curb the insolence of office.

Pennsylvania's first constitution, in its whole tenor, represented something far deeper than mere legal liberality. It mirrored the style of thought Penn had acquired in constantly pursuing the limits of understanding.

The final document was ready in April, 1682, and Penn dispatched it to his settlers in Pennsylvania for their approval. Soon after, he made plans to journey himself to his country. Guli and the children—by that time there were three—would remain in England. Later, perhaps, they would join him in America, after he had established a suitable home for them.

The impending separation cast a dark mood over Penn. The intense work on the legislative drafts had exhausted him, and his fatigue left him vulnerable to his feelings. The summer seemed to him but a long leave-taking, and he looked at Guli with the special tenderness that anticipates a long absence. He brooded over the dangers of the sea voyage, and in early August he secluded himself in his study to write a letter to Guli as if it were their last farewell:

> My dear wife! remember thou wast the love of my youth, and much the joy of my life; the most beloved, as well as the most worthy of all my earthly comforts: and the reason of that love was more thy inward than

thy outward excellencies, which yet were many. God knows, and thou knowst it, I can say it was a match of Providence's making; and God's image in us both was the first thing and the most amiable and engaging ornament in our eyes. . . .

My love, that neither sea, nor land, nor death itself can extinguish or lessen toward you, most endearedly visits you with eternal embraces, and will abide with you forever; and may the God of my life watch over you and bless you, and do you good in this world and forever. Some things are upon my spirit to leave with you . . . if I should never see you more in this world. . . .

Characteristically, Penn combines high sentiment with sturdy practicality. His letter admonishes Guli to keep careful accounts and live within her income. Penn also reminds her "to divide thy time and be regular: it is easy and sweet." Evidently he worried about her ability to manage the estate in his absence, which is why he left all financial matters in the hands of his trusted manager and accountant, Philip Ford. Penn urged Guli to influence the children toward "sweetness mixed with gravity, and cheerfulness tempered with sobriety. . . . For their learning, be liberal. Spare no cost. Be sure to observe their genius, and do not cross it as to learning."

The letter concludes with a postscript addressed to his children. Springett, Letitia, and William, Jr., were seven, four, and two at the time—too young to understand their father's exhortation. Someday, perhaps, they would be sustained by the words of a man unembarrassed by his own goodness: "Love not money, nor the world; use them only and they will serve you; but if you love them, you serve them. . . . Be gentle and humble in your conversation. In making friends, consider well first; and when you are fixed be true. . . .

Watch against anger, neither speak nor act in it; for like drunkenness it makes a man a beast and throws people into desperate inconveniences. . . . Finally, my children, love one another."

After finishing the letter, Penn evidently felt that each child should have a separate, more personal message from him. Some days later, on August 19, he wrote brief notes to each child:

My dear Springett:
 Be good, learn to fear God, avoid evil, love thy book, be kind to thy brother and sister and God will bless thee and I will exceedingly love thee. Farewell dear child.

Thy dear father,
Wm. Penn

Dear Letitia:
 I dearly love thee and would have thee sober; learn thy book, and love thy brothers. I will send thee a pretty book to learn in. The Lord bless thee and make a good woman of thee. Farewell.

Thy dear father,
Wm. Penn

Dear Bille:
 I love thee much, therefore be sober and quiet, and learn his book. I will send him one, so the Lord bless thee. Amen.

Thy dear father,
Wm. Penn

By the end of August, all arrangements had been completed, and Penn's ship, the *Welcome,* stood ready at the dock in Deal. Guli could not accompany her husband all the way to port. She rode along part of the way, but then had to return to the children. They said good-bye at a crossing of the road. Among the members of his household only Philip Ford, the estate manager, and his wife Bridget went with Penn to the dockside.

The night before his departure, Penn wrote a *Solemn Farewell to Them in the Land of My Nativity* as a farewell to his friends. The next morning he was still too deeply preoccupied with his thoughts to pay much attention when Ford stopped him as he was about to board the vessel. Ford thrust several papers at Penn for his signature. Just some household accounts, he explained.

Ford had been in charge of Penn's finances for more than a decade, and Penn trusted him implicitly. Besides, he disliked to be troubled by what he considered petty concerns. He was, after all, attuned to dealing with ideas, not with cash. Without looking at the papers, Penn signed. And he kept no copy for himself. Then he ascended the gangplank, and soon afterward the *Welcome* weighed anchor, her sails unfurled, and she set to sea.

Eliot

ARRIVALS

> Time present and time past
> Are both perhaps present in time future,
> And time future contained in time past.
> —T. S. ELIOT

The sun already stood low in the afternoon sky on October 27, 1682, as the ship bearing Penn approached its destination. The little town of New Castle, where the *Welcome* anchored, must have been a heartening sight after nearly two months at sea. Built mostly by the Dutch, the settlement consisted of a dozen or so brick houses. It probably reminded Penn of some of the smaller towns he had seen on his journeys in Holland. With painted tile set in the brick walls to accentuate the windows and the stepped gables, the little houses looked cheerful and cozy. A small fort stood at the edge of the water, flanked by the weight-house, where a large scale was kept for the benefit of traders and shipmasters wanting to weigh their goods and cargoes. A windmill rose high above the rest of the buildings, gardens spread between the houses, and the virgin forest toward the rear had been cut back several hundred feet to make way for fields and meadows.

The reddish gold of the Pennsylvania fall still suffused the landscape as the *Welcome* furled her sails and dropped anchor in the afternoon light. Penn, accustomed to England's gloomy autumn, must have been delighted at his first sight of Indian summer. From the deck of the tall ship, he could see the teeming waterfront. Nearly three thousand settlers now inhabited the area, and most of them had come to welcome him. He also had his first glimpse of the almost naked Indians, decorated with paint and feathers, who mingled freely with the rest.

The loudest shouts of welcome rose from a group of Quakers, the First Adventurers, who had preceded Penn by almost a year, jubilant that he had joined them at last.

New Castle had no dredged harbor, and the *Welcome,* being "a Ship of Great Burthen," had to anchor in the middle of the river. By the time she was secured, the sun had already slipped behind the treetops, and long shadows crept over the water. Darkness would fall soon, and it was too late to transfer to shore in small boats. Thus, Penn and his companions had to spend their first night in America still aboard ship. But the greeting shouted across the water assured them that they were no longer alone.

The light did not linger as in the English dusk. At the latitude of Pennsylvania, the autumn night falls swiftly. As the air grew cool, the crowds left the shore, the settlers riding back to their farms over woodland trails they had just recently cleared, and the Indians disappeared into the forest.

Penn watched the night settling over the shore. Here and there lamps were lit, and the windows of the little town glowed warmly in the dark. In the weeks of misery and illness during the passage, with only the sea to meet his eye, even he might have felt at certain moments that America was a mirage and they all were lost in the search for it. Now, at last, the New World lay before him. Like a latter-day Moses, he had brought his people to a Promised Land, but could not yet set foot on it. He returned to his cabin, and one more time the sound of water lapping the hull of the *Welcome* lulled him to sleep.

Quite another sound woke Penn and his companions in the morning. Again there were shouts of welcome, but now they came from all sides and from much closer. Nearly every boat and barge in the province had come down to New Castle, and they were all circling the *Welcome,* which sat in the river like a giant goose amid goslings. Even the Indians, in their tree-trunk canoes, had joined the impromptu fleet. They had heard of the white sachem and had come to see this powerful and fabled creature. Their chants mixed with the shouts of the settlers as Penn and his rumpled, travel-weary companions clambered down into the boats that bore them to shore.

At the bank stood William Markham, Penn's friend and deputy governor, who had come with the First Adventurers the year before. With him was Thomas Holme, the official surveyor, who had already begun his great task of mapping the unknown land. They solemnly greeted their proprietor. Markham and Holme, both wearing plain Quaker garb, were flanked by two men dressed in the ruffles and brocades of royal functionaries. They were John Moll and Ephraim Harman, attorneys of the King. With great ceremony, they presented Penn with the key to the fort. Then Moll held out to Penn another symbolic gift: a clod of earth with a twig implanted in it. This was the token of the land itself of which Penn now took possession.

A table and a chair were brought to the grassy clearing by the river, along with quills and an inkwell, for the formal documents of the transaction had to be executed. Under the open sky, Penn and the King's attorneys signed the formal surrender of the land to Penn's authority, with Markham and Holme affixing their names as witnesses.

Now that Penn was officially in power, new loyalties had to be affirmed. A spokesman for the resident Swedes stepped forward and declared that his countrymen "would love, serve and obey with all they had."

Penn acknowledged their homage. With his flair for ceremony, he struck the right note: solemnity without condescension. Like so many men whose authority rests within themselves, he had style. His voice and gestures conveyed a certainty and ease greatly reassuring to those who were now officially under his domination. Indeed, to the Quakers looking on, the transfer of power they had just witnessed must have seemed almost miraculous—as if God's sheltering hand had at last reached out to them. For the first time now, Quakers had a safe place on earth.

Pennsylvania was born that day. But the new land already had nearly three generations of history. A motley parade of colonists had been squabbling about possession of the Delaware region ever since the discovery of the river, in 1600, by the British sea captain De La WarR, who took the opportunity to put his name on the map. Soon after, a scraggly band of Hollanders had arrived. They had been hired by the East India Company to search for a westward passage to the South Seas. Still ignorant of America's size and shape, they were looking for an easy seaway to the Pacific, and, as a base for their explorations, they built the first settlement along Delaware Bay. A few years later, they were joined by a group of Swedes and a few Englishmen, all of whom claimed the region as their own. The animosities that resulted may account for an official Dutch document describing the Swedes as "mostly bandits."

The Swedes may indeed have been a bit rougher than the rest, for they had soon gained the upper hand, and set up an official government-sponsored trading company in the usual manner of European colonizers. But when their king, the great Gustavus Adolphus, was killed while fighting the Austrians in the Thirty Years' War, the distraught Swedes at home gave little thought and less backing to their distant outposts. This period of neglect ended in 1644, when Christina, daughter of Gustavus Adolphus, reached the age of eighteen and ascended the throne.

Exploring an unknown continent at the far edge of the world was just the kind of project to kindle the imagination of this young Queen. Before she subsided in later years into a life of lonely wandering and troubled contemplation, she had the charm, vitality, and brilliance that drew the best minds and the handsomest princes from all over Europe to her drafty palace in Stockholm. In her eager-minded restlessness, she would summon the visiting René Descartes to discuss philosophy with her at five in the morning. The great philosopher had been accustomed to stay in bed till noon, and the queen's schedule literally killed him.

To revive Sweden's exploits in America, Christina hired a Dutch adventurer named Peter Minuit, who had already proved his astuteness by buying Manhattan from the Indians for twenty-four dollars. Since the Swedes seemed to have the upper hand, Minuit had no qualms about switching allegiance and staking claims against his own country. A colonizer in the modern style, he relied on a mixture of guns and public relations. He promptly renamed the Delaware the New Sweden River, built a fortification at the present site of Wilmington, and called it Fort Cristina, in honor of his new sponsor.

But the Dutch, ensconced in Nieuw Amsterdam, took a sour view of the renegade Minuit and the Swedish settlements along the Delaware. Their earlier arrival, they felt, gave them better rights to the region. Under the command of their local governor, a peg-legged petty tyrant named Peter Stuyvesant, the Dutch sailed up the Delaware in 1655 to assault Fort Cristina. They arrived at the lucky moment when, by some fluke, the Swedish stronghold had only enough gunpowder for a single round. Under the circumstances, the Swedes thought it best to conserve their ammunition, and surrendered without even that one shot.

The Dutch didn't long enjoy their easy conquest. During one of their recurrent wars with the English in 1664, a British flotilla appeared in the Hudson River to lay siege to Nieuw Amsterdam. To the surprise of the British, the little Dutch city at the tip of Manhattan offered almost no resistance.

Happy at the prospect of getting rid of the despotic Stuyvesant, the inhabitants of Nieuw Amsterdam almost welcomed the British as liberators, and didn't mind having their town and territory renamed New York.

King Charles had sliced off part of the New York region to give as a token of royal favor to Sir George Carteret, who then named the area New Jersey, after the island of his birth. Penn's domain, granted some years after, lay between this area and the Maryland territory of Lord Baltimore.

The earliest settlers along the Delaware, unless they were lucky enough to find some abandoned Indian wigwams, lived in caves dug in the hillsides. But each group of settlers included competent carpenters and roofers, and with the tools they had brought from Europe they soon managed to build themselves houses not too different from the simple dwellings of European peasants. The English settlements had thatched roofs and walls of wattle, a weave of willow and hazel branches matted with mud. The Dutch favored brick, which they baked from the plentiful clay of the estuary lowlands, while the Swedes introduced the log cabin, which had been traditional in Scandinavia long before it became the preferred birthplace for U.S. Presidents.

The log cabin had the advantage of requiring no nails, which, like all manufactured products, were in short supply. Instead, the logs were locked together with pegs and notches, and the gaps between them were chinked with a mixture of wood chips, clay, and moss. The roofs were usually made of bark. These building materials were plentiful byproducts of land clearing, so a settler could build himself a house at no cost but his labor. Wood was abundant, and was also freely used for interior wall covering in the Dutch and English houses. Many rooms had the cheerful rosy color of fresh oak paneling not yet darkened with age.

By the time of Penn's arrival, the various nationalities living in his province had built comfortable villages that in many

ways reminded them of home. Yet it was not just homesick-
ness that made the Swedes, Dutch, and English transplant
their native styles. They simply knew no other way of building.

The only way in which these houses differed from their
counterparts in Europe was in the size of their windows. Glass
had to be imported, often broke in transit, and was very expensive. Consequently, windows were very small. Some of
the poorer colonists used no glass at all but instead made
leaded windows from bits of horn scraped thin enough to let
the light shine through. This left their houses rather dark, and
the situation was not greatly helped by the smoky strips of
pine used as indoor torches, or by the smelly fish-oil lamps
that were the most common means of illumination. But most
of the early settlers worked outdoors, did little if any reading,
and went to bed at sundown. So the lack of good indoor lighting was not felt to be a great hardship.

Keeping warm posed a more serious problem in drafty
houses, where an open fireplace was the only source of heat.
One chronicler complains that he had to skip a cold day in
his diary because the ink froze and broke his inkpot. Since
there was no plumbing—indoor or out—there was no risk of
pipes freezing.

Before going to sleep, people heated large round stones
before the fire to take to bed with them. If they had to leave
the immediate vicinity of the fireplace at other times, they
filled a warming pan with a hinged cover with live coals to
take along. Women enjoyed a thermodynamic advantage in
this respect. A Swedish settler named Per Kalm notes with
interest that they placed the hot pans under their skirts "so
that the heat therefrom might go up to the *regiones superiores*
covered by the skirts."

Kalm had sufficient opportunity for such observations, since
the Delaware area, unlike other colonies, suffered no acute
shortage of women. Most of the Pennsylvania settlers brought
their families with them, and so spared the colony the boister-

ous bands of bachelors which plagued some of the other settlements. In Virginia, for example, the plight of randy males became so desperate that the authorities organized girl-catching campaigns back home in England. With promises and blandishments, they rounded up ninety young women certified "pure and spotless," shipped them to America, and sold them at auction to eager customers, for 120 pounds of tobacco per head. Everyone was so pleased that the price went up to 150 pounds on the next shipment, and the government noted with satisfaction that this profitable trade raised the moral tone of Virginia.

Up to the time of Penn's arrival, Pennsylvania settlers and natives regarded each other with a mixture of curiosity and suspicion. Since their muskets' range, if not their accuracy, exceeded that of arrows, the settlers were usually able to discourage unfriendly Indians. Significantly, the first church built in Pennsylvania also served as a fort. Its little steeple supported a shooting gallery near the top, allowing the settlers to cover a broader zone of fire from its heights. At any rate, Indian raids were rare, and, on the whole, life at the edge of the American wilderness seemed no more dangerous than in some parts of the European countryside, where ragtag bands of brigands roamed the land and terrorized the smaller towns and hamlets. These armed marauders were stragglers from the disarrayed armies of the Thirty Years' War who had given up the fight for Christian principles to devote themselves exclusively to pillage and rape. In comparison, American Indians seemed tame, and after Penn's arrival they ceased to be a problem altogether. By treating the Indians as responsible members of the community rather than as subhuman savages, Penn transformed relations with them from sporadic hostility to durable friendship.

After chafing under European poaching laws, which made virtually all hunting an aristocratic prerogative, most of the settlers became ardent if indiscriminate huntsmen. "The Woods

of the Land," exults one of them, "are filled with Vast Numbers of Wild Creatures, as Elks, Buffalos and Stags, free and
common to any Person who can Shoot or take them without
lett, hindrance or Opposition whatsoever." In particular, he
was impressed with "various sorts of Frogs, [including] the
Bull-Frog, which makes a Roaring Noise, hardly to be distinguished from that well-known of the Beast from whom it
takes its Name."

But such reports of daily life are rare. For the most part,
the newcomers were far too busy clearing land, building
houses, and planting crops to have much time or inclination
for keeping journals, and of the few kept even fewer have
survived. In consequence, the half century of Dutch and
Swedish domination of the Delaware is sparsely chronicled.
Except for hunting and the joys of domesticity, there were
few entertainments. Not surprisingly, one of the few documents of daily life dwells fondly and lengthily on dependable
pleasures:

> Ham, beef, tongue, roast beef, fowls, with cabbage set
> round about, make a meal. Roast mutton or veal, with
> potatoes or turnips, form another. Another still is
> formed by a pasty of chickens, or partridges, or lamb.
> Beef-steak, veal cutlets, mutton chops, or turkey, goose
> and fowls with potatoes set around, with stewed green
> peas, or Turkish beans, or some other beans, are an-
> other meal. Pies of apples, peaches, cherries, or cran-
> berries, etc., form another course. When cheese and
> butter are added, one has an ordinary meal.

The writer, a Swede using the Latinized name of Acrelius,
also liked something to drink with his meals:

> French wine, Frontignac, Pontac, Port-a-Port, Lisbon
> Wine, Phial wine, Sherry, Madeira wine, Sangaree,

cherry wine, currant wine, black raspberry, cider, rum
or sugar brandy, egg dram or egg nog, bilberry dram,
tiff or flipp (made of small beer with rum and sugar),
mulled rum (with egg-yolks and allspice), hotch-pot
(warmed cider with rum in it), and sillabub (of milk-
warm milk, wine & Sugar).

Such menus may explain why John Printz, governor of the
Swedish colony, weighed more than three hundred pounds.
The rigors of the wilderness—and often they were grim enough
—apparently stopped short of those formidable Swedish kitch-
ens. The horizons of existence may have been narrow in other
respects, but the soil was fertile, the summers long, the grass
rich for grazing, and the forest full of edible creatures.

The day of Penn's arrival marked the beginning of Pennsylvania. It also marked a new turn in what had been America's first crucial conflict—the clash between Quakers and
Puritans. In a way, the struggle between these two groups had
been America's first civil war. It was one of those pathetic
and ultimately insoluble confrontations in which one group's
willingness to hurt is matched by another group's willingness
to suffer. The Puritans of New England regarded the Quakers
as Creatures of Satan and hounded them with cruel glee. The
Quakers, on their part, accepted injury and death with a
touching, if somewhat peculiar, talent for martyrdom.

Before Penn's arrival, the Puritans had been intent on driv-
ing every trace of Quakerism from the American continent,
and several earlier attempts at Quaker settlement in the north
had run afoul of the Puritans' pious fury. Penn's charter, at
last, secured legitimacy for the Quakers by placing their
colony under the auspices of the King of England. This stopped
the open virulence of Puritan persecution. But the conflict
was never resolved; it merely went underground, and its basic
issues kept rumbling beneath the surface of American history.

For the conflicting premises were irreconcilable: They represented contradictory views of human destiny. Henri Bergson, the French philosopher, observed that there are two different kinds of morality and religion: One is the product of social pressure, the other arises from inner freedom. In Puritanism and Quakerism these opposing conceptions struggled for dominance in the New World.

The Puritans, doctrinal descendants of John Calvin, got their name from their desire to purify the Church of England. But their ambitions didn't stop there. Institutional reform, to them, was just a beginning. Their basic job, as they saw it, was to get the kingdom of heaven started on earth—immediately. Their lofty aim inspired them with a chronic annoyance at human imperfection, and this, in turn, made them peevish and cruel. Had a band of militant Moslems, full of Turkish disdain for Christian compassion, landed on Plymouth Rock, they could not have been more antagonistic to the Quakers than were these brethren in Christ. Their grim encounter reveals two strands in the American fabric, which even today still pull in opposite directions.

For one thing, Quakers and Puritans arrived in the New World with entirely different expectations. In contrast to the hopeful eagerness of the Quakers, the Puritans regarded America with certain misgivings. According to one of their theories, America had been the devil's personal preserve until their arrival. The Indians, as evidenced by their nakedness, were the devil's own children. They had to be approached warily, and the whole ungodly continent had to be decontaminated with massive doses of rectitude.

The "Pilgrim Fathers" who settled New England during the two generations before Penn's arrival have long been glorified in legend. But modern historians, notably James Truslow Adams, in *The Founding of New England,* have found little evidence to sustain popular notions about the passengers of the *Mayflower.* Granted, they did not deserve Edmund Burke's malignant description of them as "miserable outcasts, not so much sent but thrown out on the bleak and barren shore of desolate wilderness, three thousand miles from all civilized intercourse." But neither were they champions of freedom, nor had they any inkling of the more humane forms of Christianity. Adams points out that their narrow theological views "stripped God of every shred of what we consider moral character." Far from espousing democratic principles, the leaders of the Massachusetts Bay settlement—Winthrop, Endicott, and Dudley—established a rigid authoritarian regime in which only one in five colonists was accorded any political rights at all. Indeed, in Adams' words, they regarded democratic self-determination as "the meanest and worst of all forms of government."

As Calvinists, they saw the relation between citizen and state as parallel to man's relation to God: they saw both as rigid structures of command and obedience. The state was the instrument compelling man to do God's will. Hence no man could set himself against the state. Obedience was the chief virtue, because, to the Puritans, man was a creature of such dark lusts that only the stern force of authority could save him from himself.

Political dissent was a crime, and even mild critics of established authority risked having their ears cut off. Everyone was accountable for his thoughts and could be questioned about them. Often the constables employed torture to help a citizen become more explicit. This form of "clarification" was sincerely believed to be for the good of the offender's own soul, as well as necessary for the preservation of public order.

The Puritans arrived at their views in a very logical fashion and with the best intentions. They wanted to leave no loopholes for evil; since man was inherently sinful, the only way to save him from perdition was to draw up a detailed catalog of human failings and stamp out every one of them. As historian Michael Walzer puts it, the Puritans wanted "to fasten upon the necks of all mankind the yoke of a new political discipline—impersonal and ideological, not founded on loyalty and affection, no more open to spontaneity than to chaos and crime."

In T. S. Eliot's phrase, the Puritans wanted "a system so perfect that nobody would have to be good." In consequence, they despised liberty and smelled the sulfur of hell in every human joy.

Neither the Puritans nor Calvin actually invented this line of thought, though Calvin certainly added some of its darker elaborations. Some aspects of Puritanism—the rigid polarization of good and evil—reach back to the very roots of Western thought. As long ago as 500 B.C. Heraclitus described the world as the interplay between opposing extremes. Good and evil, love and hate, appearance and reality, flesh and spirit, hot and cold, fire and water—these were the poles of opposition between which the Western mind sought meaning and connection. In turn, these concepts guided men's perceptions of the world. They focused on extremes and excluded the middle. Aristotle's logic, which both shaped and limited the Western imagination, rests on this exclusion.

Christianity inherited this thought pattern, this grid of overstretched abstractions balanced on a base of contradictions. The problem was to reconcile these contradictions and exclusions with the Christian idea of the harmonious Kingdom and the transcendent unity within God. St. Augustine tried to bridge the paradox by positing his City of God, where all contradictions cease. The Puritans, insistent on building an instant earthly paradise, had to take more immediate and more radical measures. They tried to escape the dilemma by cutting off one of its horns, removing contradiction by force. Deny worldly reality—scrape the flesh from the spirit—and, in the end, you may succeed in tearing evil away from good, and be left with pure virtue.

Throughout New England, the Puritans pursued this metaphysical scheme with all available means, including coercion and violence. They resurrected the old Hebrew God of Vengeance, who gloried in the righteous humiliation of sinners. In effect, the Puritans reverted to pre-Christian times. They established a God-ridden society without the mercy of Christ. "Indeed it is difficult to classify the Puritans as Christians," declares Egon Friedell in his monumental *Cultural History of Modern Times.* "They derive their beliefs mostly from the Old Testament, they name their children after Israelite heroes and prophets, suffuse their speech with Hebraic concepts, metaphors and turns of phrase, and regard themselves as the militant servants of Jehovah in Whose Name they would vanquish idolaters and infidels with fire and sword."

At first the Puritans were unopposed. They were all the more incensed when, in about 1660, the first Quakers infiltrated their region from New Jersey and Rhode Island and preached a contrary faith. Though the Quakers had no explicit doctrine, they affirmed the compassionate Christ and libertarian government. In short, they were radical subversives. No matter how many individual Quakers were silenced, the Puritans could no longer ignore the awkward fact that their ideological monopoly was being contested. Both in theology and in politics, there now were alternatives.

The rift was deep, and it virtually cut America in two. True, the southern colonies—notably Maryland, Virginia, and the Carolinas—embodied still other, mostly manorial, ways of life. But most southern colonies remained self-contained and did not engage the Puritans in ideological disputes. The Quakers, on the other hand, challenged the Puritans on all points, from basic principles down to the mood and texture of daily life.

The quarrel unrolled like a battle in heaven, and God was asked to choose sides. Each party assigned a different role to Him. The Puritan God was invariant, fixed for eternity, manifest in law and biblical dictate. The Quakers challenged this determinism. They did not envision man in prostrate subjection to the Almighty. Rather, they conceived man as a creative agent interacting with and within the mind of God: Man and God engaged in a dialectic as members of the same spiritual family. This was the meaning of the fatherhood of God: that man was creating the Kingdom of God by inhabiting it. Man was a conscious and contributory working element in God's formative design.

In this interactive relation, God spoke not in inexorable scriptural commands but through the Inner Voice—Revelation was an ongoing process. The function of the state, therefore, was not to coerce the individual toward fixed codes and orthodoxies but to encourage his creative unfolding. The instrument of salvation was not Puritan conformity but—to use Penn's own term—"soul freedom."

Quakerism thus implied a theory of evolution and emancipation—two concepts totally outside the Puritan framework. Penn's plan was to create a human environment in which this evolution could take place. He attempted to create a "new man" by changing the nature of the state—a notion that anticipates such emancipatory thinkers as Rousseau and Marx. In short, what Penn had in mind was a cultural revolution. That, and nothing less, was the aim of the Holy Experiment.

At its most fundamental level, the conflict between Quakers and Puritans centered on the relations between thought, freedom, and morality. For the Puritans, "right thinking" was a moral imperative, and thought-control thus became the duty of responsible government. In such a perspective, freedom was immoral. The Quakers believed the opposite—that morality is the result of freedom. If there is no freedom to seek alternatives, they argued, there can be no morality—only amoral obedience.

Given the conflict of their premises, the quarrel between Quakers and Puritans was both bitter and unavoidable. And since the early Quakers insisted on confronting the Puritans in their own towns, the results were often unfortunate and dramatic.

Throughout New England, Quakers expressing their opinions would be whipped naked through the streets, and the law specified that the whips should be tarred and knotted, the better to tear the flesh.

It would be unjust to the Puritans to assume that they relished such occasions. Like most decent people, they would probably have preferred not to have any awkward issues raised at all. In fact, it was nearly always the Quakers who, with irrepressible fervor and notorious lack of tact, kept forcing these confrontations. Understandably, the Puritans grew exasperated and, equally righteous in defense of their principles, resorted to sterner measures. One Quaker account, rather petulantly entitled *New England Judged by the Spirit of the Lord,* tells of beatings so brutal that even the more sportive spectators fainted at the sight of blood-smeared Quakers writhing at the whipping posts of Boston.

Still, the Quakers kept on speaking out. Unable to comprehend the odd mixture of mildness, masochism, and bravado in the Quaker character, the Puritans concluded that these traits were the marks of Satan. The Quakers were evidently emissaries of the devil, and to set an example, the government of Massachusetts decided to hang some of them. Among them was a young Quaker woman named Mary Dyer. As she stood at the gallows, Governor Endicott offered to pardon her if she would just leave the colony. Mary replied: "I cannot. In obedience to the will of God I came and in his will I abide faithful to death."

Now the Puritans felt fully vindicated. Clearly such a woman was a witch. Intercourse with the devil had warped her. How else could she conceive such delusions or cling to them with such stubborn wickedness? The hanging now seemed doubly justified, for the execution of witches was an established local practice.

It was no happenstance that a woman shared the fate of the Quaker martyrs. For the Quakers were the first settlers in America to accept women as complete human beings, not merely as lesser adjuncts to men. They were, in fact, among the first Christian sects to see women as the equals of men. Quakerism therefore attracted many women bright enough to recognize and resent their inferior status in conventional society. To them, the Quaker movement offered the only available route to full personhood.

The Quaker attitude toward women developed from logical necessity. After all, women too heard the promptings of the Inner Voice. Apparently, God also spoke to them. Since divine inspiration could not be suppressed, women had to be allowed to speak out at Quaker Meetings.

Admission to the Meeting had a far-reaching effect on women's opportunities for self-development. As long as they could speak in public, it was considered permissible, even advisable, to develop their intelligence through education. As a result, a new type of woman emerged in Quaker communities, combining articulate self-confidence with the gentleness fostered by Quaker surroundings. This particular blend of feminine charm and intellectual competence enraged the Puritans. Such women had to be silenced, and the Puritans found suitable ways of doing so.

If an outspoken Quaker woman had the misfortune to fall into the hands of Puritan authorities, she ran the risk of having her tongue burned out with a hot poker. As punishment for blasphemers, this was considered neither cruel nor unusual, but quite in keeping with current legal precepts. Thieves had their hands cut off, rapists were castrated; so, to make the punishment fit the crime, it seemed only proper that blasphemers lose their tongues. The procedure thus combined good reason with extreme pain. This too was deemed appropriate. The pain was salutary: God's instrument for inducing repentance.

Of all Quaker practices, none vexed the Puritans more than the treatment of women. After all, to teach a woman to reason and let her speak on general matters—in short, to allow her to act like a man—was striking at the very foundations of home and family. Besides, the Puritans regarded women with deep distrust. Like other religions deriving part of their emotional dynamics from sexual repression, the Puritans basically blamed women for having invented sex, which they suspected was not really part of God's creation but an underhanded trick slipped in by the devil. Eve may have learned it from the snake; but it was Woman who had sullied the purity of the cosmos. Men were by nature stalwart and virtuous, and only female lures drew them to lustful perdition.

This view prescribed a woman's role in the Puritan community. She was expected to subject herself demurely to male dominance as atonement for her inherent sinfulness. One governor of the Massachusetts Bay Colony, John Winthrop, specifically declared that woman was in bondage to her husband, noting that "his yoke is so easy and sweet to her as a bride's ornaments . . . and whether her lord smiles upon her and embraces her in his arms, or whether he frowns, or rebukes, or smites her, she apprehends the sweetness of his love in all and is refreshed, supported, and instructed by every such dispensation of his authority over her." Even wife-beating was recognized by law in some localities. One statute advises the husband to use a stick "no larger than a finger in diameter," to prevent permanent damage, and cautions him to bear in mind that, no matter how great the provocation, he might need his wife's services again.

Governor Winthrop's sentiments rested on no less an authority than that of John Knox, the great Puritan reformer, who fulminated against women as "weak, frail, impatient, feeble and foolish." Thus, by the time a Puritan girl had reached the age of ten, she had been taught to think of herself as unworthy and flawed. Her only hope was to redeem herself through selfless service, patient endurance, and unquestioning loyalty to her lord and master.

Most Puritan women repressed their resentment, developing an attitude of "feminine wile" and subtlety as their basic adaptation. Often they did so without conscious awareness of this kind of psychological self-mutilation. They internalized the social norm and molded themselves quite unconsciously according to the Puritan ideal of womanhood. A small minority, unable to relinquish personal autonomy, sought self-fulfillment beyond the limits of social expectations. Such independence of spirit was ascribed to madness or the influence of demons, and the frenzied witch hunts of Salem marked the dismal climax of what may have been the most bizarre among America's social delusions.

Almost like rival species, Quakers and Puritans struggled for the new continent, clashing over all the fundamentals: the nature of God, the function of the state, the question of freedom and authority, and the role of women. Total surrender of one or the other sect seemed the only possible outcome of so bitter a quarrel. Yet with the passage of time the edge of the conflict wore, and in some ways Quakers and Puritans even came to resemble each other. The Puritans became quite democratic in the conduct of their public affairs, while the Quakers, despite Penn's vaunted "soul freedom," grew quite puritanical in their personal lives. Boston, the Athens of America, later shone as a center of liberality, while Philadelphia became noted for a certain stodginess.

But this paradoxical rapprochement lay far in the future. On the day Penn stepped ashore at New Castle, the lines were sharply drawn and marked in blood. Until that day the Puritans, by dint of majority and ruthlessness, might have succeeded in sweeping Quakerism from America altogether. But once Penn had established a Quaker state under British protection, the Quakers' foothold was secure, and their influence soon exceeded their numbers. Their religion, with its extreme demands of individual self-direction, never found many converts, but their politics contributed a central theme to the American tradition. Their practice of religious and political tolerance prepared the ground for the democratic pluralism of a future America.

There are moments in which past and future seem to meld. Penn's landing was such a moment. The fate of a country seemed contained in it. Gathered within that instant were the years of the early settlers—the Swedes and the Dutch—and the years to come, during which the Quakers would build a vital alternative to America's dominant Puritanism. Standing there with his twig and the clod of American earth in his hand, Penn was like a prophet, making the formative connection between what was and what was yet to be.

Twelve

THE NEW LAND

Penn's proudest ambition was to build a great city as the vital center of his new land. The number of settlers in Pennsylvania would hardly populate a small town, but Penn already dreamed of a future metropolis. He even had a name for it. Casting among Greek syllables in his usual classicist fashion, he joined *philia* (love) and *adelphos* (brother) into the euphonious Philadelphia—Brotherly Love.

Penn wanted the capital of his province to be quite different from the European cities he had known. Those cities still bore the imprint of their origin as walled enclaves—defensible settlements against medieval marauders. Houses huddled close together in narrow lanes, with the market place as the only open space. But Penn wanted no fortress city. He issued specific instructions to Thomas Holme, his surveyor general: "Let every house be placed, if the person pleases, in the middle of his plot, as to the breadth way of it, that so there may be ground on each side for gardens or orchards or fields, that it may be a green country town, which will never be burnt and always wholesome."

As for the site of Philadephia, Penn and Holme chose a neck of land between the Delaware and the Schuylkill, where ships could "ride in good anchorage in both rivers" and the land was "level, dry and wholesome—a situation scarcely to be paralleled." In effect, Penn became America's first city planner. He also introduced the rectangular street pattern, not realizing that what then seemed a sensible alternative to the crooked maze of European towns would in time become a model of baneful monotony for American cities.

Less than a year after the plan was first conceived, Holme filed a progress report:

August 16, 1683

From the Surveyor General:
The City is so ordered now, by the Governour's Care and Prudence, that it hath a Front to each River, one half at Delaware, the other at Schuylkill; and though all this cannot make way for small Purchasers to be in the [water-]Fronts, yet they are placed in the next Streets, contiguous to each Front. All Purchasers of One Thousand Acres, and upwards have the Fronts, and the smaller Purchasers about half an Acre in the backward Streets; by which means the least hath room enough for House, Garden and small Orchard, to the great Content and Satisfaction of all here concerned.

By 1684, swelled by the surge of immigration that followed Penn's arrival, Philadelphia already numbered about 2,500 residents and 400 houses, "divers of them large and well-built, with good cellars, three stories, and some with balconies."

But the founder of the city still had no home of his own. During his first winter in America, while his official residence was being built, Penn stayed as guest in the houses of various settlers. His time was taken up with legislative matters. Certain revisions had to be made in the *Frame of Government,* mostly to fit the law to local conditions that Penn could not have foreseen back in England when he drafted the constitution. In dealing with his legislative assembly, Penn avoided emphasis on his status as absolute proprietor. He even underplayed his role as governor and confined himself mainly to the formal function of presiding over the General Assembly, in which he had constitutionally limited his own power. Like any member of the upper chamber, he could propose legislation, but he had denied himself the right to veto any action of the Council.

The legislative agenda was mostly minor, dealing with the naturalization of Swedish and Dutch settlers, divorce law, tax collection, and minor ordinances. Few of the council members had prior experience in politics, and in one of his letters home Penn complained about "their inability in estate, and unskilfulness in matters of government." Tactfully, Penn used his own legal expertise to educate the Council in legislative and administrative procedure.

Penn wanted his official governor's residence—Pennsbury Manor—completed before Guli and the children came to join him in America. Guli's health was still precarious, and Penn wanted to spare her the strain of moving into temporary quarters. Besides, the province of Pennsylvania still lacked any house to meet Guli's accustomed standards of scale and convenience.

Fortunately, the work on Pennsbury progressed speedily after the onset of warm weather, and it must have been a great comfort to Penn in his loneliness to anticipate the reunion with Guli and her delight with the splendid new home he was building for her. The estate was located on the Delaware some twenty miles north of Philadelphia and had been bought from the Indians by Penn's deputy, William Markham, who recorded the purchase price as follows: "350 fathams of wampum, 300 gilders, 20 white blankets, 60 fathams of duffields [wool fabric], 20 kettles, 20 guns, 20 coats, 40 shirts, 40 pairs of stockings, and quantities of hoes, knives, glasses, shoes, pipes, scissors, combs, tobacco, and twenty gallons of rum, cider, and beer." The mansion itself was to be a three-story brick house with a tile roof, standing atop a slope with a sweeping view of the countryside. With its sixty-foot front and a depth of forty feet, the house was by far the grandest structure of the domain and must have seemed truly palatial in comparison to the modest dwellings of most settlers. From the porticoed entrance, a tree-lined walk was to lead to the river, where elaborate docking facilities would provide anchorage for the boats and barges by which Penn and his visitors would travel to and from Philadelphia.

Always an ardent horticulturist, Penn took almost more interest in the planting of the grounds than in the house itself. He ordered various kinds of decorative trees to be imported from Europe, and the flower garden was designed in the formal patterns he had come to know in France, where landscape architecture also followed the convoluted shapes of the Baroque. He felt sure that Guli, who had never been to France, would be entranced at her first sight of those curlicued flowerbeds that looked like calligraphy in bloom.

Assured of the swift progress of Pennsbury, Penn took several weeks in the spring of 1683 for an extended tour of his dominion. After his return he recounted his observations in "A Letter to the Committee of the Free Society of Traders," which acted as a sort of chamber of commerce for the development of the region. The letter was intended as a spur to immigration and was widely distributed in Europe. It appeared in German as "Beschreibung der neu-erfundenen Provinz Pennsylvanien" and later in French under the title "Recueil de Diverses pièces concernant la Pennsylvanie," and contained a remarkable description of the Indians and their customs. "The Natives I shall consider in their Persons, Language, Religion, and Government," Penn writes, systematically setting up descriptive categories that would do credit to a trained anthropologist. He was clearly fascinated by the Indians' appearance: "For their Persons, they are generally tall, straight, well-built, and of singular Proportion . . . of Complexion Black, but by design, as the Gypsies in England. They grease themselves with Bear-fat clarified, and using no defence against Sun and Weather, their skins must needs be swarthy. Their Eye is little and black, not unlike a straight-look'd Jew."

Penn did in fact believe the Indians to be "of the Jewish Race—I mean the stock of the Ten Tribes. . . . I find them of like Countenance and their Children of such lovely Resemblance [to European Jews] that a man would think himself in Dukesplace or Berry Street in London when he seeth them." Drawing comparisons between London's ghetto and the settlements of the Delaware Indians may seem anthropologically naive, yet it surely betokens a certain scientific open-mindedness.

Penn's comment on the native language is strikingly modern in its perception of the link between language and available modes of thought. He notes, for example, that an ambiguous vocabulary renders conceptual clarity impossible and that the hearer must supply meanings that the language itself cannot convey: "Their Language is lofty, yet narrow . . . in Signification full, like Short-Hand in writing; one word serveth in the place of three, and the rest are supplied by the Understanding of the Hearer: Imperfect in their Tenses, wanting in their Moods, Participles, Adverbs and Conjunctions."

He describes Indian customs with equal discernment. His is by far the most thorough and certainly the most sympathetic account of American aborigines written by an early European settler. Penn comments regretfully on such Indian traits as secretiveness and vengefulness but is impressed with the Indians' generosity in giving gifts and sharing possessions.

The Indians were the first people Penn had encountered outside the Judeo-Christian framework, and he deplores that "these poor People are under a dark Night in things relating to Religion," but is reassured by the fact that the Indians believe in "God and Immortality without the help of Metaphysicks."

Penn's benevolent interest in the Indians was unique. In their rapacious colonization of America, Europeans rarely took the trouble to make intelligent observations of native cultures. For the most part, the Dutch and British were no more thoughtful than the Spanish conquistadores in taking account of native customs and ideas, and whole Indian civilizations vanished unremarked under the European assault.

Natives, as a rule, were slaughtered or baptized, and robbed in either case. Even the pious Puritans took Indian land by force or fraud whenever they could. If the Indians retaliated by massacre—the Puritans interpreted this action as a sound moral pretext for killing off the Indians.

Greed, of course, was the main motive in the usual European treatment of native Americans. Yet other factors help explain the casual atrocity of the colonizers. Never before had western Europeans experienced the sort of prolonged exposure to radically different cultures that would produce mutual accommodation and understanding. The encounter with Islam had been relentlessly hostile, and explorations like those of Marco Polo had produced little cooperative interaction and durable contact. Europeans and Indians were equally unprepared for intercultural encounters. In consequence, they usually confronted each other with murderous incomprehension.

Penn's racial policy stands as a singular exception to this dismal rule. He insisted on treating Indians under his jurisdiction with scrupulous fairness. According to his charter, he owned all Indian territory in his domain and could have taken it with armed force by right of conquest. Yet he abjured force as a matter of principle and stipulated that no land be taken from the Indians except through purchase. He even instructed his agents not to beat the price below going rates, though he refused to pay inflated demands by smart Indian speculators, who soon caught on to the wiles of bargaining. Land-sale records specified the exact terms of each trade. Usually the Indians exchanged land for such items as guns, coats, shirts, axes, drinking glasses, combs, awls, fishhooks, and sewing needles— articles that seemed to them almost miraculous in their efficiency.

Since the Indians set a high value on physical courage, they were probably as much impressed by Penn's personal daring as by his fairness. He went among the Indians unguarded and unarmed, believing his truest defense was "God's spirit within the Indians' hearts." It never occurred to him that the Indians might have other gods in their hearts, who might look approvingly on the opportune killing of a powerful and possibly troublesome stranger. Fortunately, his luck held out.

Penn became a legend among the Indians, and fond tales about him were passed along for generations among the Delawares. No white man had ever before approached the Indians with such trust. It also may have helped that Penn shared the Indians' great fondness for foot racing. An enthusiastic sprinter ever since his days at Chigwell School, Penn had kept in good physical shape. At the age of thirty-eight, he was still able to outrun some of the nimblest Indian braves—a feat that earned him profound respect.

For all his fairness, Penn's attitude toward the Indians contained a patronizing tinge, and in some ways he took up the white man's burden a little too eagerly. His cherished hope was "to reduce the savage nations, by gentle and just means, to the love of civil society and the Christian religion." Yet this missionary bent for the uplift and betterment of the benighted never overshadowed his genuine tolerance of human differences. Often he visited the Indians in their homes, and they undoubtedly sensed the genuine warmth of his sympathy.

Penn's amity with the Indians culminated in the Great Treaty concluded beneath a large elm tree at Shackamaxon, located in what is now the Kensington district of Philadelphia. Surprisingly, no documentary evidence exists of this famous occasion. But informal recollections passed on as family lore among the early settlers make it seem likely that the event actually took place.

A century later, the painter Benjamin West depicted the scene of the treaty in a widely reproduced painting that has ever since shaped the historical imagination of Pennsylvania schoolchildren. Unfortunately, West's pictorial account is more notable for sentiment than accuracy. The picture shows a style of brick building that could not have been standing at the time. It also portrays Penn in pot-bellied middle age, though he was still youthfully slim, and in a costume of a kind unknown to his period.

But the fundamental distortion of the painting lies in its spirit. It shows the Indians as simpering primitives confronted by a delegation of stiff-backed Quakers assuming expressions of almost unbearable smugness and stolidity. In all, the painting exemplifies an attitude that has added much to the confusion of treacle and truth in popular notions of American history.

What is certain is that Penn indeed met with Indian delegations, for he refers to several such meetings in his correspondence. The Indians preferred to hold these meetings outdoors, often under certain landmark trees, and they appeared on these occasions in full feathered regalia. They would seat themselves in a half circle with the chief at the center. At such meetings, Penn would negotiate land exchanges and trade agreements, and, by his own account, he was sufficiently fluent in native speech to dispense with the services of translators. Since the Indians were illiterate, agreement was often signified by tokens other than writing, usually by the ritual exchange of gifts. On one such occasion, the Indians presented Penn with a belt consisting of eighteen strings of wampum, decorated with four crosses of violet-colored beads made from clamshells. And at the meeting presumed to have taken place under the elm at Shackamaxon, the Indians reportedly pledged themselves "to live in love with William Penn and his children as long as the Sun and the Moon shall endure."

Voltaire, Penn's great admirer, said of the Shackamaxon pact that it was "the only treaty between those [Indian] nations and the Christians which was never sworn to and never broken." Indeed, as long as Penn personally conducted the affairs of his land, his racial policy created a harmony unmatched anywhere in colonial relations. Only much later, in Penn's absence, when Indian policy was administered by officials bowing to pressure from exploitative traders, did the usual tensions arise. Sharp deals poisoned the atmosphere of trust.

At this later stage, French agents entered the picture. Agitating against British interests in America, they persuaded the Indians that the Quakers were cheating them on land prices, whereupon the Indians began to massacre the unresisting Quakers as enthusiastically as they attacked more militant whites. For a while, the Quakers bravely held to their conviction that it was better to die than to kill, trusting that the Indians would be pacified by this noble attitude. But the moral point was lost on the Indians, who enjoyed raiding Quaker settlements all the more since they ran no risk of organized resistance.

Helpless against such violence, which reached a brutal peak during the French and Indian wars, the Quakers eventually resolved their dilemma by inviting non-Quakers to furnish the province with a defensive force and military supplies, as long as these items were called by some other name. Whatever may be said of this subterfuge in terms of ethical principle or logical consistency, it assured the physical survival of the Quaker colony, which had by then become a pawn in the wars between England and France. But the pacific spirit of the Holy Experiment had been damaged beyond repair, and in his final years Penn suffered the agony of seeing his province gradually transformed into a military state like the other colonies.

Still, Penn's pacifist policy had not been a failure. As long as it operated undisturbed within its own sphere, it was a remarkable success, which remains a shining page in the otherwise sordid annals of colonialism. Penn's policy of brotherhood faltered only when it fell under the shadow of a distant war, raging between European powers.

None of these distant debacles beclouded Penn's first visit to his province. High hope still prevailed. No less than thirty ships reached the new city of Philadelphia in the first year of its existence, bringing settlers from England, Holland, Germany, Sweden, Finland, Ireland, and Wales. The budding colony soon developed a cosmopolitan atmosphere and cultural diversity found nowhere else in America. This helped attract some wealthy and sophisticated settlers, among them Penn's friend Robert Turner, who arrived with no less than seventeen servants. He set up a hospitable household in Philadelphia, with an extensive library that became the meeting place for the growing number of Philadelphians with educated interests.

Those with a taste for simpler entertainment found it most readily in the taverns that soon sprang up in the new city of Philadelphia. Homesick immigrants could well imagine themselves back in England as soon as they entered those tavern rooms. Pewter mugs and tankards hung from the exposed beams, and the ceiling was low enough to put them within easy reach. The comforting smell of beer blended with tobacco smoke and the aroma of suckling pig roasting on a spit in the fireplace. Long tables and benches were shared by everyone and helped produce an easy conviviality that let the patrons forget the strangeness of the new land. Recent arrivals would bring news from home, swap stories with the older settlers, make friends, and soon feel more at ease. Especially for unmarried men, the tavern was a place of needed companionship. For many, the tavern was the only place to go in their leisure hours. There had been no time for a popular culture to develop. There was no theater, no public concerts, and there were few organized sports. Most Quakers shared the Puritans' distrust of the arts and did little to encourage them. Penn himself regarded theater and music as frivolous or worse. Under these conditions, a typical frontier pattern developed in which drinking became the chief social diversion.

Other factors created a psychological need for alcohol common in new communities. It was a pattern repeated in a later era in the saloons of the western frontier. The lives of the new settlers had been cleft by their uprooting. The sense of continuity, so vital to personal integration, had been disrupted, and alcohol sometimes helped restore a sense of unity and wholeness to fractured lives.

This psychosocial drinking pattern applied nearly everywhere in colonial America, and not even the Puritans invoked prohibitions against alcohol until much later. To a degree, the early colonies might be characterized as drug cultures centered on alcohol, and in keeping with these bibulous habits early Americans developed medical theories concerning the harmfulness of water. Colonial doctors quite logically pointed out that water might be contaminated, whereas beer, wine, and liquor were certainly more hygienic.

Penn disliked the boisterous merriment of the taverns. He himself drank sparingly and usually remained staunchly sober. Yet he recognized the importance of drinking in the social pattern of his land, and one of his reports gives considerable space to the subject:

> Our Drink has been Beer and Punch, made of Rum and Water. Our Beer was mostly made of molasses, which well boyld, with Sassafras or Pine infused into it, makes very tolerable drink. But now they make Mault, and Mault Drink begins to be common, especially at the Ordinaries and the Houses of the more substantial People. In our great Town [Philadelphia] there is an able Man that has set up a large Brew House in order to furnish the People with good Drink. . . .

But neither town nor tavern set the keynote in the colony's way of life. In the main, the province was agricultural, and the typical settler lived in a small farming village with only a few houses. The ways of working the land were still primitive, having remained almost unchanged for the past two thousand years. Crop rotation was yet unknown, and manure was thrown away instead of being used as fertilizer. As a result, the soil was soon exhausted, and farmers faced the staggering task of clearing more virgin forest to gain arable land. No machinery lightened their labor. Even the most basic of all farming tools, the plow, was woefully inefficient. The shape of the modern metal plowshare, designed to toss the loosened soil to one side, was yet to be invented a hundred years hence by an ingenious Scotsman named James Small. Early Pennsylvania farmers still used wooden plows that barely reamed a groove in the earth, and then let the dirt fall right back into the furrow. Thus, after plowing, each row had to be shoveled out. Little was known of selective breeding and nothing of efficient feed-mixing, and the oxen drawing the plow were so small and weak that four or six of them were needed in each team, which made them difficult to manage. By the same token, the cows yielded little milk. Pigs, too, were scrawny and had not much meat on them, for they were not fed at all but left to forage.

The Indians had taught the settlers to plant corn, the chief indigenous crop, but soon enough seed for wheat and oats had been imported to make these cereals abundant. Pear and apple trees were also imported as seedlings, to join such native fruit as persimmon, cherry, and strawberry. Oddly enough, there were no potatoes. Native to Peru, they did not reach North America until the eighteenth century, when they came by way of England and Ireland.

In appearance, farmers did not differ much from city people. Since the streets in town were still unpaved, they were often almost as muddy as the open fields, and most men wore boots reaching up to the knee. So did the rural women, except when dressing for the Meeting or an excursion into town. On these occasions they would display whatever finery they had brought with them from Europe. One settler lady proudly noted in her journal that she went to town in "a little round cap of Lincoln green, a petticoat of green drugget cloth with puffed and ruffled sleeves, high-heeled leather shoes with green ribbon bows and a mask of black velvet." Most women wore masks outdoors to protect their faces from sunlight, for extreme pallor was regarded as fashionable and attractive.

Rural families were kept busy to the point of exhaustion with basic survival tasks: field work, building construction, and household chores. The women preserved surplus meat by salting and smoking it to prevent heat spoilage. Processes for canning fruits and vegetables had not yet been developed, but fruit was preserved in the form of jams and jellies. These were luxuries, however, because of the high cost of sugar.

Most dwellings had no plumbing and no bathrooms. Soap was already familiar as an item of hygiene, but it was so caustic that it had to be used sparingly for fear of causing skin eruptions. Indoor bathing in a wooden tub was considered a medicinal procedure, not without risk, to be practiced only rarely. The toothbrush was already familiar in Europe, but in America, most people still cleaned their teeth with a twig dipped in brine.

In the poorer households furnishings were sparse, consisting mostly of a few rough-hewn tables and benches, for not many of the settlers had the skill of fine carpentry. Straw pallets usually served as beds. Only the wealthy could afford imported furniture from England, for the shipping space taken up by such pieces made their cost exorbitant.

Today it is difficult to imagine the pace and tone of daily life in such settings. But a lovely paragraph by the great Dutch historian J. Huizinga evokes something of these bygone ways of being:

> The contrast between suffering and joy, between adversity and happiness appeared more striking. All experience had yet to the minds of men the directness and

absoluteness of the pleasure and pain of child-life.
. . . The contrast between silence and sound, darkness and light, like that between summer and winter
was more strongly marked than it is in our lives. The
modern town hardly knows silence or darkness in their
purity, nor the effect of a solitary light or a single distant cry.

Penn had been in America hardly more than a year when it
appeared that he might soon have to go back to England. For
one thing, there was the constant worry about Guli's health.
She had been pregnant when Penn left, although, to avoid bur-
dening his mind before the great voyage, she may not have
told him so. A little girl was born early in March of 1683, but
she lived for only a week. After that, Guli became ill and remained so for a long time. Her mother had died a few months
earlier, and, having always been rather aloof and concerned
mostly with her own thoughts, Guli had not many close friends.
She felt very alone. But Thomas Ellwood, who had so deeply
loved her as a young girl, heard of her illness and came for a
while to Worminghurst to take care of her. When she would
be well enough to join her husband in America none could say.

Also, Penn's colonizing efforts were being sabotaged in London by envious rumor-mongers who accused Penn of running
his province purely for personal profit and, somewhat incon-
sistently, spread stories that he had been killed under harrowing circumstances such as one was likely to encounter in
America. Worse yet, in his death agony he had confessed himself a Catholic. Philip Ford, Penn's agent, placed advertise-
ments in the *London Gazette* to say that, when last heard from,
Penn had been quite alive. But given the transatlantic communications lag, anything might have happened in the mean-
time, and Ford's affirmations didn't convince the astounding
number of people who somehow feel vindicated by the death

of their betters. Appearing in person, Penn believed, would be the best way to spike rumors of his demise.

What finally forced the issue of Penn's return to Europe was a border clash with Lord Baltimore, the owner of Maryland. The dispute arose from an ambiguity in land titles based on inaccurate maps and inadequate surveys. Despite several ostensibly friendly attempts to negotiate the matter, the controversy had become increasingly bitter. During a diplomatic visit to the town of Upland—later renamed Chester—Lord Baltimore turned to Deputy Governor Markham, who acted as Penn's negotiator. Staring intently at Markham, his Lordship swept the horizons of Pennsylvania with his arm and declared: "Therefore, afore you and afore all, I lay claim to this place, and as far further as the degree of forty will reach!"

As any map will show, his Lordship had just appropriated the city of Philadelphia. By way of reply, Markham, with "disordered countenance," ushered his Lordship to his barge and motioned the oarsmen to cast off.

At this point, Penn and Baltimore both appealed their dispute to the King's Privy Council. But Colonel George Talbot, the surveyor general of Maryland, was in no mood to wait for replies from London. With a platoon of soldiers, he marched on Ogle's Land, a promontory within five miles of New Castle, and proceeded to build a fort on what Penn clearly considered his own territory. The mayor and magistrates of New Castle promptly marched out to the landspit to demand an explanation. Talbot merely trained his guns on the approaching delegation. Stand off! a soldier shouted at them. Stand off or be blown to bits!

Talbot had established an invasion beachhead. Penn was in a quandary. His proudest boast was that during his stay in Pennsylvania "not one soldier, or arms borne, or militia had been seen." He had found ways of dealing peacefully with the savages, but not with this English Lord who was his neighbor by favor of the same King who had granted his own domain and on whose protection he would now rely. Only at White-hall, before the royal throne, could this conflict be resolved.

Once again Penn prepared for an ocean crossing, and again he wrote solemn notes to potential survivors. One of these was addressed to the new City of Philadelphia, and it sounds as lyrical as if it had been written for Guli: "My love and my life is to you, and with you; and no water can quench it, nor distance wear it out, or bring to an end. I have been with you, cared over you and served you with unfeigned love; and you are beloved of me, and near me, beyond utterance."

In late summer he boarded the ship *Endeavor* in the harbor of Philadelphia, the city he cherished as if it were his child, and entrusted himself to the sea.

Thirteen

ADVERSITY

Give sorrow leave a while to tutor me to this submission.
                                              —SHAKESPEARE

For a brief time, all trouble was forgotten. To see Guli again
was sheer happiness. Penn stayed with her at Worminghurst
for about a week, hardly leaving the house. Those who expected him in London on urgent matters waited in vain.

That week was Penn's last season of joy for years to come.
It was perhaps the last time he could still feel that innocent
trust in an ultimate rightness, that supernal confidence which
had carried him to great attainments at a young age. Afterward
the tide turned. Silently it drew him away from himself and
into the whirlpools of adversity.

England had changed during the two years he had been
away, and Penn sensed the shift on his first visit to London.
"I found things in general with another face than I left them,"
he observed. Calling on the King and the Duke of York, Penn
perceived them as "sour and stern, resolved to hold the reins
of power with a stiffer hand than heretofore, especially over
state and church dissenters."

Shortly after Penn's return, the conflict between the Crown
and Parliament erupted anew. When the Whig party openly
called for the limitation of royal power, the King took an

uprising of the radical fringe—the so-called Monmouth Rebellion—as a pretext for crushing the entire liberal Whig movement by arbitrary arrests and summary executions.

It was a time of ceremonial book-burning, when the works of Locke and Milton were piously tossed into the flames, and John Locke had reason to fear he might be burned along with his books. Even London's famous coffeehouses were closed as "the great resort of idle and disaffected persons" who might be brewing sedition along with the newly popular Arabian bean.

One of Penn's close friends, the statesman and scholar Algernon Sidney, had fallen victim to the persecution of Whigs. At the King's behest, soldiers broke into Sidney's house, ransacked his desk, and found the manuscript of *Discourses Concerning Government,* which Sidney had been writing in secret. Proposing a "mixed monarchy" with reliable parliamentary restraints placed upon the power of the Crown, the book was far from revolutionary. In fact, along with the political writings of Locke, it was recognized after posthumous publication as a sober and circumspect treatise on a theory of government based on the separation of powers. But in the turmoil of the times, neither the moderation of his views nor the scholarly merit of his work kept Sidney from the gallows. As the historian Maurice Ashley later put it, "He died for his book."

Taking Sidney's death as a personal warning, Penn realized the difficulty of his own position. As a professional dissenter and known friend of prominent Whigs, he was suspect. His adversary, Lord Baltimore, was clearly aware of this. No doubt he would try to discredit Penn's territorial claim on political grounds. Penn also feared that the King, now striving to consolidate all power through centralized administration, would revoke the Pennsylvania charter altogether if Penn gave him cause for displeasure.

At this point, Penn's major concern was to secure his holdings, not only for personal gain but because a refuge for

Quakers and nonconformists now seemed more necessary than ever. Civil liberty and religious tolerance had nearly vanished from England as King Charles had emulated the absolutism practiced in France by his friend and financial supporter, Louis XIV. Since the law no longer furnished protection, Penn had no choice but to curry favor. He did his best to ingratiate himself at court, and to gain admission to the King's circle of close advisors he wrote an extensive brief entitled *True Interest of King and Kingdom,* which slyly flattered the monarch's autocratic ambitions while warning him not to overplay his hand. For a while, Penn even suspended his agitation for tolerance. He continued to write in support of liberty of conscience, but left his writings unpublished so as not to embarrass the King. "The times," he said, "are too rough for print."

Clearly Penn was no longer the man who had once written defiantly from prison: "I shall not budge." He had begun to count costs. Property and power had taught him to bargain, and care taught him to compromise. He could no longer afford absolute morality. Penn had lost his political innocence.

Penn had reason to be anxious. Lord Baltimore's claims to the Delaware peninsula in the southern part of Pennsylvania turned out to be far from groundless. Baltimore appeared to have prior rights to the territory, based on a royal grant preceding the Pennsylvania charter by nearly fifty years. But if that area were annexed to Maryland, Penn realized, he would lose waterways essential to the commercial prosperity of his own province. Penn therefore contrived a counterclaim based on the argument that the Delaware territory had been settled by the Dutch and therefore should be lumped with the other formerly Dutch domains that had been granted to him.

Oddly enough, Penn received unwitting support from Colonel Talbot, the Maryland commander who had staged the invasion of Ogle's Land. In another of his more impulsive moments, the colonel had murdered the royal customs collector. The King took a dim view of such temperamental excess, especially when directed against revenue officials, and since the colonel happened to be Lord Baltimore's nephew, the incident put Baltimore out of favor. Penn the pacifist thus became the main beneficiary of violence. No immediate decision seemed likely, however, for the King was too involved in his domestic difficulties to be much concerned about a petty border squabble on a distant continent. Penn's status thus remained uncertain, both at court and in America.

His position improved greatly in February, 1685, when the King suffered a stroke. The doctors did their best. They "opportunely blooded and cupped him and plied his head with red-hot frying pans." Despite or because of this therapy, the King died. His brother and successor, James II, was more cordially disposed toward Penn. As the former Duke of York, he had shared the command of the Navy with Admiral Penn and saw in William the son of a cherished comrade. But there was an even deeper bond. Penn and the new King both belonged to despised and persecuted religious minorities. James was a Catholic, which rendered his rule deeply problematic in a kingdom where Anglicanism was the official religion and where Anglican pressure for conformity now reached a point of hysteria. Quaker and Catholic were thus bound in a common cause. They both depended on a legal shift toward religious toleration. This common interest between King and Quaker now formed the basis for Penn's brief and perilous career as a courtier.

Penn's new position at court was hardly lost on the official panel of arbitrators for the Pennsylvania border dispute. They now moved for a swift decision. If Baltimore's prior claim was recognized, it meant that the new King, when Duke of York, had ceded land to Penn which wasn't actually his own. Upholding Baltimore, therefore, would embarrass both the King and his Quaker friend.

Penn, aware of the arbitrator's dilemma, chose this exact moment to submit new evidence: documents supposedly proving the existence of Dutch settlements in Delaware *before* the granting of Baltimore's charter. This history, Penn claimed, made the area part of the Dutch conquest by the Duke of York and hence a legitimate part of his own bounty.

It was a sophistical argument. Not many lawyers would consider this a strong case, and in his better moments as a legal scholar Penn would have scorned his own stratagem. Penn was displaying new talents. The paragon of principle was proving himself surprisingly adept at expediency.

If the arbitrators balked at having doubtful evidence forced on them, they could no longer evade the issue. Still, they managed to sidestep a clear decision in favor of Penn. On October 17, 1685, they handed down their opinion, denying Baltimore's claim. But they did not cede the disputed area directly to Penn. Instead, they let it revert to the King for disposition at his pleasure.

Penn was jubilant. He felt sure of the King's favor, confident that the land would eventually be joined to his. In great elation he wrote to a friend that victory had been gained "at much cost & paines." Since men of high morality go to great trouble to think well of themselves, he probably never realized the taint of his triumph or the true nature of its cost.

Penn had now reached the height of his power. At forty-one, the former rebel had become an intimate of the King and a prominent figure in the city of London. Yet the character and mood of both court and city were oddly out of step with Penn's own. Indeed, what seems most striking about Penn's position at that time is the sheer incongruence between the man and his surroundings.

London had rebounded from fire and plague with amazing swiftness. True, a great deal of rebuilding yet remained to be done, and the new dome of St. Paul's was still but a huge shell gaping open at the sky. But elsewhere Sir Christopher Wren's spires already graced the horizon; and with its population

swelled to half a million, London was reaching westward past
Piccadilly, gradually enfolding the fields of Kensington.

Street traffic had increased with the population, and in such
busy thoroughfares as the Strand or around London Bridge
police had to be employed for the first time to keep horses, carriages, and pushcarts from getting tangled in traffic jams. The
Thames partly relieved this congestion by serving as an auxil-
iary traffic artery. Along the banks, boatmen offered their
barges for hire, shouting "Oars! Oars! Will you have any oars!"
and obviously relished what to cockney ears sounded like
double-entendre. Soon the river became so crowded with all
kinds of craft that boats were constantly bumping into each
other, sometimes spilling their passengers, and the language
of their pilots grew as foul as the water. The Thames, in fact,
was little more than an open sewer for the brewers, tanners,
butchers, and millers who set up shop along its banks. One
observer complained:

> Sweepings from butcher's stalls, dung, guts and blood,
> Drowned puppies, shaking sprats, all drenched in mud,
> Dead cats and turnip tops, come tumbling down the flood.

The aroma of the river mingled readily with the social
atmosphere. As is usual in times of political oppression, most
of the population concentrated on the search for pleasure and
excitement. But in Restoration London this search assumed
somewhat grotesque aspects. For example, the corridors of
the stock exchange teemed with women negotiating transactions of their own. Far handsomer on average than common
whores, these ladies ranked among the accepted amenities of
the Royal Exchange, symbolizing perhaps the vision of life as
a trade. As for the brokers' wives, they enjoyed equal but
separate facilities at Covent Garden Church, where elegant
swains sat piously in the pews, awaiting invitations from
fashionable women.

Such customs were not incidental. They reflected a compulsive, if naive, striving for wickedness, a reaction against the Puritan fetters of a generation before. The whole orientation of London life was still a protest against coerced virtue, and venality passed as the mark of personal liberation.

True, there were also such exemplary institutions as the newly founded Royal Society, of which Penn was a member and where he might hear Mr. Newton, the director of the Royal Mint, expound his curious notions about the planets, or learn from Mr. Robert Boyle that the air had weight, and other strange facts about the behavior of gases. But the tone of the city was set neither by its few savants nor by its plentiful whores and gamblers. Rather, it reflected the nominally respectable majority: the merchants who considered discreet cheating the proper way of doing business and those solid burghers of either sex who, with energetic devotion, made sybaritism and lasciviousness the basic climate of their existence.

Yet the sheer vitality of its slightly tainted people gave London a pleasant mood of buoyancy and exhilaration. There was always a splendid show at the Royal Theater in Drury Lane and in the new Vauxhall Gardens, in Lambeth, one could hear open-air concerts on summer evenings. Above all, promenading had become a favorite pastime. Dandyism had evolved into something like a civic sport, and men and women of all ages needed a chance to show off their finery. The crowds would mill along the Strand, looking at the shops that featured such new luxuries as small brushes with long handles for cleaning one's teeth, straw hats to ward off the summer sun, stockings made of silk, and lace-trimmed fans. Usually these walks ended with a visit to one of the many taverns, where for threepence one could get one's fill of bread and hard cheese, softening the cheese by dunking it into a mug of warm ale. Or one might dine more expensively on boar, pigeon, and port. Taking his payment, the tavern owner would weigh the money on a scale to make sure none of the silver had been shaved off, and if the customer was obviously from the provinces, he probably received his change in counterfeit coin.

When tired of walking on the ankle-twisting cobblestones, Londoners now had a choice of public transport. Horse cabs cruised the streets with perforated roofs through which the passenger could shout directions at the coachman. And for those who could not afford a cab there were the precursors of buses. Drawn by eight horses, they carried as many as twenty passengers seated on wooden benches or old barrels. Wending their way through the narrow streets among the usual melee of sedan chairs, dung carts, brewer's drays, and occasional flocks of sheep, these broad-beamed conveyances were often not so much a means of travel as a cause of total standstill. In short, London had begun to exhibit the symptoms of a metropolis.

Penn remained untouched by both the charm and the tawdriness of London. As a man of invincible if rather stolid virtue, he averted his nose from the rancid odor of the city's turmoil. But by the same token he somehow failed to catch the basic tune of the times, and so the earthy grit of practical politics often eluded him.

It was this curious remoteness, this high-minded distance from the immediate that kept Penn from grasping either the potential or the danger of his own situation. As the King's confidant, he could have shaped the course of events. Instead, he let events lead him. With a strange naiveté that defies convincing explanation, Penn allowed himself to become the tool of one of the worst rulers ever to occupy England's throne. In his loyalty to James as a friend, he could not see the King as he was: narrow, inflexible, arrogant, and vengeful.

A few years earlier, the Whigs in Parliament had voted to exclude James from the royal succession because of his Catholicism. His way to the throne had been paved by the brutal suppression of the liberal Whigs and stained with the blood of Penn's friends. Now this last of the Stuart kings revenged himself on the parliamentary powers that had once opposed him, by affirming the absolutism of the Crown. Like his father, whose head had been severed by Cromwell's ax, James proclaimed the divine right of kings once again. His grandfather and namesake, James I, had spoken the creed of all the Stuarts: "As it is atheism and blasphemy to dispute what God can do, so it is high contempt in a subject to dispute what a king can do, or say that he cannot do this or that." Even then, this was the echo of a dying cause. To revive this doctrine after Cromwell seemed both madness and insolence.

The second James had come late to his reign. He was fifty-three when he ascended the throne. In his younger years he had shared his brother's liking for variety in women, though apparently with much inferior taste. Some historians suggest that by the time James assumed the government, his judgment was already impaired by the syphilitic consequences of his pastimes. His monumental stubbornness, his inability to weigh alternatives, and his gross manners may well have had medical causes. At any rate, those who knew and cherished Penn could only wonder at the close bond between him and the King. But Penn's judgment of people had always been clouded by generosity. As one writer observed, "He could criticize a theory, but could not judge a man."

Even so, Penn's position at court now enabled him to do effective work on behalf of tolerance. He devoted himself to the task with an urgency heightened by a recent experience. He had seen the burning of a nonconformist at a public execution.

Such events were meant as warnings to the populace, symbolizing the evil of crime. Yet in fact they were widely regarded as a form of popular amusement. For many Londoners, executions were a fair substitute for bear-baiting, which the Puritans had banned, not because of the pain it gave the bear, but because of the pleasure it gave the spectators. Why Penn attended this grim occasion is not known. The culprit in the case was a certain Elizabeth Gaunt, an Anabaptist, whose religious views and human sympathy had impelled her to give shelter to a Whig rebel. Now she paid for this act of treason in the customary manner. According to an account by Gilbert Burnet, Penn was visible moved when the woman at the stake grasped the straw flaming about her feet and held it against her chest and face to end her agony more quickly. The terror and compassion of that moment may have spurred Penn toward total political involvement with his preposterous King in hopes of ending such incidents forever.

Almost daily Penn was in conference at the palace. Careful strategies had to be worked out to make tolerance legislation palatable to a Parliament now consisting mostly of staunchly Anglican Tories. With the liberal Whigs such laws would have passed easily. But the Whigs had been hounded out of power because of their opposition to Stuart absolutism. By this purge, the former King had hoped to leave his successor a more supportive assembly. Paradoxically, he had produced the opposite result. True, the Tories were loyal monarchists, but they were also Anglicans, implacably hostile to Catholics. The situation was patently absurd. Parliament militated against popery, yet Mass was celebrated daily at court.

It was not a conflict that could be resolved rationally. With faith and fear as dominant factors, the spectral concepts of salvation and perdition hovered in the background of political debate. The darker elements of magic, underlying all religion, were seeping into the political process, charging almost every aspect of public affairs with explosive potential. Averting imminent disaster called for precisely the kind of political finesse so notably lacking in the new King. All the more, the monarch relied on Penn's advice and mediation.

By this time, Penn had acquired a personal manner suited to the functions of high diplomacy. He had given up his youthful insistence on Quaker habits of language and deportment. He took off his hat in the presence of others, and used "thee" and "thou" only in speaking to fellow Quakers. When the

Quakers reproached him for this, he replied: "I know of no religion which destroys courtesy, civility, and kindness."

Along with his manners, Penn's attitude also became more conventional. No longer did he allow religious fervor to sweep him beyond the limits of the practical. Now he resisted the temptation to become God's prophet, preferring instead to become God's politician. He carefully shaded the mystic glow of the Inner Light. His writings began to sound more like lawyers' briefs than the product of divine inspiration. It was as if Penn deliberately fenced in his spiritual range, keeping transcendence outside the gate.

To be near the King in the mounting crisis, Penn took up residence at Holland House, while Guli and the children remained at Worminghurst. The magnificent mansion with its rows of pointed arches stood on a hill in Kensington, just beyond London's western limit. He lived there in the sumptuous style of a viceroy, and the long hallways were filled with people seeking audience with Penn as if he himself were a branch of government. Always readily accessible to petitioners, Penn saved scores of politically endangered persons from the gallows by his personal intervention. He even succeeded in getting George Fox released from jail.

His mediation between King and Parliament brought about some lessening of religious repression. He prepared the way for the proclamation of the Acts of Indulgence, an amnesty that freed well over a thousand political prisoners, many of them Quakers. One contemporary account speaks of the "great consolation . . . to have the company of so many valuable Friends, whose faces had not been seen for many years, having been immured in prison, some of them twelve or fifteen years or upward, for no other crime but endeavoring to keep a good conscience toward God."

Yet Penn failed in his larger aim of establishing universal religious tolerance, for in this he had little support from the King and none from Parliament. Penn had naively assumed that the King was genuinely devoted to freedom of conscience. In fact, the King was interested only in the Catholic cause, and it was precisely for this reason that Parliament frustrated nearly all efforts at religious liberalization.

The cause of tolerance suffered a major setback in 1685, when the King of France, probably persuaded by his bigoted mistress, revoked the Edict of Nantes. Under this ordinance, the Protestant Huguenots had been freely tolerated in France. Now they were persecuted with vicious cruelty, and England recoiled from tales of horror drifting across the Channel. Penn himself, recalling his happy time of study at the Huguenot academy at Saumur, was appalled. "They fling water on the drowsy till they submit or run mad," Penn wrote to his friend Harrison. "The [prisoners] pray to be killed, but the King has ordered his dragoons to do anything but kill. . . ."

A new wave of fear now swept over the English. They were convinced their own King would follow the French example, suppress all Protestants, and plunge England into a new civil war. Protestants began hoarding weapons under their beds or carrying them under their clothes to defend themselves against what they expected to be an English version of the St. Bartholomew massacre. Because of his closeness to the King, Penn himself became suspect of being part of the "Popish conspiracy," and his effectiveness as a mediator declined. As political positions grew more polarized, Penn found himself caught in the King's camp. The advocate of impartial tolerance became more and more enmeshed in the King's dubious schemes.

One of these schemes was to send Penn on a diplomatic trip to Holland, where King James' daughter Mary lived as the wife of the Protestant ruler, Prince William of Orange. The purpose of Penn's mission was to convince the Protestant Dutch that the Catholic King of England meant them no harm. But William of Orange had a more realistic understanding of the character of the Stuarts, having married one of them. Instead of heeding Penn's assurances, he followed the advice of others to strengthen his fleet.

As the King's aide, Penn also revisited Oxford, the university that had once expelled him. This time he went there to return the compliment, so to speak. He went to oust the president.

The King wanted to replace the head of Magdalen College at Oxford with a man of his own choice, a Catholic bishop. Wherever possible, the King filled important positions with Catholics, and now he was trying to put Oxford under Roman influence. This was hardly the way to further the cause of religious freedom. Still, Penn lent himself to the King's scheme, presenting the King's demands to the university. Penn's writings leave no clue as to his motive. He had become taciturn and guarded. Possibly he felt that his show of loyalty to the monarch would protect his holdings in America from seizure by the increasingly erratic ruler.

Partly because of Penn's machinations, the eminently capable Dr. John Hough was supplanted at Oxford by Bishop Samuel Parker, a pious mediocrity. Penn at least had the decency to secure an adequate hearing for the opposition. When the university protested the King's appointment, Penn recognized the validity of the objections and himself presented the protest at court. But when James proved adamant, Penn deferred to the King.

He experienced the same kind of frustration when the King, disregarding Penn's advice, conducted what was probably the first public-opinion poll. Officials throughout the land were sent out to ask the populace whether they favored the King's plan to give Catholics and nonconformists access to governmental positions. Penn did not object to the poll in principle, but he realized that instead of providing confidence and assurance, such official questioning would only foment tension, evasion, and suspicion. Ignoring Penn's warning, the King ordered the poll and thereby heaped on himself such distrust on the part of the Protestant majority that rebellion seemed almost inevitable.

At this critical moment, the King made another mistake. He impregnated his wife. If the baby was a boy, it meant that another Catholic would succeed to the throne. English Protestants now panicked. They might have politely waited for James to die, trusting to his age and illness that this might happen soon. Most certainly they had not expected him, at this late date, to produce an heir. It seemed another of the King's underhanded tricks, and after the baby's birth it was rumored that the little boy wasn't really the King's son but had been smuggled into Windsor Castle in a big warming pan.

To complicate matters, there was trouble abroad. Holland and France were at the verge of war, and English Protestants feared their King would side with the French Catholics against his own daughter, the ruler of the Protestant Dutch.

James reacted to the mounting tension by compounding his errors. To Penn's dismay, he kept packing important posts with Catholic appointees and harassing prominent Anglicans with political trials on trumped-up charges. The opposition felt cornered. But, as a majority, they had ways to extricate themselves from such dilemmas. They could deliver the country to a foreign invader.

Through secret emissaries, the opposition leaders, with clandestine parliamentary support, invited the King's daughter Mary and her Protestant husband, William of Orange, the rulers of the Netherlands, to the English throne. In 1688, William and Mary sailed their newly refurbished fleet to the coast of Devon and proceeded to London in virtual triumph, while King James, his wife, and the new little Prince of Wales hastily fled to France. It was the Glorious Revolution.

Under the new rule of William and Mary, religious tolerance was soon established, along with other reforms that made England a model of political liberty.

The revolution of 1688 deserves its epithet. Perhaps no other revolution ever achieved such durable victory over the forces of despotism—a victory remarkable for having been attained without the capricious terror that normally accompanies major upheavals. Unlike the French, Russian, and Chinese revolutions in later times, it was a revolution with restraint. There were no *mitrailleurs* peppering shackled groups of men with shredded metal stuffed into cannon because, as Joseph Fouché complained, "the guillotine is too slow." Nor were entire regions deliberately starved because, as Leon Trotsky observed, "food is a weapon." It can be argued, of course, that the Glorious Revolution was no revolution at all, since it produced merely a change in governmental attitude without change in property relationships or class structure. Besides, the internal uprising was aided by an invasion from abroad. Even so, the events of 1688 revealed what is perhaps the most favorable condition for constructive social change: a belief in an alterable future defined by specific and limited objectives combined with humane constraints upon force.

At last, the ideals for which Penn had struggled all his life had triumphed. Tolerance and freedom of conscience were embedded in the law of England. But Penn had compromised himself, and now he stood in peril.

All the venom that had been built up against Penn for his friendship with the deposed Catholic King now spewed forth. He was denounced not only as a secret Papist but as a Jesuit who posed as a Quaker only to disguise his traitorous intentions. As the former King's counsellor, Penn had supposedly been plotting to betray England into the hands of the French. A friend of Penn's, William Popple, served as secretary of the Board of Trade. This post placed him in a good position to hear some of the accusations secretly made against Penn in prominent circles. Popple thought it best to inform his friend of what was said of him: "You have taken orders at Rome and there obtained a dispensation to marry; you have since frequently officiated as a priest in the celebration of Mass at Whitehall."

Penn even received warnings about the sudden change in his reputation abroad. William Sewel, an old friend, wrote from Amsterdam: "The things that are rumored about you in this part of the world in the discourse of almost everyone have struck me with sad horror. Although I never doubted the sincerity of your heart, I always feared for you because of your enemies, who have usually interpreted your best counsel in the worst way."

Penn defended himself, calling attention to his writings and his actions. Everything he had published, everything he had done belied these accusations. In his *Address to Protestants of All Persuasions* he had specifically warned that Catholicism had a long history of imposing religion by terror and that England had reason to fear Rome. Were those the words of a Papist, let alone a Jesuit?

But Penn's enemies were in no mood to sift evidence. Nor had the new King any liking for him. William III had distrusted Penn's earlier diplomatic mission to Holland, and events had proved him right, even though Penn may have acted in good faith. As for the Queen, she felt uneasy about her father's friend now that her father had become her enemy, plotting her overthrow from abroad. The royal pair were readily persuaded by Penn's detractors, and in February, 1689, the King's Privy Council issued a warrant for Penn's arrest "upon suspicion of high treason."

Penn went into hiding. He moved furtively from one address to another, meeting with Guli whenever he could manage. Guli had become very frail. The nervous strain had visibly affected her. Also, her little four-year-old girl, Gulielma Maria, had died shortly before and now lay in the family plot along with her three other dead children.

The news from America was also disheartening. Predictably

falling short of Penn's utopian expectations, the colony had been politically divided by disagreements that the inexpert legislature could not effectively settle. Oppressed in Britain, the Quakers had shown almost heroic solidarity. But in the freedom of America they proved as divisive and quarrelsome as most other groups. Penn's hopes of a spiritually cohesive community were slowly fading, and at one point he even appointed a non-Quaker, Captain John Blackwell, formerly of Cromwell's army, to be his deputy governor. An outsider, he hoped, might be able to restore harmony to the discordant ranks. But, as usual, Penn proved a poor psychologist. He failed to foresee the clash of personalities between the ex-military Blackwell, who was accustomed to obedience, and the meek but unmovable Quakers.

Blackwell's reception was an omen of things to come. When he entered the governor's mansion, the only person to welcome him was the gardener. Philadelphia merchants humiliated their new deputy governor by neglecting to pay his salary, and Blackwell soon asked Penn to relieve him of his post. Thereafter, Pennsylvania resumed its aimless drift under the indolent governance of its Council.

Penn's involvement in politics had kept him far too busy to look after his own finances. All such matters he left in charge of Philip Ford. Habitually he put his signature on whatever papers Ford laid before him, without bothering to read what he signed. Had anyone suggested that Ford, a fellow Quaker, might be less than honest, Penn would have rebuked such a remark. With his unquestioning, obstinate trust in his friends, Penn was incapable of harboring suspicion. It never occurred to him to investigate Ford's management of his affairs, and he would have considered it beneath his dignity to do so.

With Penn under indictment for treason, there was renewed danger that the province of Pennsylvania might be taken from him. This prospect carried a financial threat. Penn now had

no other source of income. His Irish estates had been confiscated by the new King as property of an outlaw even before
Penn had been tried or convicted. They were up for sale, and
meanwhile their proceeds went to the Crown. To protect
Penn's American holdings, Ford had a timely suggestion. Why
not assign the whole province to Ford? Then Ford could take
care of Penn's family in case Penn was found, tried, and beheaded. Besides, Ford's ownership of Pennsylvania would
protect the interest of the Quakers there if anything happened
to Penn. What's more, no one needed to know of the transaction, Ford explained. It could be kept secret between them.
Ford must have been remarkably persuasive, or Penn particularly despondent and suggestible, for on September 3,
1690, Penn signed a document conveying his entire colony
to his trusted servant.

Later that year it seemed that Penn's troubles were at last
coming to an end. A judicial hearing in November cleared
him of the treason charge. He immediately made plans to go
to America with Guli, who was very eager to see Pennsbury
now that the great mansion had been completed. But soon
afterward, in February, 1691, Queen Mary still suspecting
that Penn was plotting her overthrow with her exiled father
personally issued an arrest order for Penn, charging he had
"designed and endeavored to depose their Majesties and sub-
vert the government of this kingdom by procuring an invasion
of the same by the French."

Again Penn was a hunted man, his whereabouts known
only to his family and a few trusted friends. Some Quakers,
incurably naive about the perils of politics, chided Penn for
not facing the charges squarely. He answered them in a letter
dated March, 1691: "My privacy is not because men have
sworn truly, but falsely against me; 'for wicked men have
laid in wait for me, and false witnesses have laid to my charge
things that I know not.' "

There is evidence that Penn secretly went to France that

summer, seeking affidavits and testimony of his innocence from people who had known him during his time at court and who were now living in French exile. He also asked influential acquaintances to speak to the King in his behalf. "Lay my case before him," he wrote to the Earl of Romney, and "dispose him to regard me and mine under our present great difficulties. . . . I will make no ill use of his favor. I say, and that truly, that I know of no invasions and insurrections, men, money, or arms." He only hoped the King would "allow me to live quietly anywhere, either in this kingdom or in America." Romney conveyed the message and told the King that Penn was "a true and faithful servant to King William and Queen Mary, and if he knew anything that was prejudicial to them or their government, he would readily disclose it." Penn also pleaded for an audience with the King, hoping that he might personally convince the monarch of his innocence. But Penn's days of access to the throne were over. The audience was refused.

Nearly two years passed without further action. The royal pair remained deaf to repeated pleas by Penn's friends. But neither did the constabulary seem very eager to find Penn and bring him to trial. After all, William and Mary were laying the foundations of a liberal constitutional monarchy based on broad toleration of dissent. Penn had fought for the same principles. What could be more absurd than an ideological trial in which accuser and accused are in full agreement? Still, it would be impolitic to let Penn, the former intimate of King James, freely assert his influence. Under the circumstances, procrastination seemed the wisest course. It sufficed to keep Penn isolated simply by allowing the treason charge to remain in force. Penn thus lived as an outlaw in the chimerical underworld of "unpersons" who, at the displeasure of the government, had lost their legal existence.

Penn's hiding places during this period have never been located. Though not the object of an active manhunt, he was in constant danger of discovery and wisely kept no record of his whereabouts. His friends, at best, could offer only temporary refuge. A prolonged stay in any one place would have been too risky. After all, Penn's appearance was widely known and he would have been easily recognized. Even if he avoided the streets and stayed in the house, children or servants might betray the presence of the secret guest. Sheltering a criminal was a serious offense, and Penn's detection would bring ruin not only to himself but also to his host.

But there were parts of London where Penn could readily drop from sight—the sprawling slums and rat-ridden tenements overflowing with former countryfolk. These dismal districts sprang up when the rural squires of England "enclosed" the public land of their villages to graze their own sheep. This systematic plunder of the poor by the rich left many villagers destitute, unable to plant the meager crops that had supported them before. In desperate multitudes they drifted to the city, where they sank into the gin-sodden underworld that Hogarth depicted and that lives on in the sardonic saga of the *Three-penny Opera*. Here even Penn could rent some hovel with no questions asked, and since the constabulary rarely ventured into these precincts, he could feel fairly secure. The only immediate danger he experienced there, apart from ubiquitous cutthroats, was endemic disease in surroundings where personal cleanliness and public sanitation were equally unknown.

It is difficult to imagine Penn in such surroundings, but presumably that is where he spent his years of public disgrace. As in his prison days, Penn used his time for writing. One book of this period is suitably named *Some Fruits of Solitude*. The subtitle describes it precisely: *Reflections and Maxims Relating to the Conduct of Human Life*. It is a collection of contemplative epigraphs, clearly the work of a man who has little company but his own thoughts and remembrances. A few aphorisms convey the flavor of the book:

They have a right to censure that have a heart to help.
Never marry but for love; but see that thou lov'st what
is lovely.
There can be no friendship where there is no freedom.
To do evil that good may come of it is for bunglers in
politics as well as morals.
The less form in religion the better, since God is a
spirit.

The 855 maxims of this book form a personal code that sup-
plements the ethical philosophy of Penn's theological writings,
and the book has been favorably compared with the famous
Maximes of La Rochefoucauld and Benjamin Franklin's *Poor
Richard's Almanac*. The Quaker historian William Hull observes that "the contrast between Penn's emphasis on kindness
and charity and Franklin's emphasis on the shrewd and thrifty
arts of making money shows the difference between seventeenth-century idealism and eighteenth-century 'common
sense.' " Comparison of the two books indeed shows the
change from the ideal individualism of Penn's time to the
acquisitive individualism of Franklin's era.

Considering the circumstances under which the book was
written, it seems incredible that it contains no trace of bitterness. Penn makes only a single, indirect reference to his un-
deserved persecution: "The Author blesseth God for his
Retirement, and kisses that Gentle Hand which led him into
it."

In banal men, such resignation is suspect. It smacks of
spiritual blandness. Yet in Penn it seems a manifestation of
grace. Misfortune could not touch the core of his faith or
bring to the surface the sense of darkness that assails even
deeply religious persons in their contemplation of human destiny. Frequently in religious experience it is precisely this
sense of darkness that stirs the longing for redemptive symbols

and transcendent illumination. Penn's Inner Light dispelled these shadows of the soul.

The most substantial product of Penn's seclusion is *An Essay Toward the Present and Future Peace of Europe,* a work that places Penn among the earliest theorists of international law. In writing this book, Penn regained his utopian vision. No longer is he hemmed in by political prudence. Though he writes as neither a prophet nor a philosopher but simply as a legalist, the prophetic gleam once again shines from his pages. Like all visionaries, he asserts commitment to an ideal partly through negation of the empirical world; yet he remains within the framework of the practical.

Taking his departure from Grotius, who virtually originated the concept of international law in its modern form in his *De jure belli et pacis* and his postulate of "freedom of the seas," Penn advanced a bold proposition: the limitation of national sovereignty. Unchecked autonomy, Penn argued, creates conflict. A permanent supranational assembly is therefore needed to arbitrate international disputes and assure a measure of justice sufficient to forestall armed encounters. Building on an idea once suggested by Henri IV of France and his advisor Sully, Penn proposed a "Parliament of Europe" with powers of sanction against its member states. He also noted that such an agency of arbitration, equipped with authority and force, would reduce the need for large national armies, which were placing staggering economic burdens on their respective countries.

These ideas seem commonplace in retrospect, but in Penn's time they ran counter to all prevailing currents. The idea of the autonomous nation-state was just emerging as the concept dominating the political imagination, and colonization had established the notion of empire. War was the logical instrument of such ideologies, and the mystique of military glory became the secular faith that formed a savage counterpoint

to the nominal Christianity of modern Europe. What Penn
was attempting, in the face of these trends, was the structural
definition of a substitute for war. "Europe, by her incom-
parable miseries, makes this now necessary to be done," urged
Penn. But his warning went unheeded, and more than two
centuries of rampant national militarism left their harvest of
sorrow and devastation before Penn's ideas took their first tangible form in the League of Nations and the United Nations.

By working on his books during his period of hiding, Penn
apparently regained something of the personal integration—
that notable harmony of thought, feeling, and action—that
had come apart during his period as courtier. And whatever
inner strength he could muster he certainly needed now. For
the hardest blows were yet to fall.

In October, 1692, the King annexed Pennsylvania to the
territory of New York. A royal governor, Benjamin Fletcher,
took command of the province in the name of the Crown.
Strangely, the action was not taken as punishment for Penn.
It was a purely military move to unify all English colonies
against French encroachment from the St. Lawrence Valley
and the Great Lakes. Since the Quakers could not provide
for their own defense in the war against France, this action
may have saved the colony. But for Penn, it was the end of
his utopian dream. The Holy Experiment lay shattered.

At this dark moment, an old admirer, the philosopher John
Locke, offered his aid. Having returned from his Dutch exile
with the new King, and being recognized as England's leading
political theorist, Locke proposed to secure Penn's pardon.
Penn refused. He was in no way guilty. Hence no pardon
would be acceptable. He wanted exoneration.

Still, Penn's case was again brought up at court, either by
Locke or by Penn's other friends, and this time their arguments prevailed. The new King had been in power long
enough to feel secure and had no further need to abridge

justice or generosity. On the King's instruction, the warrant against Penn was rescinded, and the Secretary of State, Sir John Trenchard, personally carried the message to Penn.

At last, after nearly four years, Penn could come out of hiding and live at Worminghurst with Guli and his children. But it was a subdued homecoming. The prolonged stress had broken Guli's health. At forty-eight, her face still recalled the fine-boned beauty of her younger years, and her eyes still spoke the intensity of her spirit. But she no longer had strength enough to leave the house.

Penn had been away so long. Now, as if to recapture time lost, he stayed with Guli every moment. Invited to attend an important Quaker Meeting, Penn declined. It would have meant a day away from Guli. Perhaps he sensed there were not many days left. But Guli remonstrated. Penn later recalled her words. "O go my dearest!" she urged him. "Don't hinder any good for me. I desire thee go. I have cast my care upon the Lord. I shall see thee again."

Later, deep in winter, the roads became impassable, and few visitors found their way to Worminghurst. It was as if Penn and Guli were rewarded with a gift of stillness after all the turmoil. Their days were not marked by the clock but passed in unbroken entity as the sun traversed its low path over the fields, where the hedges stood black against the snow.

On February 23, 1694, according to an account later given by Penn himself, Guli asked her husband and her children to come to her. She looked at the children and then sent them away. Only Penn remained.

Three hours later, members of the household grew apprehensive and entered the room. They found Penn cradling Guli's head against his chest. Gently they loosened his arms that held her. They put Guli's head back on her pillow and closed her eyes.

Fourteen

AMERICA AGAIN

In creation there is not only a Yes but also a No; not
only a height but also an abyss; not only clarity but
also obscurity; not only progress and continuation but
also impediment and limitation.

—KARL BARTH

After Guli's death everything somehow seemed too late. It
was as if the core had gone from Penn's life and the rest was
but a shell.

Outwardly he functioned efficiently, soon resuming his
briskly organized, task-oriented routine. But the traces of pain
remained. From that time onward, a dry, wooden tone entered Penn's writing, a strained rigidity that hints at the
intense effort needed to maintain competence and cover the
silent, invincible grief. Penn's actions lost their luminous
thrust. His spirit was not wholly quenched, but the fire now
burned low.

For months he was ill, and only with the coming of summer did he regain his strength. His chief comfort during this
difficult time was Springett, his oldest son. Almost nineteen,
Springett was precocious, already noted for his eloquence in
French, Italian, and Latin. He resembled his mother more
than his father, having inherited Guli's pensive quietness as
well as her physical frailty, and his lack of robustness was a

great concern to his athletic father. It also worried Penn that Springett inclined toward such frivolous matters as literature and music and couldn't seem to get interested in the sterner disciplines of theology and law. Yet it was precisely the echo of Guli in Springett's character that consoled Penn with a sense of human continuity beyond the barriers of death.

During his years of disgrace Penn kept insisting that he wanted not pardon but vindication. And now, at last, a royal gesture fully restored his honor: the King and the Queen returned Pennsylvania to him as his personal property. On August 20, 1694, they signed the royal patent that re-established Penn's dominion. For Penn, it was a proud day but a wistful triumph. Guli no longer shared it.

To regain his rule, Penn had to make concessions. He had to contribute to the common defense of the American colonies. Pennsylvania was to furnish eighty men to the militia or pay the sum needed to hire the same number of mercenaries. This was clearly against Penn's principles. But the only alternative was to let Pennsylvania continue wholly under military government. Penn submitted to the compromise as the lesser evil.

The new pact also stipulated that Penn himself was to go to America to govern his province. But it was some time before Penn could bring himself to cross the ocean again. During his earlier stay in America without Guli, he had come to know the pains of loneliness. He would not again go so far away, even to his own land, without a wife. The problem now was to find one.

He seems to have approached the acquisition of a spouse in a realistic frame of mind. Love, he knew, comes rarely. At fifty, he had no time to wait for it. He remembered Guli. That was enough; for in this memory he retained what Shakespeare called "the marriage of true minds," his company in contemplation and the solace of his longing. He would not tantalize himself with hopes of another woman of Guli's quality. He probably also realized that he himself was a somewhat questionable suitor. No longer vitalized by youth, he could not hope to capture the fancy of a woman with predominantly romantic desires. At any rate, Penn organized his wife-hunting as a fairly businesslike personnel search. He canvassed Quaker Meetings with an eye to an eligible mate, and eventually spotted Hannah Callowhill.

At thirty, Hannah was getting to be an old maid by the standards of her time. Marrying a widower was the most likely of her waning prospects, and Penn's wealth and prominence probably made up for the fact that he was getting sallow and paunchy. The years of hiding, with their enforced inactivity, had robbed him of his former physical strength and grace. His stance was now slightly bent, and his enduring grief over the death of Guli had cast an air of listless abstraction over his face.

As for Hannah, she was hardly a woman to rekindle an aging man's passions. By all accounts, she appears to have been sturdy and good-hearted, plain in appearance, competent in practical matters, and with an ordinary mind. Yet Penn courted her as if she were the most charming of girls. Perhaps he sensed that, in receiving him as a suitor, Hannah had struck a bargain beneath her hopes. As if to console her for this, he allowed her the illusion of romance. It was his kind of spiritual courtesy, and it brought its own reward. For by his gallantry, by the outward expression of desire, Penn seems to have awakened a genuine feeling in himself and Hannah. It was perhaps not love, for love cannot be bidden, and no one can make the stars dance. But at least it was warmth and liking, and a gladness with each other.

10th of 7th Month 1695

Most Dear H.C.:

My best love embraces thee, which springs from that fountain of love and life, which time, distance, nor disappointments can ever wear out, not the floods of many

great waters ever quench. Here it is, dearest H, that I
behold, love and value thee and desire, above all other
considerations, to be known, received and esteemed by
thee. And let me say that the loveliness that the tender-
ing and blessed Truth has beautified thee with, has
made thee amiable in my eyes above many, and that
it is my heart, from the very first, has cleaved to
thee. . . .

    I would persuade myself thou art of the same mind,
tho' it is hard to make thee say so. Yet that must come
in time, I hope and believe; for why should I love so
well and so much when I am not well beloved?

Thy unchangeable friend,
W.P.

    Many such letters found their way from Penn's residence
in Worminghurst to Bristol, where Hannah lived in her parents'
house, on High Street. Her father was a well-to-do linen
draper, and her family was highly respected among the local
burghers. Yet the disparity of social standing between the
bourgeois Hannah and the eminent son of Sir William Penn
seemed even more of an obstacle to any possible union than
the twenty-year difference between their ages. Penn swept
aside these objections with his usual blend of directness and
persistence. He pushed through the marriage as if it were a
piece of public legislation. "The time draws near," he informed
Hannah, "in which I shall enforce this subject beyond all
scruple." The linen draper's daughter hardly knew how to
cope with such a suitor. The simplest solution was to marry
him.

    Once William and Hannah had publicly announced their
intention to wed, the tone of their correspondence changed
notably. He was sending her French recipes obtained from the
private kitchen masters of London's more elegant households,
while she recommended salt purgatives for Penn's frequent

constipation. Penn, in reply, acknowledged the effect of the salts, adding: "I am indifferent well for one that sleeps so little, only my nose frequently upon blowing bleeds a little." Evidently, the two were getting comfortable with each other.

At this stage, Penn took his children to Bristol to meet Hannah. For a week, Springett, Letitia, and William, Jr., enlivened the quiet draper's household with their exuberance and precocious conversation. Despite differences in education and social background, they responded to Hannah's warmth and friendliness and immediately took a liking to her. On returning home, Letitia wrote a separate letter to Hannah, which opens as a rather conventional thank-you note, acknowledging Hannah's hospitality. But, with a teenager's typical concern in such matters, Letitia could not forbear to act as a belated matchmaker for her father:

> If I may be so bold, I must tell thee that at my father's first coming from Bristol, though I kept it to myself, I perceived which way his inclination was going and that he had entertained an inward and deep affection for thee. . . . And therefore I was not a little anxious to see Bristol for thy sake, and I am sure I was not disappointed, for ever since my esteem for thee has increased, and my father's design been more and more pleasant to me.

In December, 1695, Penn sent to the Bristol Quaker Meeting "a few lines in his own hand wherein he signified his intention of taking Hannah Callowhill to be his wife," as the official record recalls. But the winter proved "so rude" that the roads became impassable and contact between Penn and Hannah was disrupted for a while. Still, some mail was evidently getting through, for Penn managed to send Hannah three gallons of French brandy to lessen the hardships of the cold season. In return, Penn received from Hannah two pots

of chocolate and some venison paté "of her own manufacture."
Making meat paté was easier for Hannah than writing
letters. Penn begged her to write at least twice a week, com-
plaining that her letters were too few and too brief. Hannah
protested her inexperience at writing. Penn, in return, assured
her that her letters were "excellently writ." At one point, the
long ₄gaps between Hannah's letters made Penn doubt the
sincerity of her feelings. He asked her outright: Did she feel
any aversion to him because of his age? Hannah's reply has
not been preserved, but it apparently expressed the cause of
her reluctance. She feared that with her lack of prior sexual
experience she might not be able to satisfy a man who had
been married so long.

Penn dispelled her doubts with remarkable tact, leaving
open a great range of possible adjustments:

> As our case is not common, so if the rest not be in the
> common way, we ought less to wonder. . . . Want of
> longer familiarity and inward and intimate freedoms
> before it came to the push, with natural shyness and an
> averse education to that part of life, certainly disjointed
> things at first. . . . By time, I don't doubt but that it
> shall be effectively set. I have faith, yea assurance of it,
> and if thou hast not too much, I will hazard thy having
> too little. However, dearest and best friends we shall
> ever be, and a life of Truth and tenderness and devo-
> tion I hope we shall live.

Making wedding preparations led Penn and Hannah to
their first quarrel. Penn had ordered a new coach built to take
the newlyweds from Bristol to Worminghurst—"a chariot for
four to sit in, and harness for four horses upon occasion, all
to be plain without and within, only the velvet lining to be of
an olive colour." Hannah objected to a coach "all plain without and within." She wanted a festive carriage. Another man

might have indulged the wishes of his bride on her wedding day. But Penn took the occasion to teach the future First Lady of Pennsylvania something about status and ostentation: "I am determined to keep my old plainness. . . . I'll tell thee a story; a man of quality sitting down at table at the lower end. Some formalists in breeding mightily pressed him to sit higher. At last, he to stop their troublesome civilities, told them that wherever he sat was the upper end, and so much for that affair about the coach."

Just after the wedding date was set, all the Penns succumbed to a lingering grippe. Penn recovered very slowly. "I am not so well as I could wish," he wrote Hannah during his convalescence, "and I am much fallen away, which is the best part of it." Penn, who had been so lean in younger years, had become concerned about his middle-age corpulence and was much pleased by the loss of weight.

Springett, suffering the longest from the obstinate illness, had been unable to rid himself of a nasty cough. Even so, he insisted on journeying to Bristol for his father's wedding, which finally took place on March 5, 1696. Sixty-six guests crowded the Callowhill house, and they all signed the marriage certificate, along with three of Penn's children, Springett, Letitia, and William, Jr.

Spring comes early in the English West Country. With the warm Gulf Stream washing the coasts of Cornwall and Devon, the first green returns in March, and after the long winter these first signs of the new season must have been a happy sign to the newlyweds, as they traveled eastward from Bristol in their plain coach. Only Springett's cough added a note of concern. By the time they reached Worminghurst, Springett was once again running a fever, and Hannah spent much of her honeymoon nursing her sick stepson.

"Don't thee do so," Springett protested. "Don't trouble thyself so much for such a poor creature as I am." He rapidly grew weaker, and soon it was clear that his illness was no ordinary cold. Despairingly, Penn realized that Guli's tragedy might be repeated in her son, who was so much like her. And Hannah was tormented by the thought that it was because of her that Springett had undertaken the strenuous trip to Bristol which had so worsened his condition. Springett himself had dark premonitions. "I am resigned," he told the family gathered at his bedside.

Foreseeing his end, he had one more wish. Though he was too weak even to sit up unassisted, he wanted to go out in the coach and ride through the countryside with his father—once more to see the land and the sky. Penn ordered the horses harnessed, and with his ailing son drove off into the April morning. Springett looked at the budding trees and the signs of renewed life in the freshly green meadows. Upon returning home he said: "All is mercy, dear father. Everything is mercy."

He died a few days later, on April 10th, at the age of twenty-one.

"So ended the life of my dear child and eldest son," wrote Penn, "much of my comfort and hope . . . in whom I lost all that any father can lose in a child, since he was capable of anything that became a sober young man; my friend and companion, as well as most affectionate and dutiful child."

The shared tragedy of Springett's death at the very outset of their marriage deepened the relationship between William and Hannah. Penn felt sure now that his new wife would be a fit partner for the great task of revitalizing his Holy Experiment in America. But before they could sail, Penn had to put his European affairs in order, particularly he had to reclaim his Irish estates and place them under proper management.

Before departing for Dublin, Penn had a remarkable encounter. Peter Alekseyevich, the young Muscovite prince who came to be known as Peter the Great, was already well on his way toward making Russia a major power in the world. He had heard from his Swiss tutor about the technical marvels

of the West, particularly the great ships by which the Western
nations sailed the open sea. As future ruler of a landlocked
domain, Peter listened to these stories with fascination and
became obsessed with the ambition to gain access to the sea
for his own country. He dreamed of building a great navy and
merchant fleet. Ships and commerce would awaken his country that had lain frozen in Byzantine torpor for half a millennium, and would transform a feudal state into a mercantile
empire, like the great nations of Europe.

Peter wasn't worried about the opposition he would face
from his stolid, fur-mantled boyars. He knew the ways of the
East for enforcing obedience. But to accomplish his plan, he
felt that he also had to learn the ways of the West in technical
matters. Spirited and adventurous, the future Czar of all the
Russias signed on incognito as an apprentice in the shipyards
of Holland and England to learn shipbuilding and navigation.

One of the few men in England who knew the true identity
of the Czar was Thomas Story, a young Quaker lawyer and
close friend of Penn. Believing that the Czar, so eager to explore every facet of the West, might also be interested in Penn's
political ideas, Story arranged a meeting between the two.
Since the Czar spoke broken English, Penn addressed him in
Latin, only to discover to his surprise that the education of
Muscovite princes did not include classical languages. But
they were able to converse in German, which the Czar had
learned while working in Holland and Penn had picked up
on his travels.

Peter was only twenty-six at the time, but he already had
the independence of mind which set him on his remarkable
course as the first Russian ruler to think in terms of modern
administration and geopolitics. In other ways, though, he was
far from modern. The most absolute of monarchs, in his style
of governance, he reflected the ancient traditions of oriental
despotism more than the European-Christian idea of royal
stewardship. Penn's liberal notions about constitutional re-

straint upon authority must have seemed very odd to a man who was to rule as much by the executioner's ax as by his organizational genius. Yet, strangely, this neo-Byzantine tyrant seemed particularly interested in Penn's religious ideas. He eagerly read the German Quaker literature that Penn gave him. Years later, during a military campaign, he heard that a Quaker meetinghouse had been ransacked by his soldiers. He immediately ordered full restitution of the damage and declared the Quakers to be under his personal protection.

Otherwise Penn's pacifism made little impression on the man who cut Russia's bloody path to the Baltic Sea, probably arranged the murder of his own son, and took pleasure in personally cutting off the heads of his opponents. Peter failed to grasp Penn's attempted synthesis of love and power. Like other visionaries of realpolitik from Alexander to Mao, the Czar was convinced that "all power issues from the muzzle of a gun" and that terror is the basic instrument of statecraft. "What good is a man to any kingdom," the Czar asked Penn, "if he will not wear arms?" The same question, in effect, was raised by the King of England when he demanded that Penn furnish men for the militia.

Penn's meeting with the Czar may have prompted him to reexamine his political assumptions. Up to that time he had been reluctant to carry out his military promise to the King. Now he began to argue forcefully for conscription, against the adamant Quakers in the Pennsylvania Assembly. Bitter epistles crossed the Atlantic, and much animosity arose against Penn in his own province. Ultimately, he rammed through the necessary military measures by pointing out that the independence of the province was at stake—an argument that amounts to saying that half a loaf is better than none. As one contemporary drily observed, "Penn the Quaker failed. Penn the Statesman succeeded." Once again, Penn the theologian had struck a bargain between Spirit and World and abetted the victory of expedience over principle. To the young Penn, in his years of rebellion, this would have been moral treason. To the aging governor, it was the shape of wisdom. To the reflective philosopher, it was the recognition that there is no innocent compromise and therefore all human history has a tragic cast. But Penn never spoke of that.

While Penn was pondering the need for the joint defense of the colonies, his thoughts reverted to the ideas he had formulated in his proposal for a federation of Europe. Now he projected a federation of the American colonies, and he submitted such a proposal to the British government in February, 1697. Specifically, he recommended an American Congress with delegates from all colonies "to debate and resolve on such measures as are most advisable for their better understanding and the public tranquility and safety." The matter was referred to the Royal Board of Trade, which took no action on it. The British just missed their chance to put a central American Congress under their own aegis. The idea of a United States of America, loyally proposed by Penn, was thus submerged for almost a century, until it was picked up again in Penn's own city of Philadelphia by a decidedly disloyal group of radicals and revolutionaries.

By 1699, Penn had put his affairs in Ireland in sufficient order to feel ready to sail for America, intending to remain there the rest of his life. But just as he was making final preparations for the voyage, Philip Ford, his business agent, asked him to clear up a few matters. For one thing, Ford reminded Penn that he had deeded all his American holdings to Ford while under indictment for treason. Penn felt that this secret agreement, signed under the duress of circumstances, might well be forgotten and torn up now that he was no longer in danger. But Ford had other ideas. He assured Penn that he would not press his claim to Pennsylvania under the private agreement. All Penn had to do was to pay Ford rent.

In effect, Ford was demanding hush money to keep the agreement secret. It is a measure of Penn's character that he did not recognize blackmail when confronted with it. After all, he had in fact signed the agreement, so Ford's claim was legitimate. He agreed to work out some arrangement.

Two days before his scheduled departure, Penn went to see Ford at his home. It was to be just a friendly visit to say good-bye. But Ford managed to turn this social call into a business meeting of sorts. He brought out a welter of jumbled accounts and dumped the papers in front of Penn. These documents, he claimed, proved that Penn owed Ford £14,000 for debts ostensibly incurred in the management of Penn's affairs. The paper pile, as later investigation revealed, contained all kinds of bogus bills and false claims along with legitimate accounts. Penn, always averse to bookkeeping, seemed staggered. Preoccupied with the impending voyage, he could not possibly sift through the paper mountain. He merely remarked that he had invested £30,000 of his private money in Pennsylvania without ever getting a penny in return. Surely, somewhere funds must have accrued to satisfy whatever legitimate claims were outstanding against him.

Ford did not answer immediately. He drew his wife into a corner, and the two whispered to each other while Penn waited. Then Ford stepped toward Penn. No, there were no available funds. He must insist on immediate payment of those £14,000. Penn said he did not have the money. In that case, Ford calmly suggested, he would be obliged to ask Penn to sign yet another paper. He pulled out a document already drawn and ready for signature.

What for? Penn asked.

"You might be drowned at sea," Ford said. Of course he trusted Penn, he added amiably. But what if Penn were shipwrecked? Could he then depend on those who might enter the case after Penn's death? Besides, Ford complained, he himself was a sick man and had to think of his widow. Mrs. Ford looked properly pathetic.

Penn was moved. With his customary trust in a fellow

Quaker and old friend, Penn signed the paper thrust at him. During the next two days Penn was busy preparing for his embarkation. Expecting to stay in America for the rest of his life, he had most of his household goods loaded aboard the *Canterbury*, a sturdy three-master moored at the docks of Cowes. Pennsbury, his great mansion, had long been completed, and Penn expected to fill the house with the fine English furniture that was now hoisted into the hold of the ship. Again there were solemn dockside farewells to old friends, but this time the sea would not separate Penn from his family. Hannah was with him, pregnant with their first child, and Letitia, a graceful girl in her late teens, was also coming along. Only William, Jr., who had married earlier that year, remained in England.

The winds were fair on September 3, 1699, as the *Canterbury* weighed anchor. But the good omen proved deceptive, and for a while Penn was feared lost. He was at sea for three months, beyond anyone's reach and knowledge. The log of the voyage has not been preserved, but most likely the *Canterbury* had drifted far off course.

Some basic navigational aids were already in common use. That marvelous Mongolian invention, the compass, had been introduced from the East by the merchants of Venice; and with the help of the map grid of longtitude and latitude, devised a century before by the Flemish mapmaker Gerardus Mercator, a seafarer could locate any point on earth. But one essential element was still missing: an accurate way to determine the position of a ship at sea. A shipmaster could not know what course to steer toward his destination unless he knew just where he was at any given moment. And he could not tell this from the stars unless he knew the exact time. In cloudy weather he could not read high noon from the sun, and pendulum clocks, the only accurate timepieces of the period, were useless aboard ship. The sway of the vessel threw off the pendulum. Trying to solve this problem, the German clockmaker Peter Hele came up with the idea of replacing the pendulum with a spring-loaded balance wheel. This principle formed the basis of all portable watches, but metalworking techniques at the time still lacked the refinement necessary to make such mechanisms accurate and reliable. Unable to determine their precise whereabouts, seafarers could not measure the amount of drift and correct their course accordingly. The *Canterbury* apparently went astray in this manner and spent months in search of her destination.

Luckier vessels had meanwhile taken the news of Penn's departure from England to Philadelphia, and when the *Canterbury* failed to arrive within the normal span, Penn's fate was in doubt. But anxiety gave way to jubilation when the *Canterbury* was sighted at last off the Pennsylvania shore.

Penn's colony received its proprietor with all the pomp and pageantry it could muster as he stepped ashore at Chester on the first day of December. Quaker austerity was forgotten for once, as crowds thronged the banks with banners and hundreds of brightly decorated boats surrounded the looming hull of the *Canterbury*. Penn, whose Quaker convictions could never quite subdue his taste for elegance, was dressed in his most resplendent cavalier costume, all silk, satin, and gold braid.

Only one grotesque incident marred the festivities. A stubby little cannon had been trundled to the embankment to present Penn with the traditional salute. But artillery in those days tended to perform erratically. Quite possibly the young man in charge of the piece had been overly enthusiastic in stuffing gunpowder down its mouth in hopes of making a louder noise. But the result far exceeded his expectations. The cannon exploded, shattering the arm of its attendant. A physician in the crowd rushed forward, decided that only immediate amputation of the mangled arm could save the man's life, and, like a battle surgeon, immediately set to work with a saw. But some of the brandy given to the wounded man to ease his pain spilled on the doctor's clothes and caught fire from one of the ceremonial torches. Bystanders quickly rolled the doctor on the ground to quell the flames. Despite his burns, he then continued the operation, which both doctor and patient happily survived.

Penn hardly recognized his province. Eighteen years before, he had established a precarious outpost at the edge of the wilderness. Now he entered a secure and prospering country. Philadelphia, the city that had once existed only in his vision, now numbered more than 10,000 inhabitants, and its wide, airy streets were lined with solidly built brick houses, many of them with balconies. The trees that Penn had so carefully planned as part of the city had already grown to respectable height, shading the shop windows displaying the products of Pennsylvania's flourishing household industries, such as weaving, cheese-making, candle-molding, and carpentry. Neither was there any shortage of European imports, such as shoes, boots, metal tools, knives and spoons. Forks were also on display, but they were very expensive, because it was difficult to cut the tines by the metalworking methods then in use. Consequently, forks were regarded as an affectation of the rich, while the rest ate with spoons or relied on their fingers. The wealthier colonists had their choice of other luxuries, such as brass lamps or metal-clad flagons and inkwells. Here and there, an importer proudly displayed one of the great pendulum clocks, with their finely wrought hands and dials, which were the pride of English craftsmanship and mechanical ingenuity. In short, Philadelphia was a town where one could obtain almost anything that might be found in an English city. At night, however, the streets were deserted, for there was no public lighting other than an occasional whale-oil lantern hung over the door by an obliging house-owner who could afford such civility.

Thanks to Penn's liberal immigration policy, the province had become truly cosmopolitan. English settlers were almost

matched in number by Germans, and in addition to the predominant Quakers, there were now many Lutherans, Dunkers,
Moravians, Pietists and Schwenkfelders, and even a scatter-
ing of Catholics and Jews. They had all come seeking the
tolerance of the Quakers, and the spiritual diversity of Penn's
province caused an Anglican priest to complain that "Africa
never more abounded in Monsters than Pennsylvania does
with New Sects."

Penn was not at all displeased to see the Quaker colony develop into this kind of religious patchwork. He saw religious
diversity as a safeguard against the dogmatism he abhorred.
His views in this regard anticipated those of Voltaire. "Were
there but one religion," the French skeptic suggested, "its despotism would be fearful; were there but two, they would cut
each other's throats; but there are thirty and they live in peace
and happiness."

Yet Penn's reason for inviting religious diversity went
deeper than Voltaire's scoffing pragmatism. Though convinced
that belief could not be commanded, Penn was afraid that it
might be engineered. He knew that subtle pressure for conformity debases faith more readily than the harsher compulsions he had known in England. He realized, too, that the comfort of thoughtless agreement is perhaps the greatest threat to
spiritual vitality—and he considered such vitality essential if
the state was to represent a meaningful human association.
This insight prompted a paradoxical policy: Penn felt that the
essence of Quakerism could be preserved only by diluting
Quaker influence—by forcing the Quakers into a continuing
dialogue with contrasting groups. This policy ensured that no
single tradition or institution could "represent" faith. Rather,
faith had to be attained by each person within himself.

To integrate this segmented population into a workable
community, Penn proposed open admission to Quaker schools
for children of all creeds, and compulsory attendance for both
boys and girls to the age of twelve. In effect, he established a

public school system. Of course, the schools were primitive, with children of various ages sharing a single room and a single schoolmaster. In winter, each child carried a small bundle of firewood to the schoolhouse in the morning. They all huddled around the fireplace, and instruction lasted as long as the fire. Since paper was scarce and slate expensive, children learned to write and "cipher" by scratching letters and figures on soft horn plates, which could be erased by vigorous scrubbing. Penn insisted that, in addition to the "three R's," boys should be taught "some useful trade or skill, to the end that none may be idle, but the poor may work to live, and the rich, if they become poor, may not want."

Penn's view foreshadowed the country's later reliance on public education as the main instrument both for producing new knowledge and for fitting individuals into the social process. But in his own time, Penn's belief in the benefits of schooling was not yet widely shared. Fundamentalist Christians, including many Quakers, protested against public education on the ground that all school learning was a snare of the devil. "Blessed are the pure in spirit," they would argue, convinced that all trees of knowledge bore forbidden fruit and only the simple heart and simple mind were suitable receptacles for divine inspiration. The farmers of the region had more tangible arguments against compulsory education. They felt that their children could spend their time more profitably in barn and field.

Penn prevailed against such opposition. His educational program assured a high rate of literacy which, in turn, prepared for the growth of knowledge in the New World. Though formal schooling did not extend beyond the elementary level, young men—but not women—with aptitude and curiosity were encouraged to read independently and welcomed into the homes of the more literate Quakers, where they found good libraries and an atmosphere hospitable to the exchange of ideas. Notable among the local scholars was Penn's friend

Francis Daniel Pastorius, a German immigrant from Frankfurt. He was the sort of man who wrote personal letters in the form of Latin verse and had studied at the universities of Strasbourg, Basle, and Jena before he moved to Pennsylvania and founded Germantown, in 1683, bringing his library of some five thousand volumes with him. Pastorius' home was, in effect, a private academy in which his friends read and discussed not only history, theology, and philosophy but—remarkable for their time—astronomy, physics, medicine, and agronomy. It was largely thanks to Pastorius and his group that Philadelphia became America's first center of open intellectual inquiry, and it is no accident that, in later years, the American Philosophical Society and America's first medical school were established partly under Quaker influence. Thus began the trend that eventually yielded the experimental physics of Benjamin Franklin and set the stage for the development of medicine as a rational science.

Elsewhere in America medicine was regarded differently. Disease was considered either a form of divine punishment or the justly deserved byproduct of intimacy with demons. Accordingly, any attempt to relieve pain was considered sinful. A documented incident in Edinburgh typifies this point of view, which also prevailed in Puritan America. A midwife named Agnes Sampson had discovered that certain herbs could lessen the pain of childbirth, and prepared an infusion of such herbs for women in labor. This act was considered blasphemous, since God had specifically decreed in His curse upon Eve that women should bear their children in sorrow. When it came to the attention of the authorities that a certain woman named Eufame Macalayne had experienced a remarkably easy childbirth as a result of Miss Sampson's analgesic herbs, they immediately drew up a criminal indictment. With remarkable logic they indicted not the midwife but the mother. After all, it was the mother who had experienced the relief of pain and thereby thwarted God's design. To redress the divine balance of pain, they burned the mother alive.

Medicine and religion, of course, are intimately bound together in most cultures. Since, for the Puritans, suffering signified the just wrath of God, any medical interference with illness seemed theologically unsound. Medical practice was therefore confined to military necessity: the treatment of wounds—usually with a mixture of oil and wine—and control of bleeding through arterial ligature. Under Quaker influence, this harsh view gradually changed and the way opened for a broader definition of acceptable medicine. Even so, the medical arts in America were slow to rise above the level of folk remedies.

One favored nostrum of Penn's time was Venice Treacle. It was prepared by pounding the bodies of snakes and then boiling them in white wine and a mixture of twenty herbs, with an ample dollop of opium added. No doubt this treacle provided symptomatic relief for almost anything. A more specific cure for "the Miserable Distemper called the Twisting of the Guts" was to swallow rifle bullets, a therapy probably plagued with serious side effects, since the bullets were made of lead.

Curious remnants of medieval death-idolization survived in medical lore, as in the belief that arthritis could be cured if the patient rubbed the painful part of his body against the corresponding part of a human cadaver. Almost any illness was said to be curable with moss grown on the rotting skulls of criminals left unburied for public display. This item was hard to obtain in Pennsylvania, because of the low incidence of capital crimes. The filling of dental cavities with metal inserts was already an established practice. But apparently this technique was felt to be in need of improvement. Instead of metal fillings, one medical text of Penn's period recommended an amalgam of boiled earthworms and toads reduced to ashes by dry heat, the mixture to be capped with wax.

Pennsylvania's most noteworthy contribution to medicine was in the treatment of the insane. As might be expected in any society made up of displaced dissidents, aberrant personalities were not uncommon. One contemporary, Richard Baxter, observed that Quakers were likely to have "troubled minds." But that is virtually a precondition for serious religious concern.

The Quakers' way of dealing with such problems was unparalleled in their time. It anticipated the methods of modern psychiatry in some ways, and set an ethical example for public response to social deviants. Elsewhere, witchcraft and demon possession still passed as the most likely explanation of behavior disorders, and the standard treatment was to beat or burn the devil out of the afflicted. By contrast, the Quakers' humane attitudes enabled them to perceive the obvious: that to torture the demon also hurts the person. And unlike the Puritans, they were not so eager in the pursuit of demons that they ignored human pain. Consequently, they devised gentler methods for the cure of the soul. They attempted some form of dialogue, some human contact, with the disturbed person. In doing so, they were sometimes able to gain insight into the distorted perceptions of the sufferer, and—having entered his private symbolic world—they could gradually lead him back toward the shared, "normal" framework of thought and feeling.

As the presiding member of the Council, Penn was immersed in legislative tasks. The *Frame of Government* he had so boldly forged nearly two decades before now needed extensive revision to meet the needs of a fast growing and diversified country. Besides, partisan factions had arisen that put Penn's conciliatory talent to a severe test. Almost despairing about picayune squabbles among his legislators, Penn urged them toward self-discipline and charity as the necessary basis for the exercise of public power.

Be most just, as in the sight of the all-seeing, all-search-
ing God; and before you let your spirits into an affair,
retire to Him (who is not far away from every one of
you; by whom Kings reign and princes decree justice)
that He may give you good understanding, and government of your selves, in the management thereof;
which is that which truly crowns public actions and
dignifies those that perform them. . . . Love, forgive,
help and serve one another; and let the people learn by
your example, as well as by your power, the happy life
of concord.

Penn did not always follow his own advice. Hardened by his
long immersion in practical politics under the Stuarts, he no
longer seemed to trust his ideals. Many of the reforms he now
proposed or accepted were backing off from the bold, liberal
premises of his earlier legislation. And after the experience of
being at the mercy of political circumstance, Penn now more
jealously secured his own power base in the governmental
structure. He was not averse to bending a principle to protect
his own interests. One historian, Edward Beatty, comments
wryly: "When, in his province, he found 'unruly' people bent
upon what they termed 'liberty' with no great appreciation of
his vested rights, he stigmatized their activities as 'licentious'
and invoked the law of his own constituted authority."

Penn's personal attitudes and his political conduct at that
period seem self-contradictory. Where he had once been liberal
almost to the point of anarchy, he was now sometimes as
sternly authoritarian as his Puritan adversaries. The erstwhile
champion of "soul liberty" now urged his government to
regulate even the private conduct of citizens. "Let no vice or
evil conversation go uncomplained or unpunished," he urged,
"that God be not provoked to wrath against the country."
Laws were enacted against the use of improper language,

gambling, and other forms of what Penn considered unseemly conduct. He insisted on ordinances against public entertainment, particularly theater and games, which he regarded as morally pernicious. His statutes were so restrictive that the Privy Council in London finally interfered and struck them down on the ground that they kept "Her Majesty's subjects from Innocent Sports and Diversions." The open trust of his fellowmen, which lay at the base of Penn's earlier politics, had somehow given way to a severe, though still benevolent, paternalism.

Penn seemed to have lost the traits that had marked his earlier life: exuberance and generosity of spirit. His writings of this period reflected the change. The fine logical reasoning now gave way to shallow rationalization and dogmatic assertion, and the style turned pallid. It was as if bitter memories debilitated him, overshadowing his true nature. No longer able to mediate between practical politics and private ethics, Penn reduced the unanswerable paradox to plain contradiction. This, of course, is the common tragedy of idealistic leadership. Penn succumbed to this irony of fate, apparently without realizing it.

Despite Penn's ambivalence, the province flourished. The ideas Penn had implanted in earlier times had borne fruit, and Pennsylvania's way of life reflected the finest aspects of his political imagination. Beneath the inevitable petty quarrels and clashes of interest, a spirit of communal responsibility and mutual caring persisted. There was little need for coercion. In the absence of outright poverty, there was almost no major crime, and hence little need for police action or show of public force. Even private disputes usually yielded to mediation without recourse to law, and passions soothed by understanding friends rarely reached the point of violence. The result was a social climate in which open and ethical relations between persons and groups became possible and prevalent.

Envisioning a state of human freedom and equality, Penn had set the perennial motif of the American dream and brought it as close to realization as it had ever been. There was genuinely equal opportunity, at least for white males. Even women were more emancipated than elsewhere. As equal members of the community, they were allowed to become educated. This in itself was a step of historic importance toward women's chance for self-realization. Whatever restraints remained upon a woman's life were cultural rather than political, and these barriers were so deeply ingrained that women themselves rarely recognized these limitations. But their actual options were pretty well restricted to marriage. As elsewhere, this reduced women to a condition of dependence, especially since marriage was rarely based on spontaneous choice of the partners; more often it resulted from a kind of barter between the woman's father and her future husband. Only after such agreement was reached was a young man permitted to call upon a young lady. Such conventions aided class stability and the accumulation of wealth through joint inheritance. History gives no clue to whether this curb on sexual autonomy increased or decreased the chances for marital contentment.

Despite women's access to basic education, their position and the limits on their potential were defined by the attitude of the males in their social environment. And in Pennsylvania this attitude was not too different from elsewhere. It is perhaps best expressed in a fragment from the journal of Governor Winthrop of Massachusetts, reporting on the visit of a distinguished guest from Connecticut:

Mr. Hopkins, the governor of Hartford upon Connecticut, came to Boston and brought with him his wife, a godly young woman, and of special parts, who had fallen into a sad infirmity, the loss of her understanding and reason, which had been growing on her . . . by occasion of giving herself wholly to reading and writing, and who had written many books. For if she had attended her household affairs, and such things as

belong to women, and not gone out of her way to
meddle with such things as are proper to men, whose
minds are stronger, she would have kept her wits and
might have employed them usefully and honorably in
the place God had set for her.

Small wonder poor Mrs. Hopkins lost her mind.

If women had only a limited share in the new freedoms of
Pennsylvania, another group of inhabitants was totally barred
from them. Since about 1685, Pennsylvania had eagerly imported slaves, who soon became widely accepted both as
laborers and as articles of trade. In an age that had no other
energy source for such work than live muscle, the staggering
task of large-scale land clearing fell largely to these hapless
African arrivals. And in a country where prostitution was forbidden while there were still relatively few women, the traditional role of the black female as unrestricted sexual object for
white men was soon tacitly established.

Penn's attitude toward this "pecular institution" was surprisingly complacent for a man who set such high value on human
freedom and inviolability. He was a slave-owner himself and
had no qualms about it. True, in his will he stipulated the release of his slaves after his death. Evidently he thought this a
fair and decent thing to do without incurring any inconveni-
ence in his lifetime. The question why one man's freedom
should depend on another man's death apparently did not
occur to him.

The freeing of slaves upon the demise of their master was
not uncommon in pre-Revolutionary times. It was the usual
way for the master to acknowledge the children he might have
fathered with his female slaves. Occasionally, as in the case of
Penn, a humanely inclined owner would in his last will grant
freedom to his human property even if they were not blood
relations.

Penn never came fundamentally to grips with slavery. Yet

he made an effort to check the one aspect of slave trading that seemed to him the most dehumanizing. He drew up a bill that would have permitted marriage among blacks. Through the marriage bond he hoped to develop deeper feeling among mates in place of the casual breeding that commonly took place among slaves who could not count on lasting personal relations as long as their mates or children could be sold separately. But the Council rejected Penn's proposal. They wanted no restrictions in the slave traffic, or possibly they sensed the dilemma arising from acknowledging human attributes in salable merchandise, and Penn himself failed to resolve that point.

Penn's ambivalence about slavery perplexed many of his latter-day admirers. How could a man like Penn remain so halfhearted in the face of ultimate and systematic degradation? But his indifference can be understood in the framework of his time. The moral question of black slavery had not yet crystallized in the minds of white men. There was honest doubt whether black people were really human beings. Prominent scholars debated various theories as to the nature of nonwhite creatures in the shape of men and women. It had been proposed, for example, that Indians had no soul because they did not smile. This view was popular in Spain and Portugal because, if Indians had no soul, they were not human in the Christian sense. Consequently, one could rob and kill them without compunction—a logic not lost on Cortés. Even such eminent philosophers as Juan Ginés de Sepúlveda, a man admired by Erasmus, advanced such theories.

In England, anthropological science proceeded along similar lines, but the argument centered on blacks. Were they human, or could they be traded as livestock? The discussion remained academic, however. To raise the question at the political level would have been awkward, because slavery was so helpful in the development of the colonies. In fact, slave trading was one of the few forms of newly developing free enterprise in which the British government did not interfere. In short, the problem of slavery was no different from most other social problems: They can be recognized only when economic conditions or political circumstance allow them to be recognized.

Even so, not all Quakers let slavery go unchallenged. As early as 1688, Daniel Pastorius, the founder of Germantown, arose at the Monthly Meeting and declared it contrary to Christian principles that one group of people should be held in bondage by another. It is just as wrong for whites to enslave blacks, he argued, as it is for Turks to enslave European Christians.

Pastorius had hit a live nerve. White slavery, unlike black, was a topic to arouse instant passion. But nobody had ever pointed out that, in essence, the two were identical. White slavery was a timely issue because Turkish pirates had turned it into a well-organized and profitable business. Prowling the Mediterranean, they captured French, Spanish, and preferably English and Dutch ships, holding the passengers for ransom or selling them into slavery. Blue-eyed European women fetched high prices in the harems and brothels of the Levant, a fact that seemed to stir the imaginative powers of the Western mind. Countless stage plays and romances echoed and re-echoed the plight of some fair-haired and still virtuous damsel distressed at the suggestions of her captors. So widespread and dismally vulgar was this type of literature that Voltaire finally tried to kill it with persiflage in his *Candide*. Even Mozart, in *The Abduction from the Seraglio,* treated the predicament of English girls in a Turkish harem with a mixture of compassion and farcical humor.

In alluding to this theme, Pastorius put the question of American slavery in a perspective to which the white conscience had been sensitized. As a result, the Germantown Quakers at last recognized the problem and urged Pastorius to take his case to the Yearly Meeting at Philadelphia, the highest

religious assembly in the colony. This assembly heard his argument but declined to take action, letting the matter rest until
the middle of the next century. In 1758, long after Pastorius'
death, the Yearly Meeting bestirred itself, advising all Friends
to set their slaves at liberty and "to make a Christian provision
for them." Any Quaker who continued to hold slaves would be
expelled from the denomination. Many friends released their
slaves. Others simply sold them to non-Quakers. For all the
delay and equivocation, the fact remains that during the entire
colonial period, the Quakers were the only religious group to
oppose in concrete action America's cancerous evil.

Penn's personal life during his second stay in America was
placid and happy. Soon after his arrival, Hannah's first child
was born, a boy they named John. As the only one among
Penn's children to be born in the New World, he was nick-
named "the American," and as a late child he was a particular
favorite of his father's. Yet, like all of Penn's offspring, he remained undistinguished.

The trees that Penn had long ago imported for the garden of
his manor had since grown to a fair height and shaded his
walks. By colonial standards, Penn's residence was magnificent, comparable to the ruler's palace in any of the smaller
European principalities. Dominating the landscaped slope to
the Delaware, the edifice projected the combination of simplicity and grandeur which Penn had envisioned and which
expressed his own personality.

Penn kept open house in the manner of English aristocrats.
Visitors came and went freely, sharing ample meals and beer
from Penn's private brew house. The mansion was large
enough to assure Penn's privacy amid the constant flow of
guests, and even in this almost regal setting, his household routine remained similar to his habits as a private person in England. In summer he would rise at five, in winter at seven.
Depending on the weather, he devoted the early hours to

writing or meditative walks in the morning air. At nine, just before breakfast, the entire household assembled for a brief period of silent devotion, after which Penn reviewed the day's schedule with Hannah and issued the necessary instruction to the staff. Before their noontime lunch, the entire family met to read a passage from the Bible. The afternoon was given to affairs of state and conferences with officials who came up the river from Philadelphia. Evenings were often taken up with elaborate dinners for visitors. But if the guests proved dull Penn would excuse himself around ten o'clock and retire to his private rooms to read late into the night or attend to correspondence at his large but graceful Queen Anne desk. It had a foldout writing surface surmounted by a row of pigeonholes and, above, a high set of drawers that could be closed off by two hinged panels. The desk is one of the few preserved personal possessions of Penn and can still be seen at the restored manor at Pennsbury.

For travel between Pennsbury and Philadelphia, Penn used a splendid covered barge, rowed by six oarsmen. By his own admission, he "prized [this barge] above all dead things." During a brief absence, he once instructed his estate manager to make sure "nobody uses the barge on any account, and that she is kept in dry-dock, or at least covered from the weather." The remarks reveal a facet of Penn's character not usually apparent. It is somehow endearing that a man mainly devoted to abstract principle should so love a mere object. Along with Penn's passion for landscaping, flowers, and trees, his attachment to the barge shows that this stern paragon of rectitude was no stranger to simple delight.

Penn hoped to grow old in the land he had founded. But his wish was not granted. Within two years of his arrival, a new crisis arose. France threatened the English colonies. Preparing for defense, England once again considered the revocation of Penn's charter. To avert such calamity, Penn reluctantly planned another journey to England. It was to be only a brief visit, and he wanted Hannah and his family to stay in America awaiting his return. But Hannah and Letitia had other notions. They had never really liked the social restrictions that their official position imposed on them and the rather formal life at Pennsbury. Hannah, after all, had grown up as a tradesman's daughter in a world of small concerns and lively gossip and never felt at home in the austere role of Pennsylvania's First Lady.

As for Letitia, she wanted to escape a romantic entanglement with a young man who considered himself engaged to her while she definitely did not consider herself engaged to him. Because he appeared rather single-minded and determined in regard to her, Letitia even took the trouble of asking the Philadelphia Monthly Meeting for an official written declaration that she was "clear of any engagement" and in no way "spoken for." What she wanted, apparently, was a bit of the social whirl any girl feels entitled to before settling into marriage, and in that respect London seemed more promising than Pennsbury. A trip to England, no matter on what pretext, seemed just the thing to Hannah and Letitia.

Under the pressure of both family and state affairs, Penn prepared for the voyage. On November 3, 1701, Penn, Hannah, Letitia, and their little "American" John boarded the *Dolmahoy* at Philadelphia, having secured "free use of the whole great cabin of the ship," and set out upon an ocean already churned by the approach of winter. Penn looked back to his receding land. It was the last time he saw it.

Fifteen

TWILIGHT

We are what has been.
—G. W. F. HEGEL

The crossing was swift and calm. It took only twenty-six days,
and little John, barely two, enjoyed the adventure of being
on a ship. He was, as Penn noted in a letter, "hearty and well
and exceeding cheerful all the way." Penn himself suffered
a minor accident. He lost his footing on the swaying vessel,
sprained his hip in a fall, and limped for some time after.

But greater misfortune awaited. Heartbreak, perfidy, and
loss were soon joined by illness to darken Penn's last years.
What remained to him was undiminished faith in the worth of
what he had done. And in the final balance that was enough.

While still in America, Penn had received disturbing reports
about William, Jr. His eldest surviving son, now aged twenty,
had married shortly before Penn's departure and had settled
at the Worminghurst estate with his wife. But young William
was too wild and willful to adjust to marriage, and without
Penn's parental influence he drifted into a dissolute life. Neglecting his wife and two children, he spent his time carousing
and gambling with questionable friends and ran up sizable
debts. Penn intended young William to succeed him as governor of Pennsylvania. But seeing what had become of his
son during his absence, Penn wondered if William would ever
be fit for such responsibility.

Father and son had bitter confrontations, and Penn realized that he had lost effective influence over William, who defiantly persisted in his profligacy. Sorrowfully, Penn blamed himself for having failed his son. By going off to America, Penn felt, he had left William prey to temptation. His sense of failure was deepened by the fact that he was not even able to clear the family name by paying William's debts; for Penn's financial affairs had taken a disastrous turn that left him nearly without cash.

That Penn, the holder of vast lands, should be in such fiscal straits seems almost a paradox. The particulars of his finances, if they were ever properly recorded, have long been lost. Yet even without the details of a lifetime of slovenly bookkeeping, the main causes of his virtual penury appear clear enough.

As the outright proprietor of Pennsylvania, Penn had unlimited opportunity for self-enrichment, and, for all his idealistic sense of mission, he was not averse to the notion of profit. The Catholic ideal of Christian poverty was no part of his piety. He had the typically Protestant respect for money. Yet he never allowed himself to exploit the resources that had come to him, as he believed, by Providence. English merchants had offered him large sums if he would grant them monopolies on certain imports, industries, or trade with the Indians. The kings of England had traditionally lined their own pockets in this way, and the sale of monopolies was considered altogether respectable. Yet Penn refused all such offers. He felt that special privilege embedded in the basic economic pattern of the province would undermine the human equality he considered essential to his social scheme. This, by the way, is one of the rare instances in which Penn seemed aware of the link between the economic structure and the spiritual character of a community.

In selling and renting his lands, Penn had granted unusually generous terms. Sensing his leniency, his tenants and mortgagees often reneged on payments, and Penn could not bring himself to take action against them. Besides, the distance between England and America made accounting and collection difficult. The slowness of overseas communication added confusion to the already hopelessly tangled financial records, and his debtors took this as a welcome excuse to hold up payments. When Penn protested, he found that the authorities in Pennsylvania, sympathizing with the local settlers, were none too eager to exert pressure on his behalf.

All told, Pennsylvania proved a net loss. He put more of his own fortune into the development of the colony than he ever took out, and this was as much due to his idealism as to his ineptitude in business. He invested in a dream and didn't count the returns. It remained for his heirs to grow rich on what he left them. "Oh Pennsylvania! What hast thou cost me!" Penn exclaimed in his distress. "Above thirty-thousand pounds more than I ever got by it, and my child's soul almost!"

Except for his landholdings, which he tried to preserve for his children, Penn was without means. To reduce running expenses, he took a simple dwelling in Kensington, while Hannah, pregnant with her second child, went back to Bristol to live with her parents. He implored James Logan, his deputy in America, to send him whatever funds might be available from land rents. But the colony at that time suffered a shortage of currency. It was not permitted to coin its own money, and the cash influx obtained from trade was insufficient for the capital requirements of an expanding population and economy. Money was so tight that much of the commercial life of the province had to be conducted on a barter basis. Penn agreed to take rental payments from America in the form of produce, notably flour, pork, beer, tobacco, and skins. A few shiploads arrived, and for a while these eased Penn's financial situation. But soon after, renewed warfare between England and France made shipping unsafe. Penn's cargoes were either captured by the enemy or pilfered by dishonest sea captains, who pretended that their ships had been looted by the French.

His holdings in Ireland also failed him as a source of revenue, largely because of the treachery of his trusted agent, Philip Ford. For years, it seems, Ford had been concealing and diverting receipts from these estates. While stealing the income, he showed net losses on the books and then offered to cover the deficit by making usurious loans to Penn. Since Penn seldom bothered to read the documents Ford submitted for his signature, he was unaware of being bilked.

Penn's personal generosity was another drain on his fortune. His books show continual outlays for poor neighbors in England, and outright gifts for settlers in America, for whom he bought basic supplies until they were sufficiently established to shift for themselves. Whenever Penn heard of outstanding examples of kindness and generosity in others, tears came to his eyes. Clearly, he was not the sort of man to keep track of his money.

His plight grew even more desperate after Philip Ford died in 1702. Ford had been cheating discreetly. His widow, Bridget, lacked her husband's discretion. Philip Ford, as promised, kept secret the fact that Penn had ceded to Ford his American holdings while Penn was under indictment for treason. All Ford demanded was that Penn should pay him rent. Bridget confronted Penn on different terms. She was the legal owner of Pennsylvania, she declared, and she was going to sell it.

Penn retained lawyers to stop Bridget's preposterous scheme. But the lawyers were doubtful. Bridget not only had the summary conveyance of title; there were other documents to back her. Penn assumed that he had given Ford mortgages against the debts Ford claimed to have incurred in the management of Penn's affairs. Now it turned out that those papers, which Penn had never examined, were not mortgages at all. They were deeds. Technically, Bridget had a case.

Seeing herself as the owner of Pennsylvania, Bridget maneuvered behind the scenes to undercut Penn politically. She knew that a dispute had broken out in the province between James Logan, Penn's deputy, and an opposing faction led by David Lloyd, who did not believe that proprietary government held the best promise for Pennsylvania's future. Bridget dispatched her son, Philip Ford, Jr., to America to conspire with Lloyd against Penn.

Lloyd rebuffed these approaches. Politically he was opposed to Penn, but he had high personal regard for him. He plainly told young Ford that he would not ally himself with a potential usurper.

But there were others in America who would listen to Ford. Exactly what he proposed has not been clearly established. Since his mission was conspiratorial, he was careful to leave no records of his conversations. Most likely he suggested that, once Bridget had clearly established her title as proprietor, she would sell the colony to a corporation. Presumably, Philip was trying to rally local support for this plan by offering influential persons opportune terms for buying stock.

To counter Ford's machinations, Penn thought it wise to have a member of his own family in residence at the gubernatorial mansion at Pennsbury. He would gladly have gone there himself, but Bridget's legal threats required his presence in England. With considerable apprehension, he therefore asked William, Jr., to represent him in America. Perhaps he also hoped that the great responsibility of such a mission might have a sobering effect on young William. But, taking no chances, he sent specific instructions to Logan on how to handle his presumptive heir: "Possess him; go with him to Pennsbury; advise him, contract and recommend his acquaintance. No rambling to New York! Nor mongrel correspondence. . . . He must be handled with much love and wisdom; and urging the weakness and folly of some behaviors." He asked Logan to find suitable companions for William, "such persons as are soft and kind and teaching; it will do wonders for him, and he is conquered that way."

Unfortunately, these precautions proved insufficient. Going to America without his wife and children, William saw his American sojourn as a great opportunity, but not in the sense that Penn had hoped. He shunned the company of the staid Quakers Logan had picked for him. Instead, he soon found more congenial companions and, according to Logan, "committed unmannerly and disrespectful acts." In particular, he was fond of visiting the ladies of the colony in the absence of their husbands. " 'Tis a pity his wife came not with him," Logan reported to Penn. But he clearly underestimated young Master William. The presence of his wife would have made little difference.

William was no more circumspect about his finances in America than he had been in England, and Logan in great alarm advised Penn of William's mounting debts. Penn declined responsibility: "If my son prove very expensive, I cannot bear it, but must place to his own account what he spends above moderation."

The presumptive heir to Pennsylvania seemed determined to prove his talents as a public nuisance. Carousing through the nocturnal streets of Philadelphia, William and his cronies got into a nasty fight with the night watch, and the infuriated constables insisted on dragging him into court. What had been privately rumored about young Penn's character now became public knowledge. Street brawling was not the sort of thing decorous Quakers would tolerate in a person destined for the highest position in government. A member of the Assembly, William Biles, moved for young Penn's expulsion from the colony: "He is not fit to be our governor," he exclaimed. "We'll kick him out! We'll kick him out!"

Biles was reprimanded and fined for his disrespectful outburst against the son of William Penn. But general sentiment was clearly with him. It was agreed that it would be best if young Penn quickly returned to England. William himself no doubt shared this opinion.

The prodigal son returned to Worminghurst in January, 1705, confronting his grieving father with his usual air of jaunty nonchalance. Perhaps, at that moment, Penn remembered how he had once defied his own father. But what a difference there was in character and motive. And in this difference lay Penn's heartbreak.

For the first time in his life, Penn forsook hope. All had come to naught. He could no more cope with his responsibilities as governor than he could cope with his son's extravagance. He was harassed by Bridget Ford's shameless demands, and he could not even provide for the present upkeep and future security of the six additional children whom the fertile Hannah produced during this period of his life. At the time, he was living on handouts from his father-in-law, the linen draper.

Penn had come back to England to secure his American holdings. But now, despairingly, he wanted to give them up. He petitioned the Lords Commissioners for Trade and Plantations (who were, in effect, the colonial ministry of England) to take Pennsylvania off his hands, preferably before Bridget got hold of it. In return for renouncing his title and letting the province revert to the Crown, he wanted an adequate cash settlement and "some few privileges that will not be thought unreasonable."

But even in this he failed. The government considered his offer but balked at the "few privileges." Penn would surrender the colony only if the British government agreed to uphold the civil liberties that formed the core of the Holy Experiment. Penn would abandon his province, but not its principles. The government, by contrast, felt that Penn's surrender "ought to be absolute and unconditional." On this point, negotiations stalled.

Bridget Ford had meanwhile taken her case to court, seeking to oust Penn from Pennsylvania, claiming that he was a nonpaying tenant on her land. In addition, Bridget produced a welter of documents in evidence of Penn's personal indebtedness to Ford. The sheer bulk of these papers was so confusing that the court refused to consider them. This was lucky for Bridget, for a competent examination of these accounts would have revealed their fraudulence.

Encouraged by the court decision not to audit the accounts, Bridget promptly slapped yet another suit on Penn—this one for nonpayment of rent. Because it was a simple demand for back payment, this suit came quickly to trial in November, 1707. The verdict went against Penn.

Unable to pay the stipulated amount, Penn was technically liable to confinement in debtor's prison. Yet his age and prominence shielded him from such harsh measures. He might have remained at liberty while seeking means to satisfy the court award. But Bridget, for whatever motives, would not have it so. She insisted on Penn's arrest. On January 7, 1708, Bridget brought bailiffs to have Penn dragged out of a Quaker Meeting at Gracechurch Street. Only the soothing intervention of some of the Quaker elders prevented this indignity. They persuaded the bailiffs to wait and allow Penn to surrender himself peacefully at the end of the Meeting. Thus, at the age of sixty-two, William Penn renewed his acquaintance with the jails of England.

It was Bridget's moment of triumph. But she had overplayed her hand. The sheer viciousness of her action stirred widespread sympathy for Penn. His imprisonment was soon remanded to a form of house arrest. By her cruel insistence on Penn's jailing, Bridget had publicly revealed her character. Clearly, no such person could be seriously considered as a contender for statutory power in Pennsylvania. Her claim to the proprietorship of the province was denied at a hearing before the Lord Chancellor in February, 1708, at which the Lord Chancellor specifically declared that, whatever the ultimate disposition of Pennsylvania's political status might be, "the equity of redemption still remained in William Penn and his heirs."

With future revenues from Pennsylvania now assured, a group of Quakers agreed to advance Penn the sum necessary to satisfy the court award of rental payment to Bridget. A final compromise settlement was reached under which Bridget received £7,600 and Penn was at last released from house arrest.

Penn's remaining concerns were the future of Pennsylvania and the financial security of his heirs. Once again he tried to surrender his province to the British government under acceptable terms that would guarantee the legal framework he had devised and provide an adequate fiscal settlement for himself. Late in the evening of October 13, 1712, he was writing a long letter to James Logan about the progress of these negotiations. On the fifth page, the writing stops in midsentence and a line runs off the paper. Penn had suffered a stroke.

Hannah mailed the letter the next day, adding a brief note to say that her husband had "a fit of lethargish illness" which kept him from finishing his report.

During the following weeks, Penn slowly recovered, and for a while it seemed that he would regain the ability to write. But four months later a second stroke felled him, leaving him severely impaired.

The remaining five years Penn spent in a country house at the little town of Ruscombe. He took pleasure in the company of his children, but he could no longer write or "deliver his words as readily as before." He needed the help of others to dress himself and get through the necessary routines of daily life. With the heightened self-absorption of the handicapped, he mostly gave himself to silent reflection.

His last years were quiet. The rupture in his brain gradually robbed him of his memory. After that, few people came to visit. His mindless face grew vacant. Hannah took care of him. He rarely left the house. But in warm weather he would still sit outside amid the flowers and shrubs he so loved.

During the night from July 29 to July 30, 1718, he died. In the graveyard at Jordans he lies next to Guli.

As Penn's life ebbed away in his illness, the land that had risen from his dreams also drifted into a different realm. Pennsylvania, his Holy Experiment, gradually cut loose from its religious grounding and, along with the Puritan colonies of New England, gradually transformed itself into the secular society that, by the century's end, was to become the United States of America.

Pennsylvania had been founded amid the urgency of religious crisis. But another generation grew up under conditions of calm prosperity, and the religious impulse waned. The character of the Quaker community changed. The new leaders were no longer ideologically inspired rebels, pledging their lives to the creation of utopia. They had become cautious and respectable—men who preferred "good behavior" to spiritual fervor. Salvation, in its deeper meanings, was no longer on the political agenda.

The Holy Experiment had played itself out. The last word no longer belonged to the visionaries whose passion and courage had set the stage for a new order. The last word, as the historian Michael Walzer observes, always "belongs to the worldlings . . . ordinary men eager to desert the warfare of the Lord for some more moderate pursuit of virtue." The Holy Experiment could not endure, because in human affairs the aspiration to holiness is transitory. It prevails only briefly over the ordinary interests and the "ultimately more significant secular purposes of gentlemen, merchants, and lawyers."

But though it did not endure, the Holy Experiment did not fail. Something of its transcendent concept of human association survived. It settled into laws and institutions, into the quality of daily life, and into notions of both private and political decency. In this way, the Quaker experiment prepared the ground for the kind of thinking that shaped the profound achievements of the American Revolution.

Other great idealistic upheavals resulted in their own negation. The French Revolution ended in Napoleon, the Russian Revolution in Stalin. What is remarkable about the American Revolution is that it succeeded in establishing a political pattern and a form of human existence substantially consistent with its own aims. This may be partly due to the fact that, unlike other revolutions, the American Revolution was not a denial of the previously existing order. Rather, it was the radical affirmation of an already established tradition, and men like Jefferson and Franklin were, at least in part, reaping a harvest sown by William Penn.

For all its historic portent, Penn's Holy Experiment contains a flaw that can be seen only in the long perspective that perceives history as the gradual unfolding of human emancipation, as the evolution of the spirit toward the ideal of freedom. Seen in this way, the weakness in Penn's project lay not in its being too utopian, but rather in its not being utopian enough. Quaker radicalism posited spiritual equality. But this could not be fully translated into political forms as long as property relations permitted unrestrained acquisitive individualism. Resulting economic disparities eventually negated the possibility of spiritual equality.

Penn could hardly have grasped this, for the link between economic and spiritual conditions had not yet been clearly recognized. It remained unformulated until the social philosophers of the nineteenth century gave it the fateful expression that shapes the history and marks the central conflict of our own era.

Like all utopians prior to the French Revolution, Penn reacted to political but not to economic reality. Therefore he failed to see the contradiction between spiritual community in the Quaker sense and acquisitive individualism in the modern economic sense. The politics of Quakerism—as distinct from the purely religious aspect—thus became conservative rather than radical. They jelled into traditional molds, and the horizon of spiritual freedom narrowed to the span of statutory liberties. And those who shared Penn's shining dream of total human self-realization in a non-alienating community awoke to the partly cloudy morning of America.

But Penn's personal achievement is not diminished by its location in the stream of history. On the contrary. In America, he laid the foundations for political forms that placed the state at the service of the individual—a bold reversal of the prior norm. In Pennsylvania he created the first state in which the human person was regarded as an autonomous Self, and hence the first state to allow and foster the formation of full and unlimited personalities—at least in principle.

In the three centuries since Penn, America has remained basically committed to Penn's ideal of the subservient state and the transcendent Self. Despite occasional detours into chauvinistic nationalism and other types of collectivist bondage, America has been—in a psychological and partially in a legal sense the land of the free. Only lately has this changed. The organizational demands of a mass culture based on technology have begun to erode the foundations of this freedom. In the new bureaucratic society emerging in America and the rest of the Westernized world, selfhood no longer appears as the primary political and spiritual ideal. Management efficiency is challenging the very notion of the individuated Self. As the managerial attitude pervades the modern social climate, its instruments are thrust into the innermost wellsprings of our imagination and our desires. Our symbol-mediators, the popular arts, are busy trimming the human soul to standard specifications. In a technocratic culture, human beings are interchangeable parts. In such a setting, freedom is necessarily noxious. And to those who seek consensus at the expense of spontaneity, the autonomous Self appears pernicious and illusory.

William Penn would walk uneasy in his garden at the sight of today's world, for he knew that the Inner Light burns only in free air.

Appendix

The material presented in this appendix is not an integral part of Penn's biography but may prove helpful in rounding out the larger context in which Penn's attitude and outlook took their distinctive shape. Both as theologian and as politician Penn stands at the juncture between the medieval view of society and the emergence of the modern state. The aim of this appendix is to survey in broad overview some aspects of this transition. The arguments developed here necessarily repeat certain ideas set forth in the main narrative, but here they are placed within a frame big enough to set Penn's achievement in broader perspective.

The Tides of Belief

There are modes of thought
which cannot be adequately understood
as long as their social origins
remain obscured.
        —KARL MANNHEIM

Along with the many other religions that sprang up in the sixteenth and seventeenth centuries, the Quakers were a segment of the Reformation. They formed part of that groundswell in Western history that created and enveloped all Protestant faiths—the force that pushed Europe off the dead center of feudalism, where it had been resting for almost a thousand years.

The astounding duration of the feudal system, its ability to contain the rivalry of kings and the bickering of bishops, marks it as one of the most successful social adaptations in human history. How, then, did the turmoil and violence of Penn's era arise from such calm antecedents?

267

Some factors contributing to the stability of earlier times were external. Cities were few and small. Most of the population lived in hamlets and villages virtually shut off from the rest of the world. Roads were impassable in winter and spring and often beset by bands of murderous vagrants.

Communication was also limited for other reasons. The ordinary person did not know how to read and write, so he wasn't troubled by the lack of public mails. Besides, he probably knew no one outside his own village to write to. The local baron might not be able to write either, but if he could get the parish priest to write a letter for him, and if he could spare a horse, he could send a courier with his message. Only the most urgent messages justified such an effort. With travel and communications so limited, people knew nothing of other places and other times, and such ignorance is highly conducive to social stability.

The pursuits of the village were mostly agrarian, with little specialization of crafts and no complex technology of any kind. The change of seasons was the main event affecting the life of the villagers. Except for the local baron, who dwelled in the castle with his family and retinue, most people lived in simple houses that were little more than huts. A rough-hewn table and a couple of benches—chairs were rare—might be their only furniture. Beds were an aristocratic luxury; ordinary people slept on straw pallets. The rooms were dark, for in the absence of glass (far too expensive), the narrow windows often had to be shuttered against the cold. Lamps and oil were also beyond the means of common people, and a smoky fire in the open hearth was often their only source of light and heat.

But their lives were comfortable and secure in a way largely lacking in later times. A man received food, shelter, and clothing from the lord of the village in return for a traditionally fixed amount of field labor or other specified services. He also had the right to collect firewood from his master's forests. Except in times of famine, he had no worry about sustenance, and, under the terms of traditional feudal obligation, the master took care of his "villeins" even in sickness and old age. With their basic needs so provided, ordinary people rarely saw or needed money, an advantage to those who lacked the arithmetic for counting coins. Simple barter was the usual form of trade within each village.

Neighbors knew each other from birth to death, and by such lifelong contact the entire village became a close-knit communal organism. From this sense of human relatedness sprang a reasonably cheerful conformity. As for the few mavericks whose minds and temperaments kept them from fitting smoothly into the prescribed order, both law and popular opinion were firmly repressive. Deviations from approved behavior brought down brutal penalties, even death. The severity of punishment for any kind of deviance greatly increased the solidarity and satisfaction of the obedient majority. Since they rarely ventured beyond the village and its fields, they lived out their whole lives among people whose views were identical and whose horizons were no wider than their own.

Such men were not likely to question their situation in life or think about how to improve it. In fact, the notion of possible change, of evolution and progress, hadn't yet crystallized in anyone's mind. The world was believed fixed in all its forms. Mountains, streams, animals, and men were exactly as God had created them. As for human affairs, they were obviously not perfect. But that was the result of the expulsion from Paradise, a just punishment for sin, and could not be remedied in this life.

Work was physically hard, but free from competitive pressure. Medieval men moved through their day at a pace set by their own bodily rhythms. Most of them had never seen a clock. Of course, everyone grumbled, for there were mud puddles and leaky roofs, recalcitrant spouses and incurable aches. But on the whole these people were content, partly because they couldn't imagine anything other than it was.

For all its narrowness, medieval village life offered its share of sprightly diversions. One old English calendar lists more than a hundred holy days per year, and though most of them commemorated a saint, the observance of these feasts was not entirely pious. Celebrations might start in church, but they continued in pageants and mummery on the village green, later moved to the alehouse, and often ended in the haylofts, where the usual norms of sexual access were temporarily set aside. If clergy and constables didn't joint these orgiastic merriments, they at least looked the other way. Dancing, display, gluttony, and the carnal passions were viewed indulgently. Seize the moment, for famine and pestilence always lurked near, marauders might ravage the village, and early death came as the frequent companion of childbirth or ordinary infection. To the poor in the village as to the knights and their ladies at the castle, death always seemed near, but this nearness heightened the sense of life and the fervor of its celebration. The men and women of the village may have been ignorant of the forms these sentiments took at the castle, in the fine gradation of manners and the exuberant arts that marked the best of chivalry; but in their own way, in their piety and in their ecstatic joys, they shared these feelings.

Of course, even the simplest life is touched by wonder and by sorrow. For these the church provided acceptable answers. For wonder, the search for meaning, the church had a splendid prescription: The purpose of life is to glorify God and to praise Him. As for sorrow, bear your burden with patience, for in submission to your trials you will come to know the solace of God's love. For life is but a preparation for Eternity, where each will reap his reward.

This is a generous promise, and a believing priest could make it with honesty and conviction. Buttressed by all the resources of the human imagination at that time, transfigured in the beauty of medieval art, the message of the church was the culmination of all available wisdom. The church spoke with both reason and compassion, and what it said made necessary and adequate sense under prevailing conditions.

The medieval scheme, whatever its shortcomings, encompassed and explained all forms of human existence. For the rich and noble, there was tragic ambition, grandeur, and passion. For the poor, there was the remembrance of Christ's sufferings mirrored in their own travails, and the promise of eternal reward. Together, rich and poor enacted the world epic of the Christian vision:

God, the creator, made the rich responsible for the care of the poor. Through alms and charity, the great man repented for his sins and sought expiation for his earthly grandeur. The poor and lowly represented the hope of redemption, according to church doctrine, precisely because they suffered so. This was how the traditional theodicy of feudal Europe explained injustice and misery in a world created and closely supervised by a just and loving God. Thus even the wretched had a legitimate part in the greatness of God's design.

Toil was the penance by which the poor expiated man's innate depravity. Without even the possibility of formulating ambitions or demands, the poor depended on the church to provide charity and sustenance while the rich depended on the church to confirm their merit in their own eyes.

There are few periods in history when an official philosophy so fully met social and spiritual needs. At its shining heights, in the honed logic of contemporary theology, as well as at the level of the illiterate peasant, the medieval church fashioned a world view by which all manner of men could then live. It defined a harmony of world and spirit, man and God, earth and heaven, and life and death.

By postponing the knotty question of social justice until the Last Judgment, the church greatly simplified the practical management of earthly affairs. Assuring everyone his just deserts in heaven or hell and placing the whole problem of justice *sub specie aeternitatis,* the church adroitly sidestepped the sorry fact that goodness and merit often go unrewarded on earth. By the same token, the ethically awkward difference between rich and poor was also swept under the theological rug, so the church could function as an ideal instrument of social control. An old English hymn underlines the point:

> The rich man in his castle,
> The poor man at his gate,
> God made them high and lowly
> And ordered their estate.

Proclaimed in the voice of divine authority, this argument was not questioned, and gave comfort and confidence to both rich and poor. The belief that a man's station in life is God's will and not the result of any human agency acted as a powerful social tranquilizer. Worldly and spiritual authority thus joined social form and religious faith in a harmonious blend that some historians have called the medieval synthesis.

Yet the strongest reason for the durable success of this synthesis was neither the economic security it provided nor the tranquilizing effect of a resigned faith. It was the fact that, at least in theory, the system was as fair and decent as the human imagination at that time could make it. The implied contract called for an equitable exchange of duties between man and master, ruler and subject, in a paternal relationship that echoed the great metaphor of the fatherhood of God.

To those who lived under it, the feudal order did not appear as just one of many possible human arrangements but simply as a law of nature—as *the* way in which men were meant to live. The collapse of that order was therefore all the more harrowing, and even today, nearly half a millennium later, the Western mind has not yet fully come to terms with all the implications of that change. The death spasms of feudalism were the birth pangs of the modern world.

The Reformation provided the turning point. Contrary to popular notions, it did not suddenly spring from the outraged conscience of a rebellious monk named Martin Luther. In fact, Luther seems more the culmination than the origin of the great movement that cracked the rock of St. Peter. Nor can the many upheavals lumped together under the name of the Reformation be seen in purely religious terms, though the challenge to the Catholic Church remains the predominant feature. Modern historians, notably Max Weber, Ernst Troeltsch and R. H. Tawney, have pointed out that the forces pressing toward a redefinition of the Christian faith were largely economic. The shift from the rural economy of self-sufficient villages to urban commercialism required new theological assumptions and a different authority structure.

But the change could not have come about so decisively if the church had not already been weakened by insidious internal twists. A ruinous tension had arisen between Christendom as a political institution and Christianity as a transcendent faith. Ever since the Roman emperor Constantine had in effect declared Christianity to be the Roman state religion, the church had functioned as the instrument by which the power of government was made to seem just and divinely ordained. Yet in the perennial attempt to reconcile the discordant claims of love and power, the Catholic Church developed complex and often dubious codes which led official Christianity far from its moral base in the New Testament. The part of Christianity that speaks to the hope and longing of the soul became more and more overshadowed by the doctrinal artifices designed to mesh spiritual aspiration with political necessity. Points were stretched and corruption entered.

In theory, the "temporal lords"—the kings and worldly powers—acted as agents or stewards of the spiritual authority. But after popes and bishops cornered a hefty slice of worldly power of their own, the division between spiritual and temporal power became increasingly hazy. Having itself entered the political realm, the church virtually relinquished its spiritual mission, grew outwardly rich and inwardly desolate.

The pairing of church and state now took on a different aspect. They no longer functioned as parental guardians over God's children. Firmly interlocked, church and state now formed a self-serving power complex, comparable in its stifling effect to the interlocking of industry and the military in modern patterns of governance.

The closed system stagnated. Concerned mainly with preserving feudal and clerical privilege, it could not cope with change. Yet change engulfed the old order like an obstinate weed climbing over the walls of castles and cathedrals. Powerful guilds of merchants and craftsmen formed in the growing cities, which replaced the agrarian villages as focal points of the economy. The flow of goods quickened, thanks to improved roads and larger ships. In turn, the new possibilities of trade stimulated the beginnings of factory production and led to the invention of primitive machinery and investment banking. Capital accumulated in the hands of city dwellers, and the new bourgeoisie chafed under the monopolistic trade restrictions imposed by the aristocracy and the high clergy. In short, the economic model of the agrarian village, which supported the whole concept of the medieval synthesis, no longer applied. Church and aristocracy, the old centers of authority, no longer provided acceptable guidance under the new conditions, and the growing pressure of these maladjustments slowly built up to the explosive force eventually released by Martin Luther.

In the course of its malaise, the church broke out in a rash of corruption so pestilent that it could no longer be hidden from even the most naive parishioners. It hardly troubled them that popes and cardinals kept mistresses. After all, many otherwise decent and dutiful priests did the same. But under the Medici popes of the Renaissance, life at the Vatican had assumed a distinctly unchristian character. The Holy See had tilted from the merely sybaritic to the outright perverse. In their arrogance, the Medici popes made no particular effort at discretion, and when rumors spread that Pope Alexander VI's after-dinner entertainments included elaborately staged mass matings between young girls and boys specially selected for comeliness and vigor, thoughtful Christians began to harbor serious doubt about their spiritual masters.

The taste for extravagant display also proved costly in other areas. The building of St. Peter's, for example, reduced the Vatican to near-bankruptcy. A corporation in such straits might float debentures, and the church resorted to much the same methods. It sold "indulgences"—the pardon of sins in exchange for money. Even the poorest Christians all over Europe willingly scraped up their ducats to reserve a place in paradise at prices set at confession. That way, the splendors of Michelangelo and Bernini were paid for by the inhabitants of hovels.

To broaden the market for this trade, Rome propounded the doctrine that even the souls of the departed could be released from purgatory by ransom. This was a touchy point, because the dead were past repentance, which was thought to be indispensable for forgiveness and, in the case of the living, had to accompany the gift of money. The Pope argued that as Christ's vicar he could intercede in behalf of the dead. But many clerics remained unconvinced, and the manner in which indulgences were sold only deepened their doubt.

In particular, the promotional style developed by a Dominican monk named Johann Tetzel aroused resentment. He luridly described the tortures of purgatory, picturing to his audience the souls of their departed relatives crying to them for help, pleading not to be left in torment when a small sum of money might deliver them. A growing number of sincere churchmen were troubled by these fund-raising techniques. Often in defiance of their bishops, these clerics openly grumbled about both the fiscal and the moral failings of the church and gained the sympathy of the newly emerged literate urban middle class, whose confidence in the church had also become strained.

Sensing that the time was ripe for a decisive power struggle, a number of German princes, peeved by papal arrogance and financial demands, quietly encouraged the dissident segment within the church. Bypassing the rural barons, these German rulers cast their lot with the new economic forces created in their cities by guilds, merchants, and bankers, who also strove against clerical and feudal privilege. Thanks to the protection of these princes, Luther escaped the usual consequences of heresy.

Like many others, Luther had been incensed by the sale of indulgences. He did not believe that God's mercy was a purchasable commodity, and hence considered such transactions fraudulent. He particularly questioned forgiveness without repentance in the sale of indulgences for the dead. He set forth his objection in ninety-five specific "theses," neatly wrote them out in Latin, and on All Saints' Day, October 31, 1517, nailed them to the door of the Wittenberg cathedral. This promptly endeared him to the commercial class in Germany, who deplored Rome's siphoning money from the local market, even though they may have given little thought to the nature of God's mercy.

It is ironic that Luther's profound and passionate theology of salvation by faith alone found its first adherents among those whose interest was predominantly worldly. What they needed was precisely the kind of sacred legitimation for private business that the Catholic Church had traditionally given to feudal authority. For them, the Protestantism developing out of Luther's thought was a charter of individualistic liberty in economic as well as religious pursuits. For if the affairs of the soul were defined as a private enterprise, free from institutional control by the church, so the affairs of business might also be considered private, free from control by kings and nobles.

Luther could hardly have prevailed on religious grounds alone. He and his movement might have been snuffed out like previous heresies. Only in combination with a powerful coalition of political interests could he effectively deploy his own force of intellect and character, his personal courage and canny strategy. The result was the first successful uprising against the Catholic Church in a thousand years.

Still, to account for a vast spiritual movement like the Reformation purely in materialistic terms would distort the issue and tend to impugn the blazing spiritual sincerity of the reformers. Such an interpretation, as the American historian Preserved Smith remarks, is too trivial: "To say that men by the thousands and tens of thousands suffered martyrdom for their faith simply because they objected to pay a tithe reminds one of the ancient Catholic derivation of the whole movement from Luther's desire to marry." The Reformation was a genuine spiritual rebirth as much as it was a radical socio-economic departure.

This mutual reinforcement of secular and religious motives engendered the virulence of the Reformation, the unrelenting bitterness of its wars, the austerity of the Puritans, and eventually the earnest search for a new synthesis of religion and social form, which became the central theme in the life of Penn. As an actor in the drama, Penn could not possibly grasp its total outline, for history reveals its plot only to hindsight. But as a student of religion, Penn clearly saw the radical sects of England, including the Quakers, as an integral part of the Reformation, of the continuing effort to formulate adequate Christian alternatives to the lost medieval synthesis. In his religious and political program, Penn responded not merely to the immediate problems of the Quakers. As much as any single man could, he dealt with the total crisis of his age. He saw his mission defined by the failure of the past, by the breakdown of the old harmony of church and state, and in Pennsylvania he hoped to shape a new, integral pattern of faith and community.

When Penn assumed his role as religious leader, the shape of Protestantism had already been hammered out of the basic Christian material by such powerful spiritual sculptors as Luther, Calvin, and Knox. It is a measure of the Quakers' astounding independence that they reacted as vigorously against these giants of the Reformation as they did against the Catholic and Anglican tradition. But for all their differences and despite their nearly total freedom from dogma and ritual, the Quakers' religious thinking still falls within the general frame of Protestantism and must be considered in this context.

Seen without regard to doctrinal differences between its various denominations, Protestantism sets forth a central tenet: Each man can know God through his own soul and through his own mind. This was Protestantism's essential departure from the Catholic view, which regards the church as a necessary agency mediating between man and God.

The idea of personal access to God gave rise to a wholly new concept of the human person. No longer was he simply a member in a community, a particle of a larger whole in which his role and range of action were rigidly defined. Now he was an *individual,* in the modern sense of the term, unbeholden to baron or bishop and ultimately responsible only to himself and God. He was master of his own life, free to pursue his own aims, entitled to earthly recompense according to his performance and to a voice in decisions that shaped his fate. These assumptions contain the main features of modern Western civilization: personal liberty and free enterprise, capital accumulation and democratic self-determination. The shift in theology had cleared the way to a new age, the era of bourgeois liberalism.

In this way, Protestantism indeed satisfied the spiritual requirements of the new world of commerce. By breaking up the unity of the church, the Reformation also prepared the way for the modern nation-state. In essence, the Catholic Church knew but one kingdom—the Kingdom of Christ, which was Christendom—and the emerging nation-states seemed to Rome an anti-Christian heresy to be resisted at all cost.

It took a lifetime of warfare for these great mutations to take hold. From Sweden to Turkey, Europe reeked with religious slaughter. In the end, the Protestant countries gained ascendance. They pioneered new economic forms and bred a new kind of man: not the feudal subject who conceived virtue in terms of obedient submission and pious endurance and shunned riches as a root of evil, but the self-assertive go-getter, the inventor and entrepreneur, who regarded money as the reward of virtue and considered ambitious diligence a service to God. In its more vulgar manifestations, the new Protestant ethic put God in the market.

The political implications were vast. Before the Reformation, a ruler could invoke the old Christian ideal of poverty and unworldliness as essential to the salvation of his subjects. He could justify economic suppression on spiritual grounds and so protect his own monopolies and prerogatives. The dispensations of Luther and Calvin no longer allowed this. Private ambition on the part of ordinary men was no longer deemed presumptuous. On the contrary, the new beliefs idealized economic self-reliance along with spiritual independence. Values were reversed: Poverty was no longer a virtue but a punishment for sins; prosperity was the sign of God's favor. A prominent churchman of the time, Richard Baxter, maintained seriously that to please God you had to make as much money as possible: "If God shows you a way in which you may lawfully get more than in another way, if you refuse this and choose the less gainful way, you cross one of the ends of your calling, and you refuse to be God's steward." His logic foreshadows future links between the rectory and the chamber of commerce, between missionary churches and colonial empires.

Of course, none of the Protestant denominations openly proclaimed a creed of greed. Some of them, including the early Quakers, explicitly shunned wealth. But they all extolled spiritual individualism, and in the course of events almost any kind of individualism becomes acquisitive, possessive, and aggrandizing.

The biblical point of departure for this cult of capital gains is the twenty-ninth verse of the twenty-second chapter in the Book of Proverbs: "Seest thou a man diligent in his business? He shall stand before kings." Within a few generations, the Puritans, particularly in England and America, had fashioned a whole way of life from this precept. They recognized that more energy would be available for gainful toil if less energy were diverted into sensual delight and other forms of spontaneous joy. So, to further the cause of fruitful labor, they developed an attitude in which pleasure equalled sin and virtue became dour. Respectable men in Protestant lands assumed a somber mien and donned drab clothes to show they were earnest and God-fearing. Even pretty women, judging by their pictures, took care to look properly grim. To smile would be frivolous or worse.

The herald of this gloom was John Calvin, who made his views prevail in nearly all Puritan denominations. Congregationalist, Presbyterian, Baptist, Dutch Reformed, and German Reformed Churches all drew their substance from the teaching of the God-obsessed dictator of Geneva. His influence must be at least partly credited to his lucid writing, which made the tight logic of his arguments persuasive to all those earnest preachers who seriously read theology. At the University of Paris this enormously gifted and fanatically motivated metaphysician had acquired both the literary skill and the intellectual rigor to make his dark philosophy of divine doom and precarious grace a greater force among the Puritans than the New Testament itself. As a result, Calvin accomplished the singular feat of imposing his personal compulsions on an entire culture.

Calvin was by no means the first to favor arbitrary curtailment of permissible human experience. Two thousand years before, even so urbane a thinker as Plato had wanted to squelch poetry and forbid laughter to assure more effective social control. But it remained for Calvin's followers, the Puritans, to make an unprecedented practice of psychological tyranny and to organize whole communities on the principle of spying on one's neighbor. The goal was not merely to assure right thinking but to forestall all forms of happiness other than those derived from faith, useful labor, and dutiful compliance with social expectations. The Puritan community was democratic mainly in the sense that everyone's life was open to public scrutiny. Privacy, a precondition for developing cultural variety or refining personal taste, simply was not permitted. In Geneva, during Calvin's rule, constables even had statutory power to enter the bedrooms of married couples to make sure that they copulated only in a straightforward, businesslike, and approved manner. With official scrutiny extending to virtually all aspects of life, everyone grew very prudent.

With spontaneity and delight firmly clamped into pillory, the arts could scarcely flourish. While Catholic Europe reveled in baroque, Puritan lands, for a time, produced little but plain walls and hymn tunes. Drabness was elevated to an ideal. Earlier forms of asceticism, such as that practiced by the Franciscans, aimed at simplicity but were not hostile to beauty. For the medieval Christian, art and adornment were a form of praise, the celebration of God *in* the world. To the Puritan, by contrast, art was idolatry.

Still, Puritanism didn't altogether freeze the imagination but directed it into new channels. Technological invention and financial management grew increasingly ingenious. One of the most enlivening contributions of Puritanism was the loosening of the cash flow. The Catholic Church had regarded all lending for profit as usury, and many of the early Protestants were equally convinced of the immorality of interest. But the expansion of commerce depended on credit, and banking had become too important to be left entirely to Jews or to those obliging Christians who willingly risked a spell in purgatory for a percentage. This was no trivial risk, and many prominent merchants were racked by the conflict between their lust for money and their fear of hell. Having grown rich from lending for profit, they were often overwhelmed later by panic at the possible consequences, and donated their whole fortunes to the church. This remorseful dumping of profits onto holy ground undercut incentives needed for economic growth. Characteristically, it was Calvin who solved the dilemma. His legal mind bored into the crucial passage in Deuteronomy (23:19-20) which forbade the taking of interest from "brothers," a term the Catholic Church interpreted to mean all brothers in Christ. Calvin seized upon this ambiguity. Drawing new distinctions between "brothers" and "strangers," he enlarged the biblical loophole through which Protestants could afterward go into banking without losing their souls. More than any other single act, this new dispensation pushed aside religious obstacles to the unfolding of modern capitalism. The new attitude toward money later allowed Penn to regard his American colony as both a religious and a financial venture. In this respect, the later forms of Quakerism reflected the Puritan viewpoint.

On other matters, Quakers and Puritans were in continual conflict. One might even argue that the Quakers came into existence mainly because the Puritans had sidetracked the Reformation. The great aim of the Reformation had been to free the relations between man and God. Instead, the Puritans froze them. The Quakers, by applying gentle warmth, tried to restore the flow of feeling and reassert the compassionate Christ amid the cold legalism of the Puritans.

When the Quakers made their first appearance during the rule of Cromwell's Puritans, the Reformation had clearly foundered. Luther's premises, writes the historian Zimbart de la Tour, "indeed pointed toward autonomy of conscience and the emancipation of the individual, but in their institutionalized forms they attained the precise opposite. Certainly the Puritan aftermath of the Reformation tended toward clerical dictatorship as severe as that of the Catholic church." Ernst Troeltsch, the great historian of religion, confirms this estimate: ". . . early Protestantism was an authoritative ecclesiastic civilization, a claim to regulate state and society, science and education, law, commerce and industry according to supernatural doctrines of revelation. The Puritans were as hostile to intellectual freedom as the Catholic church had been, and the cause of free inquiry did not prevail until both Protestant and Catholic powers were contained by the spread of secularism in later times."

If the Reformation had fallen short of its own aims in spiritual terms, its economic results were even more questionable. Contrary to the general notion, it is not really true that the Reformation created economic improvement for broad segments of the population formerly constrained by feudal barriers. Rather, the Reformation gave an adequate frame to the economic freedoms already won by the clever and ambitious burghers of the larger cities, who formed a rising middle class.

Under the old feudal system, even the poorest enjoyed a certain basic security. They did not have to bargain for wages or seek places of employment. But as the old agrarian barter economy gave way to the money system required for broader trade, many villagers drifted to the cities in search of opportunities to earn money. Here they lost their ancient protections. No longer part of the manorial system, they entered a free labor market. But their new freedom was hardly an advantage. They became an exploitable resource of the free enterprise created by the Reformation.

Of course, wage employment provided some of the poor with opportunities for economic betterment, and a small number of them with uncommon ambition or ability experienced the heady challenge of upward mobility. But great numbers of displaced rural folk, ignorant and indigent, dropped to the bottom of the free labor market and, if they found any work at all, invested their lives without decent recompense. They were caught in the paradox of the new economy, between the Protestant success ethic and a market structure that denied them the possibility of success. This was the unresolved dilemma that prompted G. K. Chesterton to dub the Reformation "the revolution of the rich against the poor."

Conditions in England at Penn's time alarmingly reflected these failings. Dispossessed by the so-called land enclosures, when the local squires filched the common land of the villages where the poor had previously planted crops, countless families roamed the countryside or drifted desolately into the cities. Efforts to create work opportunities for the unemployed rarely succeeded, and the internal migration placed a premium on housing and contributed to an already rampant inflation that left even the middle class pressed for money. From the scant statistics available, Maurice Ashley estimates that in 1659 as many as twenty percent of the population "lived below the line of poverty as then most harshly defined." Massive discontent found expression in an upheaval that was partly political, partly religious, and which, among a variety of other radical sects, produced the Quakers.

The rise of these sects stems from the particular form the Reformation took in England. Here the shifts of belief were further complicated by the establishment of an official state church, the Anglican Church, set up by Henry VIII for the triple purpose of winning a divorce, sacking the Catholic monasteries, and consolidating temporal and spiritual power under his own heavy hand. The result was chaotic. The new Church of England existed in uneasy and often bloody rivalry with both Catholics and Puritans. Depending on vacillating government support, Anglicans harassed Catholics or *vice versa,* while both of them turned fiercely against the Puritans, who retaliated quite thoroughly during their own spell in power under Cromwell. Too busy with such bickering, none of the major creeds paid adequate attention to England's desperate spiritual and social needs during this stressful period.

Driven by this neglect and appalled by the unchristian antics of the chief churches, considerable segments of the population thronged to the small sects that sprang up spontaneously in villages and towns throughout the land. They were usually inspired by charismatic grass-roots preachers with little or no formal theological training. Later these groups became jointly known as the enthusiastic sects. In this context, the term "enthusiastic" does not carry its common meaning of exuberance, although it surely would have been applicable in this sense also. The Greek root of the word *en-theos* literally means "God within" and refers to spontaneous

inspiration through the indwelling God, as opposed to the mediation of God through the institution and ritual of traditional
churches.

In mid-seventeenth-century England, nearly two hundred such
sects noisily touted their particular convictions. Together they
formed a lively religious counterculture to the conventional creeds
and provided an arena for experiment in which new ideas and new
patterns of human association could be tested. Their names, such
as Diggers, Levelers, Ranters, and Family of Love, give some inkling of their predilections. In their sometimes bizarre conduct and
appearance, but more notably in their sincerity and innocence, they
resembled the "hippie" cults of the present era of religious transition.

Emerging as one of these sects, Quakerism might well have
vanished with most of them, had William Penn not happened to
hear Thomas Loe that evening in Ireland. For it was Penn who
gave Quakerism the supportive structure, both theological and
political, that assured its survival. Penn transformed the faith of
the Quakers from a marginal splinter movement with doubtful prospects and a tenuous grasp of its own premises into one of the
noblest carriers of the Christian ethic.

Shoptalk and Sources

The past was real,
yet truth is relative.
—R. G. COLLINGWOOD

A library is not a quiet place. Its silence rings with argument. It is the arena for the clash of ideas and the struggle of opinions. On its shelves, bold assertions are countered by careful judgments and lies are confounded by evidence. Sometimes it's the other way 'round! for the triumph of truth is by no means automatic, even in the world of learning. But as succeeding generations of writers join each other on the shelf and their separate views of a given topic combine into "a literature," the distortions of period and personality cancel out. The true features of the past emerge and the passage of time scales human events to their proper measure.

A historical biographer pursuing his subject in these lively precincts soon learns that his sources can mislead as well as guide him, and he grows wary of the subtle traps set for him by the vagaries of historical method. Voltaire, himself a notable historian, maintained that "history is a trick we play on the dead," for we reconstruct a particular past invariably according to our own preconceptions. A man can see only with his own eyes, and we therefore see the past through the lens of the present. And since the present is unknowable (at least in an analytic sense), we are unaware of the distortions introduced.

Of course, we cling to facts and try not to twist them. But even objectivity can be a trap, the more pernicious because we often pride ourselves on falling into it. Objectivity is a valid criterion in science, for the facts of nature can be verified by experiment. But history has no such facts. It has human events—unrepeatable for

283

WILLIAM PENN: Apostle of Dissent

controlled observation. Besides, these events take place in complex human environments where causal factors can't be isolated, where many causes overlap, where desire subverts reason and chance appears more pertinent than logic. Scientific objectivism—the "factual" approach—can't even touch the surface of such a reality, let alone penetrate it. For human actions, unlike natural facts, have meanings and intentions that can be surmised only through interpretation. Hence, where human action is concerned, all truth is relative. The English historian-philosopher R. G. Collingwood points out that "there are no mere events in history. . . . What is miscalled 'event' is really an action and expresses some thought —that is, an intention or purpose—of its agent. The historian's business is therefore to identify this thought."

Scholars of a sterner persuasion may frown at such leaps beyond documentary evidence. To them this may seem a risky and disreputable dealing in guesses and probabilities. Yet to me it is precisely this element of precarious hunches—of empathy for motives and passions—that makes history both credible and understandable; and I have therefore availed myself of Collingwood's generous grant of interpretive liberty in writing this book.

I set down these rather summary remarks on my own historical method (if it can be called a method at all) to invite the reader to my shop. I want him to see how I do my work, in what frame of mind I shape my materials, and through what logic (i.e., basic assumptions) I process my information. Partly I think I owe him these explanations in return for his attention and confidence, and partly, like any other craftsman, I like talking about the tools of my trade.

Since this book deals largely with politics and religion, the reader may reasonably want to know my own position in these matters, apart from what seeps through the historic account. I make no pretense of impartiality, agreeing with Charles Pelham Curtis that "there are only two ways to be quite unprejudiced and impartial. One is to be completely ignorant. The other is to be completely indifferent. Bias and prejudice are attitudes to be kept in hand, not attitudes to be avoided."

Without launching a lengthy *apologia pro mente mea,* let me post brief notice of the essentials. Politically I incline toward liberalism in the strict classical sense. My interest in Penn arises partly from his astounding anticipation of liberal precepts that

were fully articulated only a century after him. From Penn my
bridge of thought extends directly to the present. Just as in Penn's
time older social and political forms were challenged and changed
by the concrete circumstances of daily life, the classical liberalism
that Penn himself helped inaugurate today faces the challenge of
changed conditions. In the modern industrial state with its political
management of truth, opinion, and private-life options, classical
liberalism may well need a new style of expression. Part of my aim
in writing this book was to re-examine certain roots of liberalism
in order to apply any understanding so gained to the search for
future directions.

As for religion, the other principal element in Penn's life, I have
profound sympathy for diverse attempts to formulate theories of
salvation, believing the need for such theories to be inherent in the
human condition. I also draw a distinction between ritual and
religion, regarding the latter as an open and continuing quest for
the expansion of insight. In consequence, I share Penn's distrust
of institutionalized religion and his abhorrence of dogma, if not
his partisan advocacy of a particular claim to truth.

Some readers may have noticed my tendency to ascribe the development of social forms and their concomitant ideas to economic
factors. I have often found this mode of analysis useful in the
attempt to render a plausible account of historic changes, at least in
the post-medieval period. But I do not regard the production of
goods, the patterns of financing and marketing, and the resultant
distribution of wealth as the only, or even the main, forces shaping
human relations and beliefs.

Roughly specified, this is the apperceptive lens through which I
viewed my subject and my sources. I have dispensed with detailed
source references. Exhaustive annotation is helpful in academic
research and indispensable in rigorous critical studies. On less
stringent occasions, I believe, the massive display of scholarly
appurtenances overwhelms rather than informs; it would, at any
rate, be out of keeping with the informal character of this book. To
pare the overgrowth, I have been selective in compiling the following bibliography. It will hold no surprises for scholars, but I hope
that it will efficiently aid general readers seeking fuller knowledge.

Primary sources, being of limited interest and relatively inacces-
sible to the general reader, for whom this book is intended, have not

been included in this bibliography. Those interested in detailed investigation of early documents will find them in the collections of the Historical Society of Pennsylvania (Philadelphia), the Friends Historical Library of Swarthmore College, the American Philosophical Society (Philadelphia), the British Museum (London), the Library of the Society of Friends, Friends House (London), the Public Record Office (London), and the Bodleian Library (Oxford).

ABOUT PENN

Beatty, Edward C. O., *William Penn as Social Philosopher* (New York, 1939).

Brailsford, Mabel R., *The Making of William Penn* (New York, 1930).

Bronner, Edwin B., *William Penn's "Holy Experiment"* (New York & London, 1962).

Buranelli, V., *The King and the Quaker* (Philadelphia, 1962).

Clarkson, T., *Memoirs of the Private and Public Life of William Penn* (Philadelphia, 1813–1814).

Dixon, W. Hepworth, *A History of William Penn, Founder of Pennsylvania* (New York, 1902).

Dunn, M., *William Penn: Politics and Conscience* (Princeton, 1967).

Fisher, Sidney, *The True William Penn* (Philadelphia, 1900).

Hodgkin, L. V., *Gulielma, Wife of William Penn* (London, 1947).

Hull, W. I., *William Penn, A Topical Biography* (New York, 1937).

Hunt, Rachel McAsters Miller, *William Penn—Horticulturist* (Pittsburgh, 1953).

Illick, Joseph E., *William Penn the Politician—His Relations with the English Government* (Ithaca, 1965).

Janney, S. M., *The Life of William Penn* (Philadelphia, 1882).

Myers, Albert Cook, *William Penn's Early Life in Brief* (Moylan, Pa., 1937).

Peare, Catherine Owens, *William Penn* (Ann Arbor, 1956).

Vulliamy, C. E., *William Penn* (New York, 1934).

ABOUT THE QUAKERS

Barksdale, B. E., *Pacifism and Democracy in Colonial Pennsylvania* (Stamford, 1961).

Besse, Joseph, *A Collection of the Sufferings of the People Called Quakers* (London, 1753).

Braithwaite, Charles, *The Beginnings of Quakerism*, 2nd ed. (Cambridge, 1955).

Braithwaite, Charles, *The Second Period of Quakerism*, 2nd ed. (Cambridge, 1961).

Cole, Alan, "The Quakers and the English Revolution" in Trevor Aston, ed., *Crisis in Europe 1560–1660* (New York, 1967).

Fox, George, *The Journal of George Fox*. Revised edition by John L. Nickalls (Cambridge, 1952).

Jones, Rufus M., *The Quakers in the American Colonies* (London, 1911).

Nash, G. B., *Quakers and Politics 1681–1726* (Princeton, 1968).

Sykes, John, *The Quakers* (Philadelphia, 1959).

Tolles, Frederick B., *Meeting House and Counting House: The Quaker Merchants of Colonial Philadelphia* (Chapel Hill, 1948).

Tolles, Frederick B., *Quakers and the Atlantic Culture* (New York, 1960).

FOR HISTORICAL BACKGROUND

Adams, James Truslow, *The Founding of New England* (Boston, 1921).

Andrews, Charles M., *Colonial Folkways* (New Haven, 1921).

Ashley, Maurice, *England in the Seventeenth Century* (Baltimore, 1952).

Aubrey, John, *Brief Lives (1669–1696)*, O. L. Dick, ed. (Ann Arbor, 1957).

Beard, Charles A. and Mary R., *A Basic History of the United States* (New York, 1944).

Bell, Walter George, *The Great Fire of London in 1666* (London, 1920).

Bell, Walter George, *The Great Plague in London in 1665* (London, 1924).

Boorstin, Daniel J., *The Americans*, Vol. 1, *The Colonial Experience* (New York, 1958).

Clark, George, *The Seventeenth Century* (New York, 1961).

Clark, G. N., *The Later Stuarts 1660–1714* (Oxford, 1949).

Clasen, Claus-Peter, *Anabaptism—A Social History* (Ithaca, 1971).

Clowes, G. S. Laird, *Sailing Ships, Their History and Development* (London, 1930).

Earle, Alice Morse, *Child Life in Colonial Days* (New York, 1899).

Emden, Cecil Stuart, *Pepys Himself* (Oxford, 1963).
Fiske, John, *The Dutch and Quaker Colonies in America* (Boston, 1899).
Fraser, Antonia, *Cromwell: The Lord Protector* (New York, 1973).
Heer, Friedrich, *The Intellectual History of Europe,* Vol. 2 (New York, 1968).
Hill, Christopher, *The Century of Revolution 1603–1714* (New York, 1961).
Keith, Thomas, "Women and the Civil War Sects" in Trevor Aston, ed., *Crisis in Europe 1560–1660* (New York, 1967).
Langdon, W. C., *Everyday Things in American Life 1607–1776* (New York, 1941).
Lewis, W. H., *The Splendid Century: Life in the France of Louis XIV* (New York, 1953).
Merton, Robert K., *Science, Technology and Society in Seventeenth-Century England* (New York, 1938).
Miller, John C., *The First Frontier: Life in Colonial America* (New York, 1966).
Myers, Albert C., *Narratives of Early Pennsylvania, West New Jersey and Delaware, 1630–1707* (New York, 1912).
Notestein, Wallace, *The English People on the Eve of Colonization 1603–1630* (New York, 1954).
Ogg, David, *England in the Reign of Charles II,* 2nd ed. (Oxford, 1955–1956).
Ogg, David, *England in the Reigns of James II and William III,* 2nd ed. (Oxford, 1957).
Ogg, David, *Europe in the Seventeenth Century* (New York, 1960).
Osgood, Herbert L., *The American Colonies in the Seventeenth Century* (New York, 1904).
Parry, J. H., *The Age of Reconnaissance* (New York, 1963).
Pepys, Samuel, *Diary.* Revised edition by J. P. Kenyon (London, 1963).
Plumb, J. H., *The Origins of Political Stability in England 1675–1725* (London, 1967).
Shepherd, W. R., *Proprietary Government in Pennsylvania* (New York, 1896).
Smith, Preserved, *The Social Background of the Reformation* (New York, 1920).

Stevens, Sylvester K., *Pennsylvania, Birthplace of a Nation* (New York, 1964).

Trevelyan, George Macaulay, *England under the Stuarts* (New York, 1949).

Trevelyan, George Macaulay, *Illustrated English Social History* (London, 1942).

Trevor-Roper, H. R., *The Crisis of the Seventeenth Century: Religion, the Reformation and Social Change* (New York, 1968).

Wilson, J. H., *All the King's Ladies* (New York, 1958).

Wright, Louis B., *The Cultural Life of the American Colonies 1607–1763* (New York, 1957).

FOR INTERPRETIVE BACKGROUND

Arieli, Yehoshua, *Individualism and Nationalism in American Ideology* (Baltimore, 1966).

Berman, Marshall, *The Politics of Authenticity: Radical Individualism and the Emergence of Modern Society* (New York, 1970).

Harris, Victor L., *All Coherence Gone—A study of the 17th-century controversy over disorder and decay in the universe* (New York, 1949).

Hill, Christopher, *Society and Puritanism* (New York, 1964).

James, William, *The Varieties of Religious Experience* (New York, 1902).

Jones, Rufus M., *Mysticism and Democracy in the English Commonwealth* (New York, 1965).

Knox, Ronald A., *Enthusiasm; A Chapter in the History of Religion* (New York, 1950).

Koyré, Alexandre, *From the Closed World to the Infinite Universe* (Baltimore, 1957).

Láczay, de, e., *Crystallization of the Notion of "Person"* (Unpublished monograph presented at the New School of Social Research, New York, 1971).

Little, David, *Religion, Order and Law* (New York, 1969).

Miller, Perry, *The Life of the Mind in America* (New York, 1965).

Miller, Perry, *The New England Mind; The Seventeenth Century* (New York, 1939).

Mueller, C., and Conway, C., *The Politics of Communication* (New York, 1973).

Muller, Herbert J., *Freedom in the Modern World* (New York, 1967).

Nelson, Benjamin, *The Idea of Usury* (Chicago, 1969).

Nelson, Benjamin, "Self-Images and Systems of Spiritual Direction in the History of European Civilization" in S. Z. Klausner, ed., *The Quest for Self-Control: Classical Philosophy and Scientific Research* (New York, 1965).

Nettles, Curtis P., *The Roots of American Civilization* (New York, 1946).

Tawney, Richard H., *Religion and the Rise of Capitalism* (London, 1926).

Troeltsch, Ernst, *Protestantism and Progress* (New York, 1912).

Walzer, Michael, *The Revolution of the Saints: A Study in the Origins of Radical Politics* (Cambridge, 1965).

Weber, Max, *The Protestant Ethic and the Spirit of Capitalism,* trans. by Talcott Parsons (New York, 1958).

White, A. D., *A History of the Warfare of Science with Theology in Christendom* (New York, 1960).

Willey, Basil, *The Seventeenth Century Background* (New York, 1934).

Wish, Harvey, *Society and Thought in Early America* (New York, 1950).

Ziff, Larzer, *Puritanism in America—New Culture in a New World* (New York, 1973).

Index

291

French and Indian wars, 193
French etiquette, 47
French Protestantism, 51
French Revolution, 264
Freud, Sigmund, 99
Friedell, Egon, 178
Friends, Society of, *see* Quakerism;
  Quakers
Fronde, 48

Galileo Galilei, 143
Gandhi, Mohandas K., 112
Germany, religious freedom in, 145–146
Gines de Sepúlveda, Juan, 249
Glorious Revolution, 214–215
God
  fatherhood of, 271
  medieval view of, 270
  nature of, 52–53
  Puritan idea of, 177–178
  of Reformation period, 277
Good and evil in Puritanism, 177
Great Fire of London, 63–64
Great Plague of London, 60–61
Great Treaty of Shackamaxon, 191–192
Greek thought, tolerance and, 30
Grotius, Hugo, 105, 222
Gustavus Adolphus (Gustavus II), 168
Gwynn, Nell, 39

Halley, Edmund, 3
Halley's comet, 3
Hals, Frans, 134
Hammond, John, 121, 127
Harman, Ephraim, 167
Harsnett, Samuel, 13
Harvey, William, 32
Hegel, G. W. F., 54, 254
Henley, Henry, 121
Henri IV, France, 222
Henry VIII, England, 281
Heraclitus, 177
Heresy, punishment for, 85
Hill, Christopher, 150
Hispaniola, 20–22
Hobbema, Meindert, 135
Hobbes, Thomas, 30, 134, 145, 157

Holland
  religious freedom and tolerance
    in, 134, 145–146
  trip to, 133–136
  see also Dutch
Holme, Thomas, 167, 185–186
"Holy Experiment," xiii, 3, 179, 260
  pacific spirit of, 193
  Pennsylvania charter and, 150–164
  termination of, 223, 263–264
Homer, 13
Hopkins, Mrs. Edward, 247–248
Hough, John, 213
Howel, John, 115, 128
Hubmaier, Balthasar, 86
Huizinga, Johan, 197–198
Hull, William, 221

Ignatius, St., 105
Indians and Indian language, Penn
  on, 188–191
Iniquin, Lord, 10
Inner Light or Inner Voice, doctrine
  of, 23, 85, 178–179, 266
Inquisition, Spanish, 123, 125
Insane, treatment for, 244
Institutes of Law (Coke), 118

Jamaica, seizure of, 21
James, H.M.S., 18
James II, England, 146, 219
  accession of, 204
  Catholics and, 214
Jaspers, Karl, xi, 159
Jefferson, Thomas, 264
Jerome, St., 105
Jesus Christ
  divinity of, 108–109
  suffering and death of, 98–100
John and Sarah, ship, 153
Jury, freedom of, 128
Justinian II, 15

Kafka, Franz 114
Kalm, Per, 171
Kepler, Johannes, 143
Kéroualle, Louise, 39
Killigrew, Elizabeth, 39